Two Early Tudor Lives:

THE LIFE AND DEATH OF
CARDINAL WOLSEY

THE LIFE OF SIR THOMAS MORE

new dayes begets new tides;
Life whirles bout fate, then to a graue it slydes.

*(Sir Thomas More, in the play
of that name, c. 1590)*

Two Early Tudor Lives

The Life and Death of Cardinal Wolsey

by George Cavendish

The Life of Sir Thomas More

by William Roper

Edited by Richard S. Sylvester
and Davis P. Harding

NEW HAVEN AND LONDON: YALE UNIVERSITY PRESS

Set in Janson type and printed
in the United States of America by
The Colonial Press Inc.
Clinton, Massachusetts.

Published in Great Britain, Europe, and Africa by
Yale University Press, Ltd., London.
Distributed in Latin America by Kaiman & Polon,
Inc., New York City; in Australasia and Southeast
Asia by John Wiley & Sons Australasia Pty. Ltd.,
Sydney; in India by UBS Publishers' Distributors Pvt.,
Ltd., Delhi; in Japan by John Weatherhill, Inc., Tokyo.

Contents

Introduction

BOTH these early English biographies have been wantonly treated by time and circumstance. Historians have always acknowledged their value as primary sources for studies of the lives and characters of the two protagonists, Cardinal Wolsey and Sir Thomas More. But for the historians their value understandably stops at that point. Careful research during the intervening centuries has filled in details, both about the men themselves and the tumultuous times in which they lived, details that Cavendish and Roper seem deliberately to ignore. For example, nowhere in his *Life of Wolsey* does Cavendish mention the rising political fortunes of a brilliant young lawyer named Thomas More. Yet More was destined to succeed Wolsey in high office, and Cavendish's acquaintance with him must have been more than just a casual one.[1] And nowhere in Roper's *Life of More* is mention made of the single accomplishment which earned him greater fame, both at home and abroad, than anything else he did in his life—save perhaps, in the long run, his martyrdom—the writing of the *Utopia*. Such omissions are startling, and they serve also to explain why the historians of English biography are unwilling to concede that the *Lives* are true biographies. Too much is left out. They prefer to see the *Lives* as representing a kind of bridge between the pseudo-biographies of the Middle Ages ("The Fall of Princes" genre and that of the "Saint's Life") and the genuine "modern" biography that delineates the whole man.

The kind of emphasis these two *Lives* have received in the past has had one unhappy consequence. It has frightened off

1. Cavendish had married Margery Kemp, the daughter of Mary and William Kemp, in the early 1520's. Mary Kemp was the sister of More's first wife, Jane. Thus Cavendish's wife was More's niece by marriage.

viiiINTRODUCTION

the critics. Literary critics are notoriously skeptical of works that they have been led to suppose have only an historical importance. Consequently, they have been disposed to leave the *Lives* snug in the domain tradition has assigned to them—the related fields of history and biography. There have been, of course, other factors tending to inhibit a proper literary appreciation of the *Lives*. The modern ear, conditioned by the tight, highly organized structures of modern prose, does not easily adapt itself to the long, rambling, discursive, and often syntactically difficult sentences which characterize the styles of both Cavendish and Roper. For example, that grammatical vice—the indefinite antecedent—holds no terrors for them. But, on the whole, they write with simplicity and dignity, and if we today find their writing sometimes obscure, we should have the grace to remember that both authors, being gentlemen born and bred, had been brought up on the Latin language and literature and could not altogether forego its influence when they undertook to write in the vernacular.

There is another, and more practical, reason why the *Lives* have not had a wider reading public. Inexpensive texts have been hard to come by, and most of the editions have been highly unreliable. Fortunately, this situation no longer obtains. In 1935 Dr. Elsie Vaughan Hitchcock edited Roper's *More* for the Early English Text Society, and in 1959 the same Society published Cavendish's *Life of Wolsey*.[2] The time now seems ripe for a modernized version of the *Lives* that will reach out to an audience not narrowly restricted, as heretofore, to specialists and antiquarians. The *Lives* deserve a better fate. Readers may not agree with the opinion of the co-editors of the present volume that both biographies are artistic masterpieces, but at least they have now been provided with a convenient opportunity to judge for themselves.

Cavendish tells us, on the flyleaf of the autograph manu-

2. William Roper, *The Lyfe of Sir Thomas Moore, knighte*, Original Series, No. 197 (Oxford, 1935); George Cavendish, *The Life and Death of Cardinal Wolsey*, ed. R. S. Sylvester, Original Series, No. 243 (Oxford, 1959). The present modernized versions have been based, with the permission of the Early English Text Society, on these texts.

script[3] of his *Life of Wolsey*, that he "began his book on the fourth of November" (probably 1556) and marked it as "finished and compiled" on June 24, 1558. Born in late 1499 or early 1500, he had entered Wolsey's service about 1522 as the Cardinal's gentleman usher. In this capacity he functioned as a personal attendant upon his master, supervising the preparations connected with Wolsey's many progresses and receptions, making sure that the pomp and ceremony to which the Cardinal was so devoted would be fittingly and comfortably maintained. His duties are reflected in many of the vignettes of his biography, where he himself plays an important part in his own narrative. We see him, for example, riding as an advance courier on Wolsey's trip to France or making the necessary arrangements for the banquet at Hampton Court honoring the French embassy. While Wolsey lived, it was Cavendish and his fellow ushers who prepared the way for the advent of the great prelate, a public function that formed the real-life analogue for Cavendish's later role as the author who would, more powerfully than any other of the Cardinal's biographers, introduce the figure of his master into the pages of history and literature.

Formal as Cavendish's position must have been in such an entourage, we note in his *Life* a gradually developing intimacy between him and Wolsey. The Cardinal was indeed proud and arrogant, but he was not the man to disvalue the kind of devotion which Cavendish gave him. Both Cavendish and Wolsey came from Suffolk, where the circumstances of the Cardinal's birth could justly be said to be meaner than those of his future biographer.[4] It may well be that Wolsey's full appreciation of his good and faithful servant came only after his fall in that long and tortuous year of disappointed hopes that Cavendish records in such painstaking detail. During this year occurred those conversations between master and servant

3. MS. Egerton 2402 in the British Museum. For a more expanded treatment of the biographical and critical material presented below, see the E.E.T.S. edition already cited and also R. S. Sylvester, "Cavendish's *Life of Wolsey*: The Artistry of a Tudor Biographer," *Studies in Philology*, 57 (1960), 44–71.

4. Cavendish refers to Wolsey's father (an Ipswich butcher) as an "honest poor man"; his own father (d. 1524) was Clerk of the Pipe in the Royal Exchequer under both Henry VII and Henry VIII.

from which Cavendish drew much of the material that he used in describing Wolsey's early career; and it is in this portion of his narrative that Cavendish speaks most compellingly to the modern reader. As servant after servant forsakes the Cardinal's train, we come to rely more and more on the sympathetic, eyewitness account of the young gentleman usher who so poignantly feels and so movingly relates the troubles that have overtaken his master.

Out of the knowledge bred in such an intimacy grew Cavendish's portrait of Wolsey. Yet it is important to recall that this was a knowledge that had been matured and mellowed, perhaps even, in some details, distorted, by the passage of time. Cavendish can be mistaken on a point of fact, but he seldom errs artistically. When he left the service of the great after Wolsey's death in 1530, he took back to Suffolk with him a host of memories. We know from his prologue that he had long meditated the composition of his biography, and the skilful organization of his recollections amply testifies to the concentration that he was able to achieve in the process. The composition of his book may well have been, to his mind, the final significant gesture of his own life. He added a postscript to his manuscript in November 1558 which predicted ruin for the kingdom in the coming reign of Elizabeth and, as far as we can tell from the extant documentary evidence, he seems himself to have died a year or two later.

Historians have been, for the most part, singularly gracious in the judgments they have expressed regarding Cavendish's *Life*. Although they find him at times incorrect in his facts and may lament the occasionally confused sequence of events in his narrative, they nevertheless value the *mémoire*-like quality of his finest moments and pay at least implicit tribute to the calm impartiality of his portrait of Wolsey. The *Life of Wolsey* stands out uniquely among sixteenth-century accounts of the Cardinal, for it is no exaggeration to say that both Protestant and Catholic writers of the period tend to treat Wolsey as the most despicable of men. For a Protestant chronicler like Edward Hall, the Cardinal epitomized the corrupt luxury of the Roman Babylon from which the reformers revolted; for a Catholic like Harpsfield, and perhaps also for Roper, Wolsey was the author of Henry VIII's divorce and thus directly responsible for the disaster, in Catholic eyes, of the English Reformation. Cavendish's own portrait, although basically sympathetic, is at once more balanced, more understanding, more controlled, and more profoundly human. He is both witness and judge, both artist and historian; beneath his admiring delineation of the grand power that Wolsey at his best could wield so magnificently runs a subtle, ironic insight into the tragic personality of the man behind the robes.

The balanced complexity of this portrait is most readily discernible in the broad structural lines controlling the basic movement of Cavendish's *Life*. He writes in the medieval tradition of the "Fall of Princes," viewing Wolsey's career in terms of a sharply dichotomized pattern—"rising and falling, triumph and trouble, South and North," as he phrases it in his prologue. With an almost mathematical precision[5] he splits Wolsey's career, as Roper was to do More's, into two symmetrically balanced halves; the first part covers all of Wolsey's triumphant rise and the second comprehends his "tragic fall" as it was worked out in the last year of his life. The reader will note how scenes within either one of these halves echo scenes in the other. The journey South to France contrasts with the journey North to York; the matter "framed" against Queen Catherine becomes metamorphosed into the matter "framed" against Wolsey; the young Earl of Northumberland, whom the Cardinal so scathingly rebukes in the first part, appears again as the royal agent who will carry out Wolsey's arrest.

Yet this symmetry is by no means rigidly mechanical. The correspondences flow easily into one another and they are never formalized by the narrator himself. Even minute details cast their shadows. All the trappings of splendor, so gorgeously portrayed in the first half of the *Life*, reappear as items in the inventories taken by the King's officers. The buckram bag, in which Wolsey does not quite manage to conceal his hair shirts,

---

5. Wolsey's fall from power, marked by his delivery of the Great Seal to the Dukes of Norfolk and Suffolk, occurs on p. 101. The text of the *Life* comprises 193 pp. So too with Roper, where More's resignation comes on the twenty-eighth page of a 57-page text.

replaces the richly embroidered valise that once carried his "vesture cardinal"; and the great man himself, who once rode gloriously through the streets of London, now grovels in the mire before a mere messenger of the King.

One need not insist on the immediate relevance of any of these or other parallels, but their overall effect in the narrative can hardly be denied. Taken together, they draw Wolsey's life, delicately and indirectly, into a highly concentrated and intensely realized portrait. History may not have admitted such precise correspondences, but the art of George Cavendish's narrative most assuredly does. We apprehend, through his careful portrayal, the misery that lurks beneath the surface of even the most triumphant moments of the Cardinal: in the early masque scene, Wolsey fails to recognize the King, and Henry remains an unknown quantity to him until, on his deathbed, he grasps the brutal essence of the man who has "given him over in his gray hairs." So, too, the Cardinal's banquet for the French embassy, richly splendid in its silver light, pales to artificiality before the golden flesh-tones of Henry's subsequent entertainment. The details themselves, even the very masque scene, can be found in the pages of the Tudor "history-graphers," but the organization of them is Cavendish's own. Mere chronicling, as he often reminds us, was no part of his "intendment."

The precarious balance that is thus manifested in the structure of Cavendish's book is also the dominant motif in his delineation of Wolsey's personality. Like More, a child prodigy, Wolsey is nevertheless not gifted with the finely articulated insight that Roper's hero seems to have possessed from the moment of his birth. More's saintly character is essentially static, his vision assured from the time when he first saw himself as others saw him at the dramatic performances in Morton's household. But for Wolsey the achievement of insight is a dynamic process; he is long deluded, complacently self-satisfied in his pseudo-knowledge of both himself and the King. His actions through most of Cavendish's *Life* are all too human as he bows, at the outset of his career, to the will of the King and seldom realizes, as More does so profoundly, that such abject acquiescence is ultimately soul-destroying. The self-awareness that he eventually acquires comes to him only in his final hours of pitiful misery as he sees that Henry, "rather than he will either miss or want any part of his will or appetite, will put the loss of one half of his realm in danger."

So it is that we come to see the tragedy of the great Cardinal's life. His rise and fall move with the circular rhythms of Fortune's wheel, the alternating patterns that control the medieval genre in which Cavendish writes. If we come to admire Wolsey it is not because, like More, he is so different from other men, but because, like most of us, he is so desperately mortal. The power that his personality generates in Cavendish's narrative is quantitatively greater than the grandeur that ordinary men might achieve, but he too is fallible, limited, caught in the temporal process that forms the stuff of tragedy.

One might object that Cavendish could scarcely have been aware that his biography had such manifold implications. His readers may rather think of him as much like the young gentleman usher whose artless naïveté he so frequently displays in his narrative. Against such a view, we may point to the text itself to illustrate Cavendish's consciousness of the tradition in which he writes[6] and of the distinction, already mentioned, which he makes between his own "history" and the history written by the chroniclers. True, he is indeed the naïve observer, sympathetic but uncomprehending, who muses over Master Cromwell's obscure machinations and who is enthralled by the courtly charm of Castle Crecqui. Cavendish himself may have resembled this youthful figure when he served in Wolsey's household, but it is impossible now to ascertain the degree of verisimilitude preserved in the self-portrait. But, more significantly, it is crucial to recognize the difference between the words of this young gentleman usher and the aging voice which is heard uttering the gloomy moralizations that, from time to time, interrupt the course of the narrative. These chorus-like laments—O tempora, O mores—belong to the old Fall of

6. Note his allusion (p. 14) to "the wise sort of famous clerks that hath exclaimed her (Fortune) and written vehemently against her dissimulation."

Princes tradition, but they scarcely seem essential to the dramatic story that Cavendish is telling. We could dispense with the moralizing, but in so doing we would fail to recognize that the difference between the youthful Cavendish and the aged one is, in its own way, a reflection of the perspective in which the character of Wolsey himself is to be viewed. Paradoxical as it may seem, the young gentleman-usher is no more deceived than is his mighty master; and the courageous retainer who refuses, at the end of the *Life*, to accept Henry VIII's offer of service has already acquired a good deal of the wisdom that Wolsey could achieve only in death. The moral weight of the narrative, and the maxims that appear in the choral laments, are part of the burden which George Cavendish bore with him when, having received "his money, his stuff, and his horse," he returned to his "own country."

Like Cavendish's *Life of Wolsey*, Roper's *Life of More* is, strictly speaking, neither history nor biography. It too is designed to preserve the image of a great man in terms of his personality and character. For Roper, what More accomplished was not nearly so important as the kind of man he was. Let other men praise his accomplishments and supply the historical details to round out the story of his life. From his privileged position in the More household, a quiet voice from Chelsea, Roper would simply show forth the man as he knew him, both in the time of his prosperity and in the days of his sore tribulation.

For twenty years following More's execution in 1535, Roper remained discreetly silent. There was, on the evidence of the *Life* itself, good reason for his reticence. Henry VIII could hardly be accounted one of the most tolerant men of his age. Not until Catholicism was restored to England with the ascension of Mary to the throne in 1553 did Roper dare to discharge the debt he felt he owed to the memory of Sir Thomas More. When Mary was crowned Queen, Roper was in his mid-fifties and had already well exceeded the life expectancy of the average sixteenth-century Englishman. For a man who loved and reverenced More, who felt that there was "no man living that of him and his doings understood so much," the racking thought that he might not live to finish his task must have been almost intolerable. So, during the reign of Mary, he sat down and recorded, honestly and dispassionately, his impressions of the More he knew. "There is nothing," writes R. W. Chambers, More's best biographer, "to shake our confidence in his [Roper's] complete honesty."

Nor can anyone question Roper's proud assertion that he knew Sir Thomas better than any other living man. Roper probably entered More's service sometime during the year 1518 and, as he says in the preamble to his story, he "was continually resident in this house by the space of sixteen years and more." The bond between the two men was strengthened when, in 1521, three years after he had become a member of the household, Roper married Margaret, More's favorite daughter. But the most decisive evidence of More's fondness for Roper comes from the *Life* itself. Time after time More opens his heart to his young companion, and it is during their intimate discourse, man to man, that the reader achieves his clearest insights into the workings of More's mind. More obviously loved Roper. He could therefore indulge the luxury of teasing him, perhaps the most certain sign of his affection. This in itself tells us a good deal about More and something about Roper.

Like Cavendish, Roper performs a dual function; he is not only the author of the living drama he re-enacts, but also a participant in it. To what extent the real and fictional Ropers are to be identified, we cannot of course ever know. Judging from the historical records,[7] Roper was shrewd, business-like, and efficient, almost grasping. But this side of Roper hardly emerges in the biography. The fictional Roper is simple, direct, unsophisticated—Lemuel Gulliver in sixteenth-century dress. Roper may have had his private reasons for adopting this fictional guise, but that is no great matter. Aesthetically, it avails. The fact of More's greatness, of his indomitable integrity, is

---

7. As Miss Hitchcock (p. xxxvii) notes, Roper "does not seem to have suffered seriously from Henry's displeasure against More and his family." In fact, he held the lucrative office of Prothonotary for fifty-four years, from 1524 until his death in 1577.

imposed upon us by the failure of his closest friend to understand the motives that led him to embrace martyrdom. Roper's
fictional guise thus inevitably enhances our growing awareness
of More's tragic isolation.

One must not underestimate Roper. His so-called "artless-
ness" is as fictional as the role in which he casts himself. No
one should take seriously his modest disclaimer in the Prologue; he is simply following an old convention and readers
who tend to pass off the *Life* as little more than a compilation
of notes for some future and more gifted biographer had better
take a hard second look. The book from start to finish is finely
articulated. It is, as Professor Chambers has said, "one of the
most perfect little biographies in the language." This is high
praise and from a responsible source.

The key concept—the key word, in fact—is "conscience."
The first time the word occurs is in the opening sentence and
thereafter it appears again and again until More has reached his
personal crisis. The word itself may be said to recapitulate the
action of the story. More's conscience first becomes an issue
when, as a "beardless boy" in Parliament, he upsets the plans
of King Henry VII to exact a "three-fifteenths" subsidy from
the people to promote the marriage of his daughter Margaret
to James IV of Scotland. From this time on, there is not a
single anecdote or episode in the book that does not reflect in
some way More's conscience or integrity of character.

The crisis comes, as it had to come, over the King's "great
matter"—the vexed question of his divorce from Catherine of
Aragon and proposed remarriage, the same crisis which had
brought the great Wolsey tumbling down. No mere King, no
matter how powerful or wilful, no Parliament, could abrogate
the overriding laws of God, as set forth in the Bible and expounded by its holy interpreters. So King Henry, typically and
brazenly, tried the last expedient. He appointed More to the
post of Lord Chancellor, hoping (as Roper clearly implies) to
bribe Sir Thomas into a token acquiescence. The ruse failed,
and the long, bitter struggle, which was to end on Tower Hill,
began.

What helps to make this story tragic is that More was not

essentially of the stuff of which heroes are made. His kind of greatness was thrust upon him. He loved life. He loved his friends and children, and may even have loved his wife, although in the biography his attitude towards her savors more of tolerant good humor than of affection.[8] More, in fact, had a genius for friendship. Even the King and Queen sought him out, and with such zeal that the time came when More, in order to escape from the royal solicitude to the tranquillity of Chelsea, found it convenient to assume the role of court-bore. The strategy worked, and More entered happily into a period of domestic exile. In Roper's pages, this is the only occasion when Sir Thomas could be accused of anything approaching Machiavellian duplicity.

One incident which Roper relates not only reveals More's characteristic warmth and amiability but also provides the reader with an insight into Roper's calculated art. The passage must be quoted in full.

And for the pleasure he took in his company would his grace suddenly sometimes come home to his house at Chelsea, to be merry with him. Whither on a time, unlooked for, he came to dinner to him; and after dinner, in a fair garden of his, walked with him by the space of an hour, holding his arm about his neck. As soon as his grace was gone, I rejoicing thereat told Sir Thomas More how happy he was, whom the King had so familiarly entertained, as I had never seen him to do to any other except Cardinal Wolsey, whom I saw his grace once walk with, arm in arm.

"I thank our Lord, son," quoth he, "I find his grace my very good lord indeed, and I believe he doth as singularly favor me as any subject within this realm. Howbeit, son Roper, I may tell thee I have no cause to be proud thereof,

---

8. Roper did not like his mother-in-law. Over financial matters he fought her bitterly in the courts after Sir Thomas' death. His description of her, therefore, may easily mirror his prejudice. It is only fair to add, however, that there is other contemporary evidence that would suggest that Dame Alice was by no means a perfect wife, not evil but also not conciliatory.

for if my head could win him a castle in France (for then was there war between us) it should not fail to go."

The comparison between the King's walking in More's garden, "holding his arm about his neck," and his strolling with Wolsey arm-in-arm drives home a central contrast between the two men. The passage also reveals More's habitual realism, the same realism which saved the life of his daughter Meg, when in the midst of fervent prayers to the Almighty God for her survival, it came into More's mind that "a glister should be the only way to help her." The enema was administered and, to the astonishment of her physicians, the girl recovered. At the crucial moment, the humanist had triumphed over the man of God—or perhaps it would be more gracious to say that there was a happy collaboration. But the question is academic. Meg lived to enjoy the dubious privilege of being the last person to embrace her father before he disappeared behind the gates of the Tower.

It is wrong to say, as some critics have said, that the book is lacking in drama. There is in fact drama on every page. In a society dominated by men and women, who, like Wolsey, were devoted to a principle of expediency, More's rectitude is constantly beset by forces from without and within, forces which ultimately he could not cope with. The most dangerous force is that exerted by Henry VIII, whose conscience was not queasy. Indeed, that is one of the reasons why Henry, who genuinely liked More, brought him to the block.

But Sir Thomas himself—and here he stands in direct contrast to Wolsey—does not underestimate the character of Henry VIII, not even from the beginning. The pattern of conflict which begins with Henry VII ends when the son of Henry VII executes him. But this is only part of the pattern. He wins over Henry when the axe falls on Tower Hill, but perhaps his most important victory is the conquest of himself. More was a complicated person. He had always had deep-seated religious impulses; and Roper makes it clear enough that More felt guilty before God because he had not given himself over to a life of sequestration. This sense of guilt is well brought out by Roper. For four years after he qualified himself as a lawyer, "he gave himself to devotion and prayer in the Charterhouse of London." He habitually wore a hair shirt against his skin (Wolsey usually preferred to keep his hair shirts safely tucked away in a bag, conveniently transportable), and, according to Roper, Sir Thomas was given to the practise of mortifying his flesh by periodic self-flagellation. The truth seems to be that More had lost his sense of direction. He did not know where to turn. Imprisoned in the Tower, he makes an important confession to Meg:

> But I assure thee on my faith, my own good daughter, if it had not been for my wife and you that be my children, whom I accompt the chief part of my charge, I would not have failed long ere this to have closed myself in as strait a room and straiter too.

As a good humanist, More had made his choice, rightly or wrongly. He had chosen the Court and a life of virtuous activity in a world he was already prepared to reject.

"Whom I accompt the chief part of my charge." Torn between the conflicting obligations he felt he owed to his God and those he owed to his prince, More turned to Chelsea and his beloved family. Chelsea was the focal point of his life, his small paradise. We have already seen to what lengths More was willing to go in order to return to his family. In Roper's version, we cannot in fact see the saint for the man. The saint is there but he is implicit in the man, and it is essentially More's humanity which Roper emphasizes.

It is in this light that we must read one of the more poignant passages in the book—More's departure from Chelsea for his trial at Lambeth.

> And whereas he evermore used before, at his departure from his wife and children, whom he tenderly loved, to have them bring him to his boat, and there to kiss them all, and bid them farewell, *then* would he suffer none of them forth of the gate to follow him but pulled the wicket after him, and shut them all from him; and with an heavy heart, as by his countenance it appeared, with me

and our four servants there took he his boat towards Lambeth. Wherein sitting still sadly a while, at the last he suddenly rounded me in the ear and said: "Son Roper, I thank our Lord the field is won."

The shutting of the wicket-gate is of course highly suggestive. Having made his decision, More is excluding himself from the world of Chelsea, and all it represents to him, a world to which he will not again return. Roper's observation is characteristic. "I wist not what he meant." Some years later, however, he had second thoughts. "But as I conjectured afterwards, it was for that the love he had to God wrought in him so effectually that it conquered all his carnal affections utterly."

More's tragedy was that he went to the scaffold thinking that no man or woman knew what he meant—least of all, his wife Alice. When she comes in his last days to visit him in the Tower, he treats her kindly and tolerantly as usual but he never makes any attempt to explain to her why he is doing what he does. He has had more than his fill of misunderstanding, and he knows his wife. It may also be said that, to a degree, she knows him. Her final appeal to him is couched in terms she knew he would understand.

> "And seeing you have at Chelsea a right fair house— your library, your books, your gallery, your garden, your orchard, and all other necessaries so handsome about you; where you might in the company of me, your wife, your children, and household be merry, I muse what a God's name you mean here still thus fondly to tarry."

But More had already made up his mind when he had closed the wicket-gate behind him.

A word should be said about the magnificent conclusion of this biography, astonishing as it is in its reticence. Roper does not linger, in the manner of a John Foxe[9] or a professional hagiographer over the details of the execution. He describes it in a few terse paragraphs. Then, instead of the passionate eulogy one might expect at this point, Roper translates the reader

9. Foxe's famous *Book of Martyrs* was published in 1563.

abruptly to the court of the Emperor Charles in Europe and records a conversation between the Emperor and Sir Thomas Elyot, alleged to have been England's ambassador to that court. To a shocked ambassador the Emperor relates the news of More's death, and he adds: "And this will we say, that if we had been master of such a servant, of whose doings ourself have had these many years no small experience, we would rather have lost the best city of our dominions than have lost such a worthy counsellor!"

It would be an insensitive reader who did not recall at this point the wistful observation More had made earlier to Roper before he entered the King's service. "If my head could win him a castle in France," he had said, "it should not fail to go."

Although their roots lie in different literary traditions, both *Lives* exhibit a remarkably similar structural development. Even more remarkable, however, is the element of counter-balance, of inverted parallel. Wolsey, as portrayed by Cavendish, is in every respect the precise antithesis of More, as he is portrayed by Roper. And this fundamental antithesis is reflected in episode after episode, anecdote after anecdote, verbal parallel after verbal parallel. It is also reflected stylistically. The color and pageantry, the pomp and ceremony, which give the *Life of Wolsey* its typical tone and atmosphere are wholly absent from the *Life of More*. This is as it should be. More was no Wolsey and had dedicated himself to another mode of living. It is, in fact, almost as if Roper's *More* were designed as a veiled commentary on the character and career of the great Cardinal. The two *Lives*, in any case, complement one another. Read together, each works for the other, generating substantial ironies and deepening the sense of tragedy which hovers, like a gathering storm cloud, over the lives of the protagonists. Neither Wolsey's stern policy of expediency nor More's moral rectitude is of avail. *Indignatio principis mors est.*

A Note on the Texts

THE texts of Cavendish and Roper as presented here are based on the editions of the Early English Text Society (see above, Introduction, n. 2). Spelling has been modernized for all words that have not changed their meaning since 1557 and glosses have been provided in those cases where contemporary significations are no longer current. With words that are now archaic in both form and meaning, the original spelling has been retained and glosses appended. We have sought to facilitate the reader's comprehension of the text by repeating, at fairly regular intervals, glosses to words that have occurred earlier in the narratives. The glosses to Cavendish are considerably fuller than those for Roper, a procedure necessitated by the fact that the *Life of Wolsey* has been modernized directly from the autograph manuscript. The *Life of More,* on the other hand, is extant only in scribal copies from the later sixteenth century, and its usages are thus closer to modern practice. The punctuation and capitalization have been completely modernized and a minimal number of historical and explanatory notes have been provided. The reader who wishes fuller annotation may refer to the Early English Text Society editions.

R. S. S.
D. P. H.

Yale University
June 1, 1961

The Life and Death of Cardinal Wolsey

by George Cavendish

The Prologue

MESEEMS it were no wisdom to credit every light tale, blazed by the blasphemous mouths of rude commonalty,[1] for we daily hear how with their blasphemous trump[2] they spread abroad innumerable lies, without either shame or honesty, which, *prima facie*,[3] showeth forth a visage[4] of truth, as though it were a perfect verity and matter indeed. Wherein there is nothing more untrue; and among the wise sort so it is esteemed, with whom these babblings be of small force and effect. Forsooth, I have read the exclamations of divers worthy and notable authors made against such false rumors and fond opinions of the fantastical commonalty, who delighteth nothing more than to hear strange things, and to see new alterations of authorities, rejoicing sometime in such new fantasies, which afterwards giveth them more occasion of repentance than of joyfulness. Thus may all men of wisdom and discretion understand the temerous madness of the rude commonalty and not giving[5] to them too hasty credit of every sudden rumor, until the truth be perfectly known by the report of some approved and credible person, that ought to have thereof true intelligence.

I have heard and also seen set forth in divers printed books some untrue imaginations after the death of divers persons, which, in their life, were of great estimation, that were invented rather to bring their honest names into infamy and perpetual slander of the common multitude than otherwise.

The occasion thereof that maketh me to rehearse[6] all these things is this, that for as much as I intend, God willing, to

1. common people.   2. trumpet.   3. at their first appearance.
4. semblance.   5. *not giving:* not give.   6. relate.

3

write here some part of the proceedings of the said Legate[7] and Cardinal Wolsey, Archbishop of York, and of his ascending and descending to and from honorous[8] estate; whereof some part shall be of mine own knowledge and some of other persons' information. Forsooth, this Cardinal was my lord and master, whom in his life I served, and so remained with him, after his fall continually during the term[9] of all his trouble until he died—as well in the South as in the north parties[1]— and noted all his demeanor and usage[2] in all that time, as also in his wealthy triumph and glorious estate. And since his death I have heard divers sundry surmises and imagined tales made of his proceedings and doings, which I myself have perfectly known to be most untrue. Unto the which I could have sufficiently answered according to the truth; but, as me seemeth then, it was much better for me to suffer and dissimull[3] the matter and the same to remain still as lies, than to reply against their untruth, of whom I might for my boldness sooner have kindled a great flame of displeasures than to quench one spark of their malicious untruth. Therefore, I commit the truth to Him that knoweth all truth; for whatsoever any man hath conceived in him when he lived or since his death, thus much I dare be bold to say without displeasure to any person or of affection:[4] that in my judgment I never saw this realm in better order, quietness, and obedience than it was in the time of his authority and rule; ne[5] justice better ministered with indifferency,[6] as I could evidently prove if I should not be accused of too much affection or else that I set forth more than truth. I will therefore here desist to speak any more in his commendation and proceed first to his original beginning, ascending by Fortune's favor to high honors, dignities, promotions, and riches.

Finis quod. G. C.

Truth it is, Cardinal Wolsey, sometime Archbishop of York,

7. Papal Legate, or special representative of the Pope in England. Wolsey held this office from 1518 until his death.   8. honorable.
9. *during the term:* for the duration.   1. parts.
2. *demeanor and usage:* bearing and customary behavior.   3. dissemble.
4. *of affection:* out of affection (for Wolsey).   5. nor.   6. impartiality.

was an honest poor man's son, born in Ipswich within the County of Suffolk.[7] And, being but a child, was very apt to learning, by means whereof his parents, or his good friends and masters, conveyed him to the University of Oxford, where he prospered so in learning that (as he told me his own person)[8] he was called the "boy" bachelor, forasmuch as he was made bachelor of art at fifteen years of age, which was a rare thing and seldom seen.

Thus prospering and increasing in learning, [he] was made fellow of Magdalen College, and after appointed (for his learning) to be schoolmaster there. At which time the Lord Marquess Dorset[9] had three of his sons at school there with him, committing as well unto him their virtuous education as their instruction and learning. It pleased the said Marquess, against[1] a Christmas season, to send as well for the schoolmaster as for his children, home to his house for their recreation in that pleasant and honorable feast. They being then there, my lord their father perceived them to be right well employed in learning for their time; which contented him so well that he, having a benefice in his gift being at that time void, gave the same to the schoolmaster in reward for his diligence at his departing after Christmas upon his return to the University. And having the presentation thereof, [he] repaired to the ordinary[2] for his institution and induction. Then, being fully furnished of all necessary instruments[3] at the ordinary's hands for his preferment, [he] made speed without any further delay to the said benefice to take thereof possession.

And being there for that intent, one Sir Amias Paulet,[4] knight, dwelling in that country thereabout, took an occasion of displeasure against him, upon what ground I know not. But, sir, by your leave, he was so bold to set the schoolmaster by the feet[5] during his pleasure; the which was afterward neither forgotten ne forgiven; for when the schoolmaster mounted the

7. in late 1472 or early 1473.   8. *his own person:* himself.
9. Thomas Grey, first Marquis (1451–1501). He had been instrumental in deposing Richard III and thus enjoyed the favor of Henry VII.
1. in preparation for.   2. the bishop's deputy.   3. documents.
4. (d. 1538). He was restricted to the Temple by Wolsey from 1518 or 1519 until 1524.   5. *by the feet:* in the stocks.

dignity to be Chancellor of England, he was not oblivious of the old displeasure ministered unto him by Master Paulet, but sent for him and, after many sharp and heinous words, enjoined him to attend upon the council until he were by them dismissed, and not to depart without license, upon an urgent pain and forfeiture.[6] So that he continued within the Middle Temple the space of five or six years or more; whose lodging there was in the Gatehouse next the street, the which he re-edified [7] very sumptuously, garnishing the same on the outside thereof with cardinals' hats and arms, badges and cognisaunces[8] of the Cardinal's, with divers other devices, in so glorious a sort that he thought thereby to appease his old unkind displeasure.

Now may this be a good example and precedent to men in authority (which will sometime work their will without wit), to remember in their authority how authority may decay; and whom they punish of will [9] more than of justice may after be advanced in the public weal to high dignities and governance, and they based [1] as low, who will then seek the means to be revenged of old wrongs sustained wrongfully before. Who would have thought then that when Sir Amias Paulet punished this poor scholar that ever he should have attained to be Chancellor of England, considering his baseness in every condition? [2] These be wonderful works of God and Fortune. Therefore I would wish all men in authority and dignity to know and fear God in all their triumphs and glory, considering in all their doings that authorities be not permanent, but may slide and vanish as princes' pleasures do alter and change.

Then, as all living things must of very necessity pay the due debt of nature, which no earthly creature can resist, it chanced the Lord Marquess to depart out of this present life. After whose death the schoolmaster, considering then with himself to be but a small beneficed man, and to have lost his fellowship in the college (for, as I understand, if a fellow of that college be once promoted to a benefice he shall by the rules of the

6. upon . . . forfeiture: with the threat of sharp punishment and forfeiture of his estates.   7. rebuilt.   8. crests, coats of arms.
9. of will: willfully.   1. debased, demoted.   2. respect.

house be dismissed of his fellowship), and perceiving himself to be also destitute of his singular good lord, thought not to be long unprovided of some other succors[3] or staff to defend him from all such storms as he lately sustained.

And in his travail thereabout, he fell in acquaintance with one Sir John Nanfant,[4] a very grave and ancient knight, who had a great room[5] in Calais under King Harry the Seventh. This knight he served, and behaved him so discreetly and justly that he obtained the special favor of his said master; insomuch that for his wit, gravity, and just behavior, he committed all the charge of his office unto his chaplain. And, as I understand, the office was the Treasurership of Calais, who was, in consideration of his great age, discharged of his chargeable[6] room and returned again into England, intending to live at more quiet. And through his instant[7] labor and especial favor his chaplain was promoted to the King's service and made his chaplain. And when he had once cast anchor in the port of promotion, how he wrought I shall somewhat declare.

He, having then a just occasion to be in present sight of the King daily, by reason he attended and said Mass before his grace in his privy closet and, that done, he spent not the day forth in vain idleness, but gave his attendance upon those whom he thought to bear most rule in the council and to be most in favor with the King; the which at that time were Doctor Foxe, Bishop of Winchester,[8] then Secretary and Lord Privy Seal, and also Sir Thomas Lovell,[9] knight, a very sage counsellor and witty, being master of the King's wards and Constable of the Tower. These ancient and grave counsellors in process of time, after often resort, perceived this chaplain to have a very fine wit, and what wisdom was packed in his head, thought [him] a meet and an apt person to be preferred to witty affairs.[1]

It chanced at a certain season that the King had an urgent

3. succor, help.
4. An error for Sir Richard Nanfant (d. 1507), the Deputy of Calais.
5. office.   6. involving responsibility.   7. insistent, urgent.
8. Richard Foxe (1448?–1528), Bishop of Winchester from 1501.
9. Sir Thomas Lovell (d. 1524), Chancellor of the Exchequer under both Henry VII and Henry VIII.
1. *witty affairs:* matters requiring considerable intelligence.

occasion to send an ambasset[2] unto the Emperor Maximilian,[3] who lay at that present[4] in the low country of Flanders, not far from Calais. The Bishop of Winchester and Sir Thomas Lovell, whom the King most highly esteemed as chief among his counsellors—the King consulting and debating with them upon this ambasset—saw that they had a convenient occasion to prefer the King's chaplain, whose excellent wit, eloquence, and learning they highly commended to the King. The King giving ear unto them, and being a prince of an excellent judgment and modesty, commanded [5] to bring his chaplain (whom they so much commended) before his grace's presence to prove the wit of his chaplain. At whose repair the King fell in communication with him in matters of weighty gravity and, perceiving his wit to be very fine, thought him sufficient to be put in authority and trust with this ambasset; commanded him thereupon to prepare himself to this enterprized journey, and, for his dispatch, to repair to his grace and his trusty counsellors aforesaid, of whom he should receive his commission and instructions. By means whereof he had then a due occasion to repair from time to time into the King's presence, who perceived him more and more to be a very wise man and of good intendment.[6]

And having his dispatch, took his leave of the King at Richmond about noon and so came to London with speed, where then the barge of Gravesend was ready to launch forth both with a prosperous tide and wind. Without any farther abode, he entered the barge and so passed forth. His happy speed was such that he arrived at Gravesend within little more than three hours, where he tarried no longer than his post horses were provided, and travelling so speedily with post horses that he came to Dover the next morning early, whereas the passengers were ready under sail displayed to sail to Calais. Into which passenger[7] without any farther abode he entered, and sailed forth with them that he arrived at Calais within three hours;

2. embassy.
3. Maximilian I (1459–1519), Holy Roman Emperor from 1493 on. Cavendish exaggerates the speed of Wolsey's mission, which probably occurred in August 1508.   4. time.   5. i.e. commanded them.
6. understanding.   7. passenger boat.

and having there post horses in a readiness, departed incontinent,[8] making such hasty speed that he was that night with the Emperor. Who, having understanding of the coming of the King of England's ambassador, would in no wise defer the time, but sent incontinent for him (his affection unto King Harry the Seventh was such that he rejoiced when he had an occasion to show him pleasure).

The ambassador, having opportunity, disclosed the sum of his ambasset unto the Emperor, of whom he desired speedy expedition, the which was granted so that the next day he was clearly dispatched with all the King's requests fully accomplished. At which time he made no further tarriance, but with post horses rode incontinent that night toward Calais again, conducted thither with such number of horsemen as the Emperor had appointed. And, at the opening of the gates there, where the passengers were as ready to return into England as they were before in his advancing; insomuch that he arrived at Dover before ten of clock before noon and, having post horses in a readiness, came to the court at Richmond that night.

Where he, taking his rest for that time until the morning, at which time after he was ready, [he] repaired to the King at his first coming out of his grace's bedchamber toward his closet to hear Mass. Whom, when he saw, checked[9] him for that he was not passed on his journey. "Sir," quod he, "if it may stand with your highness's pleasure, I have already been with the Emperor and dispatched your affairs (I trust) to your grace's contentation." And with that delivered unto the King the Emperor's letters of credence. The King, being in a great confuse[1] and wonder of his hasty speed, with ready furniture[2] of all his proceedings, dissembled all his imagination and wonder in that matter and demanded[3] of him whether he encountered with his pursuivant, the which he sent unto him (supposing him not to be scantly[4] out of London) with letters concerning a very necessary cause neglected in his commission and instructions, the which the King coveted much to be sped. "Yes, forsooth, sir," quod he, "I encountered him yesterday by

8. immediately.   9. rebuked.   1. confusion.
2. furnishing, accomplishment.   3. asked.   4. hardly, barely.

the way and, having understanding by your grace's letters of your pleasure therein, have notwithstanding been so bold upon mine own discretion (perceiving that matter to be very necessary in that behalf) to dispatch the same. And for as much as I have exceeded your grace's commission I most humbly require[5] your gracious remission and pardon." The King, rejoicing inwardly not a little, said again, "We do not only pardon you thereof but also give you our princely thanks both for the proceeding therein and also for your good speedy exploit," commanding him for that time to take his rest and to repair again after dinner for the further relation of his ambasset. The King then went to Mass; and after, at convenient time, he went to dinner.

It is not to be doubted but that this ambassador hath been since his return with his great friends, the Bishop of Winchester and Sir Thomas Lovell, to whom he hath declared the effect of all his speedy progress; nor yet what joy they conceived thereof. And after his departure from the King in the morning his highness sent for the Bishop and Sir Thomas Lovell, to whom he declared the wonderful expedition of his ambassador, commending therewith his excellent wit, and in especial the invention[6] and advancing of the matter left out of his commission and instructions. The King's words rejoiced these worthy counsellors not a little, for as much as he was of their preferment.

Then when this ambassador remembered the King's commandment and saw the time draw fast on of his repair before the King and his council, [he] prepared him in a readiness and resorted unto the place assigned by the King to declare his ambasset. Without all doubt he reported the effect of all his affairs and proceedings so exactly with such gravity and eloquence that all the council that heard him could do no less but commend him, esteeming his expedition to be almost beyond the capacity of man. The King of his mere motion[7] and gracious consideration gave him at that time for his diligent and faithful service the Deanery of Lincoln,[8] which at that time

5. request.   6. discovery.   7. *mere motion:* own accord.
8. Wolsey was collated to this office on February 2, 1509.

was one of the worthiest spiritual promotions that he gave under the degree of a bishoprick. And thus from thence forward he grew more and more into estimation and authority and [was] after promoted by the King to be his almoner.

Here may all men note the chances of Fortune, that followeth some whom she listeth[9] to promote, and even so to some her favor is contrary, though they should travail never so much with urgent diligence and painful study, that they could devise or imagine; whereof, for my part, I have tasted of the experience.

Now ye shall understand that all this tale that I have declared of his good expedition in the King's ambasset, I received it of his own mouth and report, after his fall, lying at that time in the great park of Richmond, I being then there attending upon him; taking an occasion upon divers communications to tell me this journey with all the circumstance, as I have here before rehearsed.

When death, that favoreth none estate,[1] king or kaiser, had taken that prudent prince King Harry the Seventh out of this present life (on whose soul Jesu have mercy), who for his inestimable wisdom was noted and called in every Christian region the second Solomon, what practices, inventions, and compasses[2] were then used about that young prince, King Harry the Eighth, his only son, and the great provision made for the funerals of the one, and the costly devices for the coronations of the other with that virtuous Queen Catherine, then the King's wife newly married.[3] I omit and leave the circumstance thereof to historiographers of chronicles of princes, the which is no part mine intendment.[4]

After all these solemnities and costly triumphs finished, and that our natural, young, lusty, and courageous prince and sovereign lord, King Harry the Eighth, entering into the flower of pleasant youth, had taken upon him the regal scepter and the imperial diadem of this fertile and plentiful realm of England, which at that time flourished in all abundance of wealth and riches, whereof he was inestimably garnished and fur-

9. pleases.   1. *none estate:* no rank in society.   2. crafty contrivances.
3. Henry VIII was crowned, with Catherine, on June 25, 1509. He had married her on June 11.   4. intention.

nished, called then the golden world, such grace of plenty reigned then within this realm.

Now let us return again unto the almosyner[5] (of whom I have taken upon me to write), whose head was full of subtle wit and policy. Perceiving a plain path to walk in towards promotion, [he] handled himself so politickly[6] that he found the means to be one of the King's council and to grow in good estimation and favor with the King; to whom the King gave an house at Bridewell in Fleet Street, sometime Sir Richard Empson's,[7] where he kept house for his family.[8] And he daily attended upon the King in the court, being in his especial grace and favor, who had then great suit made unto him as counsellors most commonly have that be in favor. His sentences[9] and witty persuasions in the council chamber was always so pithy that they always, as occasion moved them, assigned him for his filed[1] tongue and ornate eloquence to be their expositor unto the King's majesty in all their proceedings. In whom the King conceived such a loving fancy, especially for that he was most earnest and readiest among all the council to advance the King's only will and pleasure[2] without any respect to the case. The King therefore perceived him to be a meet instrument[3] for the accomplishment of his devised will and pleasure, called him more near unto him, and esteemed him so highly that his estimation and favor put all other ancient counsellors out of their accustomed favor that they were in before. In so much as the King committed all his will and pleasure unto his disposition and order. Who wrought so all his matters that all his endeavor was only to satisfy the King's mind, knowing right well that it was the very vein and right course to bring him to high promotion.

The King was young and lusty, disposed all to mirth and pleasure and to follow his desire and appetite, nothing minding to travail in the busy affairs of this realm. The which the almosyner perceived very well; took upon him therefore to dis-

5. almoner.   6. cunningly.
7. Sir Richard Empson, once a favorite minister of Henry VII, had been executed in 1510.   8. retinue.   9. views.   1. polished.
2. *the King's . . . pleasure:* the will and pleasure of the king alone.
3. *meet instrument:* fitting tool.

burden the King of so weighty a charge and troublesome business, putting the King in comfort that he shall not need to spare any time of his pleasure for any business that should necessary[4] happen in the council, as long as he, being there, having the King's authority and commandment, doubted not to see all things sufficiently furnished and perfected. The which would first make the King privy of all such matters (as should pass through their hands) before he would proceed to the finishing or determining of the same, whose mind and pleasure he would fulfil and follow to the uttermost, wherewith the King was wonderly[5] pleased. And whereas the other ancient counsellors would (according to the office of good counsellors) divers times persuade the King to have sometime an intercourse[6] into the council, there to hear what was done in weighty matters, the which pleased the King nothing at all, for he loved nothing worse than to be constrained to do anything contrary to his royal will and pleasure. And that knew the almosyner very well, having a secret intelligence of the King's natural inclination, and so fast as the other counsellors advised the King to leave his pleasure and to attend to the affairs of his realm, so busily did the almosyner persuade him to the contrary; which delighted him much and caused him to have the greater affection and love to the almosyner. Thus the almosyner ruled all them that before ruled him, such did his policy and wit bring to pass.

Who was now in high favor but Master Almosyner? Who had all the suit but Master Almosyner? And who ruled all under the King but Master Almosyner? Thus he persevered still in favor. At last in came presents, gifts, and rewards so plentifully that (I dare say) he lacked nothing that might either please his fancy or enrich his coffers, Fortune smiled so upon him. But to what end she brought him, ye shall hear after. Therefore let all men to whom Fortune extendeth her grace not to trust too much to her fickle favor and pleasant promises, under color whereof she carrieth venomous gall. For when she seeth her servant in most highest authority and that he as-

4. of necessity.   5. wonderfully.
6. *have . . . intercourse:* make sometimes an entrance.

sureth himself most assuredly in her favor, then turneth she her visage and pleasant countenance unto a frowning cheer[7] and utterly forsaketh him, such assurance is in her inconstant favor and sugared promise. Whose deceitful behavior hath not been hid among the wise sort of famous clerks[8] that hath exclaimed [9] her and written vehemently against her dissimulation and feigned favor, warning all men thereby the less to regard her, and to have her in small estimation of any trust or faithfulness.

This almosyner, climbing thus hastily up Fortune's wheel, that no man was of that estimation with the King as he was for his wisdom and other witty qualities. He had a special gift of natural eloquence with a filed tongue to pronounce the same, that he was able with the same to persuade and allure all men to his purpose. Proceeding thus in Fortune's blissfulness, it chanced that the wars between the realms of England and France to be open, but upon what occasion I know not.[1] In so much as the King, being fully persuaded and resolved in his most royal person to invade his foreign enemies with a puissant army to delay their hault brags[2] within their own territory; wherefore it was thought very necessary that this royal enterprise should be speedily provided and plentifully furnished in every degree of things apt and convenient for the same. The expedition whereof the King's highness thought no one man's wit so meet for policy and painful travail as his well-beloved almosyner was, to whom therefore he committed his whole affiance[3] and trust therein. And he, being nothing scrupulous in anything that the King would command him to do, and although it seemed to other very difficile,[4] yet took he upon him the whole charge and burden of all this business, and proceeded so therein that he brought all things to a good pass and purpose in a right decent order, as of all manner of victuals, provisions, and other necessaries convenient for so noble a voyage and puissant army.

7. look.   8. scholars.   9. cried out against.
1. Henry VIII had joined the Holy League formed by Pope Julius II against France in 1511. Cavendish here describes the French campaign of 1513.   2. *delay . . . brags:* check their haughty boasting.
3. reliance.   4. difficult.

All things being by him perfected and furnished, the King not minding to delay or neglect the time appointed, but with noble and valiant courage advanced to his royal enterprise, passed the seas between Dover and Calais, where he prosperously arrived. And after some abode there of his grace, as well for the arrival of his puissant army royal, provision, and munitions, as to consult about his princely affairs, marched forward in good order of battle through the Low Country until he came to the strong town of Thérouanne. To the which he laid his assault and assailed it so fiercely with continual assaults that within short space he caused them within to yield the town. Unto which place the Emperor Maximilian repaired unto the King our sovereign lord with a puissant army, like a mighty and friendly prince, taking of the King his grace's wages as well for his own person as for his retinue. The which is a rare thing seldom seen, heard, or read, that an Emperor to take wages and to fight under a King's banner.[5]

Thus after the King had obtained the possession of this puissant fort and set all things in due order for the defence and preservation of the same to his highness's use, he departed from thence and marched toward the city of Tournai and there again laid his siege. To the which he gave so fierce and sharp assaults that they within were constrained of fine force[6] to yield up the town unto his victorious majesty. At which time he gave the almosyner the bishoprick of the same see for some part of recompense of[7] his pains sustained in that journey. And when the King had established all things there agreeable to his princely pleasure, and furnished the same with noble valiant captains and men of war for the safeguard of the town against his enemies, he returned again into England, taking with him divers worthy prisoners of the peers of France, as the Duke of Longville, the County Clermount, and divers other taken there in a skirmish most victoriously.[8] After whose return immediately the See of Lincoln fell void by the death

---

5. Maximilian, who was usually in financial straits, received £25 per day for his services.   6. *fine force:* absolute necessity.   7. for.
8. The French peers were captured in the famous "Battle of the Spurs," so named because the French quickly took to flight on horseback.

of Doctor Smith,[9] late Bishop of that dignity; the which benefice and promotion his grace gave unto his almosyner, Bishop-elect of Tournai, who was not negligent to take possession thereof and made all the speed he could for his consecration. The solemnization whereof ended, he found the means to get the possession of all his predecessor's goods into his hands, whereof I have seen divers times some part thereof furnish his house. It was not long after that Doctor Bainbridge,[1] Archbishop of York, died at Rome, being there the King's ambassador unto Pope Julius; unto which benefice the King presented his new Bishop of Lincoln, so that he had three bishopricks in one year given him.

Then prepared he again of new[2] as fast for his translation from the See of Lincoln unto the See of York. After which solemnization done, and he being in possession of the Archbishoprick of York, and *Primas Angliae*,[3] thought him sufficient to compare with Canterbury;[4] and thereupon erected his cross in the court and in every other place as well in the presence of the Bishop of Canterbury and in the precinct of his jurisdiction as elsewhere. And for as much as Canterbury claimeth superiority and obedience of York as he doth of all other bishops within this realm, for as much as he is *Primas Totius Angliae*,[5] and therefore claimeth as a token of an ancient obedience of York to abate[6] the advancing of his cross in the presence of the cross of Canterbury; notwithstanding York, nothing minding to desist from bearing of his cross in manner as is said before, caused his cross to be advanced and borne before him, as well in the presence of Canterbury as elsewhere. Wherefore Canterbury, being moved therewith, gave York a certain check for his presumption, by reason whereof there engendered some grudge between Canterbury and York. And York, perceiving the obedience that Canterbury claimed to

9. Wolsey was nominated to Lincoln on January 1, 1514, although Dr. William Smith, his predecessor, did not die until January 2. He was consecrated on March 26.
1. Christopher Bainbridge (1464?-1514) was reputed to have been poisoned at Rome by his chaplain. He had been English ambassador there since 1509.   2. *of new:* anew.   3. Primate of England.
4. William Warham (1450?-1532), Archbishop of Canterbury from 1503 and Chancellor from 1504 to 1515.   5. Primate of all England.
6. desist from.

have of York, intended to provide some such means that he would rather be superior in dignity to Canterbury than to be either obedient or equal to him. Wherefore he obtained first to be made priest cardinal and *legatus de latere*,[7] unto whom the Pope sent a cardinal's hat with certain bulls for his authority in that behalf.

Yet by the way of communication[8] ye shall understand that the Pope sent this hat as a worthy jewel of his honor, dignity, and authority, the which was conveyed hither in a varlet's budget,[9] who seemed to all men to be but a person of small estimation. Whereof York, being advertized[1] of the baseness of the messenger and of the people's opinion and rumor,[2] thought it for his honor meet that so high a jewel should not be conveyed by so simple a messenger. Wherefore he caused him to be stayed by the way immediately after his arrival in England, where he was newly furnished in all manner of apparel with all kind of costly silks, which seemed decent for such an high ambassador. And that done he was encountered upon Blackheath and there received with a great assembly of prelates and lusty gallant gentlemen, and from thence conducted and conveyed through London with great triumph. Then was great and speedy provision and preparation made in Westminster Abbey for the confirmation of his high dignity, the which was executed by all the bishops and abbots nigh or about London in rich miters and copes and other costly ornaments, which was done in so solemn a wise as I have not seen the like unless it had been at the coronation of a mighty prince or king.

Obtaining this dignity, [he] thought himself meet to encounter with Canterbury in his high jurisdiction before expressed; and that also he was as meet to bear authority among the temporal powers as among the spiritual jurisdictions. Wherefore, remembering as well the taunts and checks before sustained of Canterbury (which he intended to redress), having a respect to the advancement of worldly honor, promotion, and great benefits, found the means with the King that he was made

7. Wolsey received the cardinalate in November 1514. For his legacy, see above, p. 4.   8. *by . . . communication:* as a matter of conversation.
9. *varlet's budget:* servant's bag.   1. notified.   2. gossip.

Chancellor of England; and Canterbury thereof dismissed, who had continued in that honorable room and office since long before the death of King Harry the Seventh.

Now he being in possession of the chancellorship, endowed with the promotion of an archbishop and cardinal, legate also *de latere,* thought himself fully furnished with such authorities and dignities that he was able to surmount[3] Canterbury in all ecclesiastical jurisdictions, having power to convocate Canterbury and other bishops within his province, to assemble at his convocation, in any place within this realm where he would assign; taking upon him the correction of all matters in every diocese, having there through all the realm all manner of spiritual ministers, as commissaries,[4] scribes, apparitors,[5] and all other officers to furnish his courts; visited also all spiritual houses and presented by prevention[6] whom he listed to their benefices. And to the advancing of his legantine honor and jurisdiction,[7] he had masters of his faculties[8] and masters *cerimoniarum*[9] and such other like officers to the glorifying of his dignity. Then had he two great crosses of silver, whereof one of them was for his archbishoprick and the other for his legacy, borne always before him whithersoever he went[1] or rode by two of the most tallest and comeliest priests that he could get within all this realm. And to the increase of his gains he had also the Bishoprick of Durham[2] and the Abbey of Saint Albans *in commendam.*[3] Howbeit after, when Bishop Foxe of Winchester died, he surrendered Durham into the King's hands and in lieu thereof took the Bishoprick of Winchester.

3. overrule.   4. representatives of a bishop in his diocese.
5. officers of an ecclesiastical court.
6. A technical term of Canon Law designating the right of an ecclesiastical superior to take precedence over or forestall an inferior in performing his duties. Here it refers to the fact that Wolsey named men to benefices before the monastery or abbey in which the vacancy occurred had a chance to act.
7. *legantine . . . jurisdiction:* honor and jurisdiction as papal legate.
8. spiritual prerogatives.   9. of ceremonies.   1. walked.
2. given to Wolsey in February 1523.
3. St. Albans was the richest abbey of England and it was held by the Cardinal from December 1521. The term *"in commendam"* describes the tenure of a benefice held by a clerk or layman (with enjoyment of its revenues) until a proper incumbent was provided for it. Such holdings had been forbidden by the Lateran Council of 1512–17.

Then he had also as it were in farm,[4] both Bath and
Worcester and Hereford, because the incumbents thereof were
strangers,[5] born out of this realm, continuing always beyond
the seas in their own native countries, or else at Rome, from
whence they were sent by the Pope in legation into England
to the King. And for their reward at their departure the prudent King Harry the Seventh thought it better to reward them
with that thing he himself could not keep than to defray[6] or
disburse anything of his treasure. And then they being but
strangers, thought it more meet for their assurance and to have
their jurisdictions conserved and justly used, to permit the
Cardinal to have their benefices for a convenient[7] yearly sum
of money to be paid them by eschance[8] in their countries, than
to be troubled or burdened with the conveyance thereof unto
them. So that all their spiritual promotions and jurisdictions
of their bishopricks were clearly in his demesnes[9] and disposition to prefer or promote whom he listed[1] unto them.

He had also a great number daily attending upon him both
of noblemen and worthy gentlemen of great estimation and
possessions, with no small number of the tallest yeomen that he
could get in all this realm, in so much that well was that nobleman or gentleman that might prefer any tall and comely yeoman unto his service.

Now to speak of the order of his house and officers, I think
it necessary here to be remembered. First, ye shall understand
that he had in his hall daily three special tables furnished with
three principal officers, that is to say a steward, which was
always a doctor[2] or a priest; a treasurer, a knight; a comptroller,
an esquire; which bare always within his house their white
staves. Then had he a cofferer,[3] three marshalls, two yeomen
ushers, two grooms and an almosyner. He had also in the hall

4. *as it . . . farm:* i.e. as if he let them at a fixed rent. Bath and Wells
was held by Hadrian de Castello from 1504 to 1518 when Wolsey himself
received it. Hereford belonged to Castello from 1502 to 1504 but thereafter was held by Englishmen. Worcester was occupied by three "strangers" during Wolsey's period of power.   5. foreigners.   6. expend.
7. suitable.   8. exchange.
9. *in his demesnes:* to be considered among his landed properties.
1. pleased.   2. probably a doctor of the law.
3. an officer who ranked immediately beneath the comptroller and
had the supervision of the other officers.

kitchen two clerks of his kitchen, a clerk comptroller, a surveyor of the dresser,[4] a clerk of his spicery.[5] Also there in his hall kitchen he had two master cooks, and twelve of other laborers and children,[6] as they called them, a yeoman of his scullery, with two other in his silver scullery, two yeomen of his pastry,[7] and two grooms.

Now in his privy[8] kitchen he had a master cook who went daily in damask, satin, or velvet with a chain of gold about his neck; and two grooms with six laborers and children to serve in that place. In the larder there a yeoman and a groom; in the scalding house[9] a yeoman and two grooms; in the scullery there two persons; in the buttery two yeomen and two grooms with two other pages; in the pantry two yeomen, two grooms and two pages; and in the ewry[1] likewise; in the cellar[2] three yeomen, two grooms, and two pages, besides a gentleman for the mouth.[3] In the chaundery[4] three persons; in the wafery[5] two; in his garderobe[6] of beds a master and ten other persons; in the laundry a yeoman, a groom, and three pages; of purveyors,[7] two, and one groom; in the bakehouse a yeoman and two grooms; in the woodyard a yeoman, and a groom; in the garner, one; in the garden a yeoman and two laborers. Now at the gate he had of porters two tall yeomen and two grooms; a yeoman of his barge; in the stable he had a master of his horses; a clerk of the stable; a yeoman of the same; a saddler, a farrier, a yeoman of his chariot; a sumpterman,[8] a yeoman of his stirrup; a muleteer; sixteen grooms of his stable, every of them keeping four great geldings; in the almosory[9] a yeoman and a groom.

Now will I declare to you the officers of his chapel and singing men of the same. First, he had there a dean, who was

4. who superintended the preparation and serving of food.
5. room where spices were kept.   6. i.e. kitchen pages or serving boys.
7. pastry-kitchen.   8. private.
9. room in which utensils etc. were scalded.
1. room where pitchers and jugs were kept.   2. the wine cellar.
3. perhaps a wine-taster, certainly the gentleman in charge of the storing and serving of beverages.
4. room where candles were kept.   5. wafer-kitchen.   6. wardrobe.
7. victualers, caterers.
8. a man who took care of the "sumpter" or pack mules.
9. almonry, from which alms were dispensed.

always a great clerk and a divine; a sub-dean; a repeater[1] of the choir; a gospeller; a pistoler;[2] and twelve singing priests. Of seculars he had first a master of his children, twelve singing children, sixteen singing men, a servant to attend upon the said children. In the revestry[3] a yeoman and two grooms. Then were there divers retainers of cunning[4] singing men that came at divers sundry principal feasts. But to speak of the furniture[5] of his chapel passeth my capacity to declare the number of the costly ornaments and rich jewels that were occupied[6] in the same continually. I have seen there in a procession worn forty-four copes of one suit,[7] very rich, besides the sumptuous crosses, candlesticks, and other necessary ornaments to the comely furniture of the same.

Now shall ye understand that he had two cross-bearers and two pillar-bearers;[8] and in his chamber all these persons, that is to say, his high chamberlain, his vice-chamberlain, twelve gentlemen ushers, daily waiters; beside two in his privy chamber. And of gentlemen waiters in his privy chamber he had six; and also he had of lords nine or ten, who had each of them allowed two servants; and the Earl of Derby[9] had allowed five men. Then had he of gentlemen, as cupbearers, carvers, sewers,[1] and gentlemen daily waiters, forty persons. Of yeomen ushers he had six; of grooms in his chamber he had eight; of yeomen of his chamber he had forty-six daily to attend upon his person; he had also a priest there, which was his almosyner,[2] to attend upon his table at dinner. Of doctors and chaplains attending in his closet to say daily Mass before him, he had sixteen persons; a clerk of his closet. Also he had two secretaries and two clerks of his signet and four counsellors, learned in the laws of this realm.

And for as much as he was Chancellor of England, it was necessary for him to have divers officers of the Chancery to attend daily upon him for the better furniture[3] of the same.

1. rehearser, trainer.   2. readers of the gospels and epistles.   3. vestry.
4. knowledgeable, expert.   5. furnishings, equipment.   6. in use.
7. kind of cloth.
8. Wolsey had introduced these pillars as symbols of his office.
9. Edward Stanley (1508–1572), who was one of Wolsey's wards during his minority.   1. servers.   2. almoner.   3. furnishing.

That is to say, he had a clerk of the crown,[4] a riding clerk,[5] a clerk of the hamper,[6] a chaffer of wax;[7] then had he a clerk of the check[8] as well to check his chaplains as his yeomen of the chamber. He had also four footmen, which were apparelled in rich running coats[9] whensoever he rode any journey. Then had he an herald at arms; also a sergeant at arms, a physician, a pottecarye,[1] four minstrels, a keeper of his tents, an armorer, an instructor of his wards, two yeomen in his garderobes, and a keeper of his chamber in the court. He had also daily in his house the Surveyor of York, and a clerk of the green cloth,[2] and an auditor. All this number of persons were daily attendant upon him in his house, down-lying and up-rising, and at meals. There was continually in his chamber a board kept for his chamberlains and gentlemen ushers, having with them a mess[3] of the young lords and another for gentlemen. Besides all this there was never an officer and gentlemen or any other worthy person in his house but he was allowed some three, some two servants, and all other one at the least, which amounted to a great number of persons.

Now have I showed you the order of his house, and what officers and servants he had, according to his checker roll, attending daily upon him, besides his retainers and other persons, being suitors, that most commonly were fed in his hall. And whensoever we shall see any more such subjects within this realm that shall maintain any such estate and household, I am content he be advanced above him in honor and estimation. Therefore here I make an end of his household, whereof the number were about the sum of five hundred persons, according to his checker roll.

4. officer of chancery whose chief duty was the issuing of writs for summons or elections to Parliament.
5. one of six chancery clerks who controlled the grants passing under the great seal.
6. clerk of the hanaper, who dealt with the fees for sealing and enrolling documents.   7. who prepared the wax for sealing documents.
8. keeper of the check-roll, who supervised other servants in the performance of their duties.
9. coats worn when they "ran" as part of the cardinal's entourage.
1. druggist.   2. a financial officer of the royal household.
3. common table.

You have heard of the order and officers of his house; now do I intend to proceed forth unto other of his proceedings; for, after he was thus furnished in manner as I have before rehearsed unto you, he was twice sent in ambasset unto the Emperor Charles the Fifth[4] that now reigneth, and now father unto King Philip,[5] our sovereign lord. For as much as the old Emperor Maximilian was dead, and for divers urgent causes touching the King's majesty, it was thought good that in so weighty a matter and to so noble a prince that the Cardinal was most meet[6] to be sent on so worthy an ambasset. Wherefore he, being ready to take upon him the charge thereof, was furnished in all degrees and purposes most likest a great prince, which was much to the high honor of the King's majesty and of this realm. For first in his proceeding he was furnished like a Cardinal of high estimation, having all thing thereto correspondent and agreeable; his gentlemen, being in number very many, clothed in livery coats of crimson velvet of the most purest color that might be invented, with chains of gold about their necks. And all his yeomen and other mean[7] officers were in coats of fine scarlet, guarded[8] with black velvet an hand broad. He being thus furnished in this manner, was twice sent unto the Emperor into Flanders, the Emperor lying then in Bruges; who entertained our ambassador very highly, discharging him and all his train of their charges.[9] For there was no house within all Bruges wherein any gentleman of the lord ambassador's lay or had recourse, but that the owners of the houses were commanded by the Emperor's officers that they, upon pain of their lives, should take no money for anything that the Cardinal's servants should take or dispend[1] in victuals —ne although[2] they were disposed to make any costly banquets—furthermore commanding their said hosts to see that they lacked no such things as they desired or required to have for their pleasures. Also the Emperor's officers every night

---

4. Charles V, who became Emperor on June 28, 1519.
5. Philip II of Spain (1527–1598), husband of Queen Mary.
6. suitable.   7. inferior.   8. trimmed.
9. *discharging . . . charges:* i.e. paying all their expenses.   1. expend.
2. *ne although:* not even if.

went through the town from house to house whereas any Englishmen lay and resorted and there served liveries for all night, which was done after this manner.

First, the Emperor's officers brought into the house a cast[3] of fine manchet bread,[4] two great silver pots with wine, and a pound of fine sugar; white lights and yellow; a bowl or goblet of silver to drink in and every night a staff torch.[5] This was the order of their liveries every night. And then in the morning when the officers came to fetch away their stuff, then would they accompt[6] with the host for the gentlemen's costs spent in that night and day before. Thus the Emperor entertained the Cardinal and all his train[7] for the time of his ambasset there. And that done, he returned home again into England with great triumph, being no less in estimation with the King than he was before but rather much more.

Now will I declare unto you his order in going to Westminster Hall daily in the term season. First, before his coming out of his privy chamber, he heard most commonly every day two Masses in his privy closet. And there then said his daily service with his chaplain and, as I heard his chaplain say (being a man of credence and of excellent learning), that the Cardinal, what business or weighty matters so ever he had in the day, he never went to his bed with any part of his divine service unsaid, yea not so much as one collect; wherein I doubt not but he deceived the opinion of divers persons.

And after Mass he would return in his privy chamber again and, being advertized[8] of the furniture[9] of his chambers without with noblemen and gentlemen with other persons, would issue out into them apparelled all in red in the habit of a Cardinal; which was either of fine scarlet or else of crimson satin, taffeta, damask, or caffa,[1] the best that he could get for money; and upon his head a round pillion[2] with a neck of black velvet, set to the same in the inner side. He had also a tippet[3] of fine sables about his neck, holding in his hand a very fair orange

3. quantity of bread made at one time.
4. *manchet bread:* the finest white bread.   5. tall, thick candle.
6. settle accounts.   7. entourage.   8. notified.
    9. complement of occupants.   1. a rich silk cloth.   2. priest's hat.
3. fur scarf.

whereof the meat or substance within was taken out and filled up again with the part of a sponge wherein was vinegar and other confections against the pestilent airs; to the which he most commonly smelt unto, passing among the press[4] or else when he was pestered with many suitors. There was also borne before him first the Great Seal of England, and then his Cardinal's hat by a nobleman or some worthy gentleman right solemnly, bareheaded. And as soon as he was entered into his chamber of presence where was attending his coming to await upon him to Westminster Hall, as well noblemen and other worthy gentlemen as noblemen and gentlemen of his own family; thus passing forth with two great crosses of silver borne before him, with also two great pillars of silver, and his sergeant at arms with a great mace of silver gilt. Then his gentlemen ushers cried and said, "On my lords and masters, make way for my lord's grace!"

Thus passed he down from his chambers through the hall; and when he came to the hall door there was attendant for him his mule, trapped[5] altogether in crimson velvet and gilt stirrups. When he was mounted, with his cross-bearers and pillar-bearers also, upon great horses trapped with red scarlet, then marched he forward with his train and furniture[6] in manner as I have declared, having about him four footmen with gilt pole–axes in their hands; and thus he went[7] until he came to Westminster Hall door. And there lighted[8] and went after this manner up through the hall into the Chancery. Howbeit, he would most commonly stay a while at a bar made for him a little beneath the Chancery and there commune sometime with the judges and sometime with other persons. And that done he would repair into the Chancery, and sitting there until eleven of the clock, hearing suitors and determining of divers matters. And from thence he would divers times go into the Star Chamber, as occasion did serve, where he spared neither high nor low, but judged every estate according to their merits and deserts.

4. crowd, throng.   5. adorned with trappings.
6. "equipment," i.e. the crosses, pillars, etc.   7. proceeded.
8. alighted.

He used every Sunday to repair to the court, being then for the most part at Greenwich in the term, with all his former order, taking his barge at his privy stairs, furnished with tall yeomen standing upon the baylles,[9] and all gentlemen being within with him. And landed at the Crane in the Vintry, and from thence he rode upon his mule with his crosses, his pillars, his hat, and the Great Seal, through Thames Street until he came to Billingsgate or thereabouts. And there took his barge again and rowed to Greenwich, where he was nobly received of the lords and chief officers of the King's house, as the treasurer and controllers with other; and conveyed unto the King's chamber, his crosses commonly standing (for the time of his abode in the court) on the one side of the King's cloth of estate.[1] He being thus in the court, it was wonderly[2] furnished with noblemen and gentlemen, much otherwise than it was before his coming. And after dinner among the lords, having some consultation with the King or with the council, he would depart homeward with like sort.[3] And this order he used continually as opportunity did serve.

Thus in great honor, triumph, and glory he reigned a long season, ruling all thing within this realm appertaining unto the King by his wisdom, and also all other weighty matters of foreign regions with whom the King and this realm had any occasion to intermeddle. All ambassadors of foreign potentates were alway dispatched by his discretion, to whom they had always access for their dispatch. His house was also always resorted[4] and furnished with noblemen, gentlemen, and other persons with going and coming in and out, feasting and banqueting all ambassadors divers times and other strangers right nobly.

And when it pleased the King's majesty for his recreation to repair unto the Cardinal's house (as he did divers times in the year), at which time there wanted no preparations or goodly furniture with viands[5] of the finest sort that might be provided for money or friendship. Such pleasures were then devised for the King's comfort and consolation as might be

9. bulwarks.   1. *cloth of estate:* royal canopy.   2. wonderfully.
3. *with like sort:* in like manner.   4. resorted to.   5. food and drink.

invented or by man's wit imagined. The banquets were set forth with masques and mummeries[6] in so gorgeous a sort and costly manner that it was an heaven to behold. There wanted no dames or damsels meet or apt to dance with the maskers or to garnish[7] the place for the time, with other goodly disports.[8] Then was there all kind of music and harmony set forth with excellent voices both of men and children.

I have seen the King suddenly come in thither in a masque with a dozen of other maskers all in garments like shepherds, made of fine cloth of gold and fine crimson satin paned,[9] and caps of the same with visors of good proportion of visonamy;[1] their hairs and beards either of fine gold wires or else of silver, and some being of black silk, having sixteen torches bearers[2] besides drums, and other persons attending upon them with visors and clothed all in satin of the same colors. And at his coming and before he came into the hall, ye shall understand that he came by water to the water gate without any noise, where against his coming was laid charged many chambers.[3] At whose landing they were all shot off, which made such a rumble in the air that it was like thunder. It made all the noblemen, ladies, and gentlewomen to muse what it should mean, coming so suddenly, they sitting quietly at a solemn banquet under this sort.

First ye shall perceive that the tables were set in the chamber of presence, banquet-wise covered, my lord Cardinal sitting under the cloth of estate and there having all his service all alone. And then was there set a lady and a nobleman or a gentleman and a gentlewoman throughout all the tables in the chamber on the one side, which was made and joined as it were but one table. All which order and devise[4] was done and devised by the Lord Sands,[5] Lord Chamberlain with the King, and also by Sir Harry Guildford,[6] Controller with the King. Then immediately after this great shot of guns, the Cardinal

6. theatrical performances.   7. adorn.   8. pastimes.
9. made of strips of cloth.   1. physiognomy, face.   2. torchbearers.
3. small cannon.   4. plan.
5. William Sandys (d. 1540). He became Lord Chamberlain on April 15, 1526.
6. Sir Henry Guildford (1489–1532). Maser of the Revels from 1513 and a great favorite of Henry VIII.

desired the said Lord Chamberlain and Controller to look[7] what this sudden shot should mean (as though he knew nothing of the matter). They thereupon, looking out of the window into Thames, returned again and showed him that it seemed to them that there should be[8] some noblemen and strangers[9] arrived at his bridge as ambassadors from some foreign prince. With that quod the Cardinal, "I shall desire you because ye can speak French to take the pains to go down into the hall to encounter and to receive them according to their estates,[1] and to conduct them into this chamber, where they shall see us and all these noble personages sitting merrily at our banquet, desiring them to sit down with us and to take part of our fare and pastime."

They went incontinent[2] down into the hall, where they received them with twenty new torches, and conveyed them up into the chamber with such a number of drums and fifes as I have seldom seen together at one time in any masque. At their arrival into the chamber two and two together, they went directly before the Cardinal where he sat, saluting him very reverently. To whom the Lord Chamberlain (for them) said, "Sir, for as much as they be strangers and can speak no English they have desired me to declare unto your grace thus: They, having understanding of this your triumphant banquet, where was assembled such number of excellent fair dames, could do no less, under the supportation of your grace,[3] but to repair hither to view as well their incomparable beauty as for to accompany them at mumchance,[4] and then after to dance with them, and so to have of them acquaintance. And, sir, they furthermore require of your grace license to accomplish the cause of their repair." To whom the Cardinal answered that he was very well contented they should so do.

Then the maskers went first and saluted all the dames as they sat and then returned to the most worthiest and there opened a cup full of gold with crowns and other pieces of coin to whom they set divers pieces to cast at. Thus in this manner perusing

---

7. see.   8. *should be:* were.   9. foreigners.   1. social rank.
2. at once.   3. *under . . . grace:* with your grace's support or permission.
4. a dice game.

all[5] the ladies and gentlewomen, and to some they lost, and of some they won. And this done, they returned unto the Cardinal with great reverence, pouring down all the crowns in the cup, which was about two hundred crowns. "At all," quod the Cardinal, and so cast the dice and won them all at a cast, whereat was great joy made. Then quod the Cardinal to my Lord Chamberlain, "I pray you," quod he, "show them that it seems me how there should be among them some nobleman, whom I suppose to be much more worthy of honor to sit and occupy this room and place than I; to whom I would most gladly (if I knew him) surrender my place according to my duty." Then spake my Lord Chamberlain unto them in French, declaring my Lord Cardinal's mind. And they, rounding him[6] again in the ear, my Lord Chamberlain said to my Lord Cardinal, "Sir, they confess," quod he, "that among them there is such a noble personage; among whom, if your grace can appoint him[7] from the other, he is contented to disclose himself and to accept your place most worthily." With that, the Cardinal, taking a good advisement[8] among them, at the last, quod he, "me seems the gentleman with the black beard should be even he." And with that he arose out of his chair and offered the same to the gentleman in the black beard (with his cap in his hand). The person to whom he offered then his chair was Sir Edward Neville,[9] a comely knight of a goodly personage that much more resembled the King's person in that masque than any other. The King, hearing and perceiving the Cardinal so deceived in his estimation[1] and choice, could not forbear laughing, but plucked down his visor and Master Neville's and dashed out[2] with such a pleasant countenance and cheer that all noble estates there assembled, seeing the King to be there among them, rejoiced very much.

The Cardinal eftsoons[3] desired his highness to take the place of estate,[4] to whom the King answered that he would go first

5. *perusing all*: stopping before each of.
6. *rounding him*: whispering to him (i.e. Sandys).
7. *appoint him*: point him out.   8. look.
9. another of Henry's favorites, who held many offices in the royal household. He was executed in 1538 during the Poles' conspiracy.
1. calculation.   2. *dashed out*: broke forth.   3. then.   4. honor.

and shift[5] his apparel; and so departed and went straight to my lord's bedchamber, where was a great fire made and prepared for him, and there new apparelled him with rich and princely garments. And in the time of the King's absence, the dishes of the banquet were clean[6] taken up and the table spread again with new and sweet-perfumed cloths, every man sitting still until the King and his maskers came in among them again, every man being newly apparelled. Then the King took his seat under the cloth of estate, commanding no man to remove but sit still as they did before. Then in came a new banquet before the King's majesty and to all the rest through the tables; wherein I suppose was served two hundred dishes or above of wonderous costly meats and devices, subtly devised. Thus passed they forth the whole night with banqueting, dancing and other triumphant devices,[7] to the great comfort of the King and pleasant regard of the nobility there assembled.

All this matter I have declared at large because ye shall understand what joy and delight the Cardinal had to see his prince and sovereign lord in his house so nobly entertained and pleased; which was always his only study, to devise things to his comfort, not passing of[8] the charges or expenses. It delighted him so much the King's pleasant princely presence, that nothing was to him more delectable than to cheer his sovereign lord, to whom he ought[9] so much obedience and loyalty; as reason required no less, all things well considered.

Thus passed the Cardinal his life and time from day to day and year to year in such great wealth, joy, triumph and glory, having always on his side the King's especial favor; until Fortune (of whose favor no man is longer assured than she is disposed) began to wax something wroth with his prosperous estate—thought she would devise a mean to abate his high port;[1] wherefore she procured Venus, the insatiate[2] goddess, to be her instrument to work her purpose. She brought the King in love with a gentlewoman that, after she perceived and felt the King's good will towards her, and how diligent he was

5. change.   6. completely.   7. pastimes.   8. *passing of:* caring about.
9. owed.   1. *mean . . . port:* way to bring down his proud bearing.
2. never satisfied.

both to please her and to grant all her requests, she wrought the Cardinal much displeasure, as hereafter shall be more at large declared. This gentlewoman, the daughter of Sir Thomas Boleyn,[3] being at that time but only a bachelor knight, the which after, for the love of his daughter, was promoted to higher dignities. He bare at divers several times for the most part all the rooms of estimation[4] in the King's house as Controller, Treasurer, Vice–chamberlain, and Lord Chamberlain. Then was he made Viscount Rochford, and at the last created Earl of Wiltshire and Knight of the noble Order of the Garter. And for his more increase of[5] gain and honor, he was made Lord Privy Seal and most chiefest of the King's privy council, continuing therein until his son[6] and daughter did incur the King's indignation and displeasure. The King fantasied[7] so much his daughter Anne that almost everything began to grow out of frame and good order.

To tell you how the King's love began to take place and what followed thereof, I will do even as much as in me lieth declare you.[8] This gentlewoman, Mistress Anne Boleyn, being very young, was sent into the realm of France, and there made one of the French Queen's women, continuing there until the French Queen died.[9] And then was she sent for home again and, being again with her father, he made such means[1] that she was admitted to be one of Queen Catherine's maids; among whom, for her excellent gesture[2] and behavior, [she] did excel

3. Sir Thomas Boleyn (1477–1539), who had quarrelled with Wolsey as early as 1515 and whose rise in the royal favor became rapid after 1522. Anne was probably born in 1507; she became Queen in 1533 and was executed in 1536.
4. *rooms of estimation:* important offices. Boleyn became controller in 1520 and treasurer in 1522. He apparently did not hold the offices of vice-chamberlain and chamberlain. A knight of the garter in 1523, he was made Lord Rochford in 1525, Earl of Wiltshire on December 8, 1529, and Lord Privy Seal on January 24, 1530.
5. *his . . . of:* the greater increase of his.
6. George Boleyn, executed on a charge of treason and incest on May 17, 1536, two days before his sister.   7. doted on.
8. *declare you:* to tell you.
9. Claude, the consort of Francis I, died in 1524, but Anne had returned to England by January 1522. The Percy episode occurred before October of that year.   1. *made such means:* so managed it.
2. bearing.

all other, in so much as the King began to kindle the brand of amours, which was not known to any person, ne scantly³ to her own person.

In so much [that] my Lord Percy,⁴ the son and heir of the Earl of Northumberland, who then attended upon the Lord Cardinal, and was also his servitor;⁵ and when it chanced the Lord Cardinal at any time to repair to the court, the Lord Percy would then resort for his pastime unto the Queen's chamber, and there would fall in dalliance⁶ among the Queen's maidens, being at the last more conversant⁷ with Mistress Anne Boleyn than with any other; so that there grew such a secret love between them, that at length they were insured⁸ together, intending to marry. The which thing came to the King's knowledge, who was then much offended; wherefore he could hide no longer his secret affection, but revealed his secret intendment unto my Lord Cardinal in that behalf, and consulted with him to infringe the precontract⁹ between them.

In so much that after my Lord Cardinal was departed from the court and returned home unto his place at Westminster, not forgetting the King's request and counsel, being in his gallery, called there before him the said Lord Percy unto his presence, and before us his servants of his chamber, saying thus unto him: "I marvel not a little," quod he, "of thy peevish folly, that thou wouldest tangle and insure thyself with a foolish girl yonder in the court, I mean Anne Boleyn. Dost thou not consider the estate that God hath called thee unto in this world? For after the death of thy noble father thou art most like to inherit and possess one of the most worthiest earldoms of this realm. Therefore it had been most meet and convenient¹ for thee to have sued for the consent of thy father in that behalf and to have also made the King's highness privy thereto, requiring² then his princely favor, submitting all thy whole proceeding in all such matters unto his highness; who would not only accept thankfully your submission, but would,

3. *ne scantly:* nor hardly.
4. Henry Algernon Percy, sixth Earl of Northumberland (1502?–1537), who was brought up in Wolsey's household.   5. attendant, retainer.
6. amorous play.   7. intimate.   8. engaged.
9. *infringe the precontract:* break the engagement.
1. *meet and convenient:* fitting and suitable.   2. asking.

I assure thee, provide so for your purpose therein that he would advance you much more nobly and have matched you according to your estate and honor. Whereby ye might have grown so by your wisdom and honorable behavior into the King's high estimation that it should have been much to your increase of honor.

"But now behold what ye have done through your wilfulness. Ye have not only offended your natural father but also your most gracious sovereign lord, and matched yourself with one such as neither the King ne[3] yet your father will be agreeable with[4] the matter. And hereof I put you out of doubt that I will send for your father, and at his coming he shall either break this unadvised contract or else disinherit thee forever. The King's majesty himself will complain to thy father on[5] thee and require no less at his hands than I have said; whose highness intended to have preferred her unto another person, with whom the king hath travailed[6] already, and being almost at a point[7] with the same person (although she knoweth it not) yet hath the King, most like a politick[8] and a prudent prince, conveyed[9] the matter in such sort that she, upon the King's motion,[1] will be (I doubt not) right glad and agreeable to the same."

"Sir," quod the Lord Percy (all weeping), "I knew nothing of the King's pleasure therein (for whose displeasure I am very sorry). I considered that I was of good years and thought myself sufficient to provide me of a convenient[2] wife whereas my fancy served me best, not doubting but that my lord my father would have been right well persuaded. And though she be a simple maid, and having but a knight to her father, yet is she descended of right noble parentage. As by her mother she is nigh of[3] the Norfolk blood; and of her father['s] side lineally descended of the Earl of Ormond, he being one of the Earl's heirs general. Why should I then (sir) be anything

3. nor.   4. to.   5. of.   6. labored, negotiated.
7. *being . . . point:* having almost made an agreement.
8. politically sagacious.   9. managed.
1. *upon . . . motion:* when she hears the king's plan.   2. suitable.
3. *nigh of:* near to. Thomas Boleyn had married Elizabeth Howard, daughter of Thomas Howard, afterwards second Duke of Norfolk. Anne's paternal grandfather married Margaret Butler, daughter of Sir Thomas Ormond, later seventh Earl of Ormond.

scrupulous to match with her, whose estate of descent is equivalent with mine, when I shall be in most dignity? Therefore I most humbly require your grace of your especial favor herein; and also to entreat the King's most royal majesty most lowly[4] on my behalf for his princely benevolence in this matter, the which I cannot deny or forsake."

"Lo, sirs," quod the Cardinal, "ye may see what conformity or wisdom is in this wilful boy's head! I thought that when thou heardest me declare the King's intended pleasure and travail herein, thou wouldest have relented and wholly submitted thyself and all thy wilful and unadvised fact[5] to the King's royal will and prudent pleasure to be fully disposed and ordered by his grace's disposition as his highness should seem good."[6] "Sir, so I would," quod the Lord Percy, "but in this matter I have gone so far before so many worthy witnesses that I know not how to avoid[7] myself nor to discharge[8] my conscience. "Why, thinkest thou," quod the Cardinal, "that the King and I know not what we have to do in as weighty a matter as this?" "Yes," quod he. "I warrant thee; howbeit, I can see in thee no submission to the purpose." "Forsooth, my lord," quod my Lord Percy, "if it please your grace, I will submit myself wholly to the King's majesty and grace in this matter, my conscience being discharged of the weighty burden of my precontract." "Well then," quod the Cardinal, "I will send for your father out of the north parties,[9] and he and we shall take such order for the avoiding of[1] this thy hasty folly[2] as shall be by the King thought most expedient. And in the mean season,[3] I charge thee and in the King's name command thee that thou presume not once to resort into her company, as thou intendest to avoid the King's high indignation." And this said, he rose up and went into his chamber.

Then was the Earl of Northumberland[4] sent for in all haste in the King's name, who, upon knowledge of the King's pleasure made quick speed to the court. And at his first coming out

4. humbly.   5. *unadvised fact:* rash deed.
6. *as . . . good:* as should seem good to his highness
7. withdraw.   8. relieve.   9. parts.
1. *the avoiding of:* disembarrassing thee from.
2. *this . . . folly:* this hasty folly of thine.   3. time.
4. The fifth Earl (d. 1527).

of the North he made his first repair unto my Lord Cardinal, at whose mouth he was advertized in[5] the cause of his hasty sending for, being in my Lord Cardinal's gallery with him in secret communication a long while. And after their long talk my Lord Cardinal called for a cup with wine and, drinking together, they brake up;[6] and so departed the Earl, upon whom we were commanded to wait and to convey him to his servants. And in his going away, when he came to the gallery's end, he sat him down upon a form[7] that stood there for the waiters sometime to take their ease.

And being there set, called his son the Lord Percy unto him and said, in our presence, thus in effect: "Son," quod he, "thou hast always been a proud, presumptuous, disdainful, and a very unthrift[8] waster. And even so hast thou now declared thyself. Therefore what joy, what comfort, what pleasure, or solace should I conceive in thee that thus without discretion and advisement[9] hast misused[1] thyself, having no manner of regard to me thy natural father, ne in especial unto thy sovereign lord, to whom all honest and loyal subjects beareth faithful and humble obedience; ne yet to the wealth[2] of thine own estate, but hath so unadvisedly insured[3] thyself to her for whom thou hast purchased thee the King's displeasure, intolerable for any subject to sustain! But that his grace of his mere[4] wisdom doth consider the lightness of thy head and wilful qualities of thy person, his displeasure and indignation were sufficient to cast me and all my posterity into utter subversion[5] and desolation. But he, being my especial and singular good lord and favorable prince, and my Lord Cardinal my good lord, hath and doth clearly excuse me in thy lewd fact,[6] and doth rather lament thy lightness, than malign the same; and hath devised an order to be taken for thee, to whom both thou and I be more bound than we be able well to consider.

"I pray to God that this may be to thee a sufficient monition[7] and warning to use[8] thyself more wittier[9] hereafter; for thus I assure thee, if thou dost not amend thy prodigality, thou wilt

5. *advertized in:* informed of.   6. *brake up:* separated.   7. bench.
8. unthrifty, profligate.   9. advice.   1. misconducted.
2. well-being.   3. engaged.   4. utter, total.   5. ruin.
6. *lewd fact:* villainous deed.   7. admonition.   8. conduct, behave.
9. more intelligently.

be the last Earl of our house. For of thy natural inclination thou art disposed to be wasteful-prodigal and to consume all that thy progenitors hath with great travail gathered together and kept with honor. But having the King's majesty my singular good and gracious lord, I intend (God willing) so to dispose my succession that ye shall consume thereof but a little; for I do not purpose (I assure thee) to make thee mine heir for, praises be to God, I have more choice of boys who, I trust, will prove themselves much better and use them more like unto nobility; among whom I will choose and take the best and most likeliest to succeed me.

"Now, masters and good gentlemen," quod he unto us, "it may be your chances hereafter when I am dead to see the proof of these things that I have spoken to my son prove as true as I have spoken them. Yet, in the mean season, I desire you all to be his friend and to tell him his fault when he doth amiss, wherein ye shall show yourselves to be much his friends." And with that he took his leave of us, and said to his son thus, "go your ways and attend upon my lord's grace your master and see that you do your duty." And so departed and went his ways down through the hall into his barge.

Then after long debating and consultation upon the Lord Percy's assurance,[1] it was devised that the same should be infringed[2] and dissolved and that the Lord Percy should marry with one of the Earl of Shrewsbury's daughters,[3] as he did after; by means whereof the former contract was clearly undone. Wherewith Mistress Anne Boleyn was greatly offended, saying that if it lay ever in her power she would work the Cardinal as much displeasure (as she did indeed after). And yet was he nothing to blame, for he practised[4] nothing in that matter but it was the King's only device.[5] And even as my Lord Percy was commanded to avoid her company, even so was she commanded to avoid the court and she sent home again to her father for a season, whereat she smoked;[6] for all this while she knew nothing of the King's intended purpose.

1. engagement.   2. broken.
3. Mary Talbot, whom Percy married in late 1523 or early 1524. The marriage was a most unhappy one.   4. connived.
5. the . . . device: the plot of the King alone.   6. fumed.

But ye may see when Fortune beginneth to lower[7] how she can compass[8] a matter to work displeasure by a far-fetch.[9] For now mark, good reader, the grudge, how it began, that in process[1] burst out to the utter undoing of the Cardinal. O Lord, what a God art thou, that workest thy secrets so wondersly![2] Which be not perceived until they be brought to pass and finished. Mark this history following, good reader, and note every circumstance, and thou shall espy at thine eye the wonderful works of God against such persons as forgetteth God and his great benefits. Mark, I say, mark them well.

After that all these troublesome matters of my Lord Percy's was brought to a good stay,[3] and all things finished that was before devised, Mistress Anne Boleyn was revoked[4] unto the court, where she flourished after in great estimation and favor; having always a privy indignation unto the Cardinal for breaking of the precontract made between my Lord Percy and her, supposing that it had been his own device and will[5] and none other, not yet being privy to[6] the King's secret mind,[7] although that he had[8] a great affection unto her. Howbeit after she knew the King's pleasure and the great love that he bare her in the bottom of his stomach, then began she to look very hault and stout,[9] having all manner of jewels or rich apparel that might be gotten with money. It was therefore judged by and by through all the court of every man that she, being in such favor with the King, might work masteries[1] with the King and obtain any suit of him for her friend. And all this while, she being in this estimation in all places, it is no doubt but good Queen Catherine, having this gentlewoman daily attending upon her, both heard by report and perceived before her eyes the matter how it framed[2] against her (good lady); although she showed (to Mistress Anne, ne[3] unto the King) any spark or kind of grudge or displeasure, but took and accepted all things in good part and with wisdom and great

7. frown.   8. arranged, devise.   9. *by a far-fetch:* in a roundabout way.
1. *in process:* in the course of time.   2. wonderfully.   3. state.
4. called back.   5. *device and will:* idea and desire.
6. *privy to:* aware of.   7. intention.
8. *although . . . had:* i.e. although she knew that he had etc.
9. *hault and stout:* high and mighty.   1. *work masteries:* do wonders.
2. was framed.   3. nor.

patience dissimuled[4] the same, having Mistress Anne in more estimation for the King's sake than she had before; declaring herself thereby to be a perfect Griseld,[5] as her patient acts[6] shall hereafter more evidently to all men be declared.

The King waxed so far in amours with this gentlewoman that he knew not how much he might advance her. This perceiving, the great lords of the council, bearing a secret grudge against the Cardinal because that they could not rule in the commonweal (for him)[7] as they would, who kept them low and ruled them as well as other mean[8] subjects; whereat they caught an occasion to invent a mean[9] to bring him out of the King's high favor and them into more authority of rule and civil governance. After long and secret consultation among themselves how to bring their malice to effect against the Cardinal, they knew right well that it was very difficile[1] for them to do anything directly of themselves. Wherefore they, perceiving the great affection that the King bare lovingly unto Mistress Anne Boleyn, fantasying[2] in their heads that she should be for them a sufficient and an apt instrument to bring their malicious purpose to pass, with whom they often consulted in this matter. And she, having both a very good wit and also an inward desire to be revenged of[3] the Cardinal, was as agreeable to their requests as they were themselves. Wherefore there was no more to do but only to imagine[4] some pretensed[5] circumstance to induce[6] their malicious accusation. In so much that there was imagined and invented among them divers imaginations and subtle devices how this matter should be brought about. The enterprise thereof was so dangerous that, though they would fain have often attempted the matter with the King, yet they durst not; for they knew the great loving affection and the especial favor that the King bare to the Cardinal, and also they feared the wonder wit[7] of the Cardinal. For this they understood very well, that if their matter that they should propone[8] against him were not grounded upon a just

4. dissembled.   5. Griselda, as in Chaucer's *Clerk's Tale*.
6. saintly deeds.   7. i.e. because of him.   8. low.
9. *invent a mean:* find a way.   1. difficult.   2. imagining.   3. on.
4. conceive.   5. alleged, pretended.   6. introduce.
7. *wonder wit:* amazing intelligence.   8. propose.

and an urgent cause, the King's favor being such towards him and his wit such, that he would with policy[9] vanquish all their purpose and travail and then lie in a wait[1] to work them an utter destruction and subversion. Wherefore they were compelled, all things considered, to forbear their enterprise until they might espy a more convenient time and occasion.

And yet the Cardinal, espying the great zeal that the King had conceived in this gentlewoman, ordered himself to please as well the King as her, dissimuling[2] the matter that lay hid in his breast, and prepared great banquets and solemn feasts to entertain them both at his own house. And thus the world began to grow into wonderful inventions[3] not heard of before in this realm. The love between the King and this gorgeous lady grew to such a perfection that divers imaginations were imagined,[4] whereof I leave to speak until I come to the place where I may have more occasion.

Then began a certain grudge to arise between the French King and the Duke of Bourbon,[5] in so much as the Duke, being vassal to the house of France, was constrained for the safeguard of his person to flee his dominion and to forsake his territory and country, doubting[6] the King's great malice and indignation. The Cardinal, having thereof intelligence, compassed[7] in his head that if the King our sovereign lord (having an occasion of wars with the realm of France) might retain the Duke to be his general in his wars there; in as much as the Duke was fled unto the Emperor, to invite him[8] also to stir wars against the French King. The Cardinal, having all this imagination in his head, thought it good to move the King in this matter. And after the King was once advertized hereof, and conceived[9] the Cardinal's imagination and invention, he dreamed of this matter more and more, until at the last it came in question among the council in consultation. So that it was

9. political cunning.   1. *in a wait:* in ambush.   2. dissembling.
3. *grow . . . inventions:* be filled with remarkable innovations.
4. *divers . . . imagined:* various opinions were entertained.
5. Charles, Duke of Bourbon (1489–1527), whose revolt from Francis I began in the early 1520's. His negotiations with Charles V and Henry VIII took place in 1523.   6. fearing.   7. plotted.   8. i.e. Charles V.
9. comprehended.

there finally concluded that an ambasset[1] should be sent to the Emperor about this matter; with whom it was concluded that the King and the Emperor should join in these wars against the French King and that the Duke of Bourbon should be our sovereign lord's champion[2] and general in the field, who had appointed him a great number of good soldiers over and besides the Emperor's army, which was not small, and led by one of his own noblemen, and also that the King should pay the Duke his wages and his retinue monthly. In so much as Sir John Russell[3] (which was after Earl of Bedford) lay continually beyond the seas in a secret place assigned, both for to receive the King's money and to pay the same monthly to the Duke. So that the Duke began fierce war with the French King in his own territory and dukedom, which the French King had confiscate and seized into his hands, yet not known to the Duke's enemies that he had any aid of the King our sovereign lord. And thus he wrought the French King much trouble and displeasure; in so much as the French King was compelled of fine force[4] to put harness on his back[5] and to prepare a puissant army royal, and in his own person to advance to defend[6] and resist the Duke's power and malice. The Duke, having understanding of the King's advancement,[7] was compelled of force to take Pavia, a strong town in Italy, with his host[8] for their security; whereas the King besieged him and encamped him[9] wonderous strongly, intending to enclose the Duke within this town that he should not issue.[1] Yet notwithstanding the Duke would and did many times issue and skirmish with the King's army.

Now let us leave the King in his camp before Pavia and return to the Lord Cardinal, who seemed to be more French than imperial. But how it came to pass I cannot declare[2] you, but the King, lying in his camp, sent secretly into England

1. embassy.   2. military representative.
3. Sir John Russell (1486?–1555), created Earl of Bedford in 1550.
4. *of fine force:* of necessity.   5. *put . . . back:* take up arms.
6. defend himself against.   7. advance.   8. army.
9. surrounded him. In actual fact Bourbon was not with the imperial army that was besieged by Francis I at Pavia. He led an attacking force which broke the siege.
1. *that . . . issue:* so that he could not come forth.   2. tell.

a privy person,[3] a very witty,[4] to treat of a peace between him and the King our sovereign lord, whose name was John Jokin.[5] He was kept as secret as might be that no man had intelligence of his repair,[6] for he was no Frenchman but an Italian born, a man before of no estimation in France or known to be in favor with his master, but to be a merchant, and for his subtle wit elected to entreat of such affairs as the King had commanded him by ambasset. This Jokin, after his arrival here in England, was secretly conveyed unto the King's manor of Richmond and there remained until Whitsuntide, at which time the Cardinal resorted thither and kept there the said feast very solemnly. In which season my lord caused this Jokin divers times to dine with him, whose talk and behavior seemed to be witty, sober and wonderous discreet. Who continued in England long after until he had (as it seemed) brought his purposed ambasset[7] to pass which he had in commission. For after this there was sent out immediately a restraint unto Sir John Russell into those parties[8] where he made his abiding beyond the seas, that he should retain and keep back that month['s] wages still in his hands, which should have been paid unto the Duke of Bourbon (until the King's pleasure were to him further known). For want of which money at the day appointed of payment, the Duke and his retinue were greatly dismayed and sore disappointed, when they saw that their money was not brought unto them as it was wont to be.

And being in so dangerous a case[9] for want of victuals, which was wonderous skant[1] and dear, there was many imaginations[2] what should be the cause of the let[3] thereof. Some said this and some said they wist never what; so that they mistrusted[4] no thing less than the very[5] cause thereof. In so much at the last, what for want of victual and other necessaries which could not be gotten within the town, the captains and soldiers began to grudge and mutter; and, at the last, for lack

3. *privy person:* confidential agent.   4. *a very witty:* a very clever one.
5. Jean Joachim de Passano, who arrived in London on June 22, 1524.
6. *that . . . repair:* so that no one knew the cause of his coming.
7. *purposed ambasset:* intended mission.   8. parts.   9. situation.
1. *wonderous skant:* exceedingly scarce.   2. conjectures.
3. stoppage (of the money).   4. suspected.   5. true.

of victual were like all to perish. They, being in this extremity, came before the Duke of Bourbon their captain and said: "Sir, we must be of very force and necessity compelled to yield us into the danger[6] of our enemies; and better it were for us so to do than here to starve like dogs." When the Duke heard their lamentations and understood the extremity that they were brought unto for lack of money, [he] said again unto them: "Sirs," quod he, "ye are both valiant men and of noble courage, who hath served here under me right worthily; and for your necessity,[7] whereof I am participant, I do not a little lament. Howbeit I shall desire you as you are noble in hearts and courage so to take patience for a day or twain; and if succor come not then from the King of England, as I doubt nothing[8] that he will deceive us, I will well agree that we shall all put ourselves and all our lives unto the mercy of our enemies."

Wherewith they were all agreeable. And expecting[9] the coming of the King's money the space of three days (the which days past), the Duke, seeing no remedy, called his noblemen and captains and soldiers before him and, all weeping, said: "O ye noble captains and valiant men, my gentle companions, I see no remedy in this necessity but either we must yield us unto our enemies or else famish. And to yield the town and ourselves—I know not the mercy of our enemies. And as for my part I pass not of[1] their cruelties, for I know very well that I shall suffer most cruel death if I come once into their hands. It is not for myself therefore that I do lament, but it is for your sakes, it is for your lives, it is also for the safeguard of your persons; for so that ye might escape the danger of your enemies' hands I would most gladly suffer death. Therefore, good companions and noble soldiers, I shall require you all, considering the dangerous misery and calamity that we stand in at this present,[2] to sell our lives most dearly rather than to be murdered like beasts. If ye will follow my counsel we will take upon us this night to give our enemies an assault to their camp, and by that means we may either

6. power.   7. difficult plight.
8. *as . . . nothing:* for I have no fear.   9. awaiting.
1. *pass not of:* am not concerned about.   2. present moment.

escape or else give them an overthrow. And thus it were better
to die in the field like men than to live in captivity and misery
as prisoners."

To the which they all agreed. Then, quod the Duke, "ye
perceive that our enemies hath encamped us with a strong
camp and that there is no way to enter but one, which is so
planted with great ordnance[3] and force of men that it is not
possible to enter that ways to fight with our enemies without
great danger. And also ye see that now of late they have had
small doubt[4] of us, in so much as they have kept but slender
watch. Therefore my policy and device shall be this: that
about the dead time of the night when our enemies be most
quiet at rest, shall issue from us a number of the most deliver-
est[5] soldiers to assault their camp; who shall give the assault
right fiercely even directly against the entry of the camp,
which is almost invincible. Your fierce and sharp assault shall
be to them in the camp so doubtful[6] that they shall be compelled to turn the strength of their entry that lieth over against
your assault to beat you from the assault. Then will I issue
out at the postern[7] and come to the place of their strength
newly turned; and there, or they beware,[8] will I enter and
fight with them at the same place where their guns and strength
lay before, and so come to the rescue of you of the sault.[9]
And winning their ordnance, which they have turned, and
beat them with their own pieces, and then we, joining together
in the field, I trust we shall have a fair hand of them." This
device pleased them wonderous well. Then prepared they all
that day for the purposed device,[1] and kept them secret and
close without any noise or shot of pieces within the town,
which gave their enemies the less fear of any trouble that
night, but every man went to their rest within their tents and
lodgings quietly, nothing mistrusting[2] that after ensued.

Then when all the King's host was at rest, the assailants
issued out of the town without any noise, according to the

3. cannon.   4. *small doubt:* little fear.   5. agile.
6. pressing (so as to cause fear of the outcome).   7. small back gate.
8. *or they beware:* before they know what is happening.   9. first assault.
1. *purposed device:* intended stratagem.   2. suspecting.

former appointment, and gave a fierce and cruel assault at the place appointed, that they within the camp had as much ado to defend as was possible to resist. And even as the Duke had before declared to his soldiers, they within were compelled to turn their shot that lay at their entry against the assailants. With that issued the Duke and with him about fifteen or sixteen thousand men or more, and secretly in the night, his enemies being not privy[3] of his coming until he was entered the field. And at his first entry he was master of all the ordnance that lay there and slew the gunners and charged the said pieces and bent them against his enemies, whom he slew wondersly[4] a great number. He cut down tents and pavilions and murdered them within them or they wist of their coming, suspecting nothing less than the Duke's entry. So that he won the field[5] or ever the King could arise to the rescue, who was taken in his lodging or ever he was armed.

And when the Duke had obtained the field and the French King taken prisoner, his men slain and his tents robbed and spoiled, which was wonderous rich; and in the spoil, searching of the King's treasure in his coffers, there was found among them the league newly concluded between the King of England and the French King under the Great Seal of England. Which once by him perceived, he began to smell the impediment of his money, which should have come to him from the King, having (upon due search of this matter) further intelligence that all this matter and his utter undoing was concluded and devised by the Cardinal of England. And the Duke, conceiving such an indignation hereupon against the Cardinal that, after he had established all things there in good order and security, he went incontinent[6] unto Rome, intending there to sack the town and to have taken the Pope prisoner; where, at his first assault of the walls, he was the first man that was there slain. Yet notwithstanding his captains continued there the assault and, in conclusion, won the town and the Pope

---

3. aware.   4. wonderfully.
5. The Battle of Pavia was fought on the night of February 24–25, 1525.
6. immediately.

fled unto Castle Angel, where he continued long after in great calamity.[7]

I have written thus this history at large because it was thought that the Cardinal gave the chief occasion of all this mischief. Ye may perceive what thing so ever a man purposeth, be he prince or prelate, yet notwithstanding God disposeth all things at His will and pleasure. Wherefore it is great folly for any wise man to take any weighty enterprise of himself, trusting altogether to his own will, not calling for grace to assist him in all his proceedings. I have known and seen in my days that princes and great men [who] would either assemble at any parliament or in any other great business first would most reverently call to God for His gracious assistance therein; and now I see the contrary. Wherefore me seems that they trust more in their own wisdoms and imaginations than they do to God's help and disposition. And therefore often they speed thereafter[8] and their matters take such success. Therefore not only in this history but in divers others ye may perceive right evident examples. And yet I see no man in authority or high estate almost[9] regard or have any respect to the same (the greater is the pity and the more to be lamented). Now will I desist from this matter and proceed to other.

Upon the taking of the French King many consultations and divers opinions were then in argument among the council here in England. Whereof some held opinion that if the King would invade the realm of France in proper[1] person with a puissant army royal he might easily conquer the same, considering that the French King and the most part of the noble peers of France were then prisoners with the Emperor. Some again said how that were no honor for the King our sovereign lord (the King being in captivity). But some said that the French King ought by the law of arms to be the King's prisoner; for as much as he was taken by the King's captain general (the Duke of Bourbon) and not by the Emperor's, so that some moved the King to take war thereupon with the Emperor,

7. Bourbon did not in fact attack Rome until May 6, 1527. Clement VII was not allowed to leave the Castello San Angelo until December.
8. *speed thereafter:* come to such an end afterwards.
9. scarcely, even.   1. his own.

unless he would deliver the French King out of his hands and possession; with divers many other imaginations and inventions even as every man's fantasies served them, too long here to be rehearsed, the which I leave to the writers of chronicles.

Thus continuing long in debating upon this matter, and every man in the court had their talk as will without wit led their fantasies. At the last it was devised by means of divers ambassets sent into England out of the realm of France, desiring the King our sovereign lord to take order with the Emperor for the French King's delivery as his royal wisdom should seem good.[2] Wherein the Cardinal bare the stroke.[3] So that after long deliberation and advice taken in this matter it was thought good by the Cardinal that the Emperor should redeliver[4] out of his ward the French King upon sufficient pledges; and that the King's two sons, that is to say the Dauphin and the Duke of Orleans, should be delivered in hostage for the King their father, which was in conclusion brought to pass.

Then after the King's delivery out from the Emperor's use[5] and the King's our sovereign lord's security for the recompense of all such demands and restitutions as should be demanded of the French King, the Cardinal, lamenting the French King's calamity and the Pope's great adversity (which yet remained in Castle Angel) either as a prisoner or else for his defense and safeguard (I cannot tell whether),[6] travailed[7] all that he could with the King and his council to take order as well for the delivery of the one, as for the quietness of the other. At last, as ye have heard heretofore, how divers of the great estates[8] and lords of the council lay in a wait[9] with my Lady Anne Boleyn to espy a convenient time and occasion to take the Cardinal in a brake,[1] thought it then that now is the time come that we have expected,[2] supposing it best to cause him to take upon him the King's commission and to travel beyond the seas in this matter; saying (to encourage him

---

2. *as . . . good:* as should seem good to his royal wisdom.
3. *bare the stroke:* achieved a triumph.   4. surrender.   5. control.
6. which.   7. (he) labored.   8. noblemen.   9. *in a wait:* in ambush.
1. snare, trap.   2. awaited.

thereto) that it were more meet for his high discretion, wit and authority to compass[3] and bring to pass a perfect peace among these great and most mighty princes of the world than any other within this realm or elsewhere.

Their intents and purpose was only but to get him out of the King's daily presence and to convey him out of the realm, that they might have convenient leisure and opportunity to adventure[4] their long-desired enterprise; and by the aid of their chief mistress (my Lady Anne) to deprave[5] him so unto the King in his absence that he should be rather in his high displeasure than in his accustomed favor, or at the least to be in less estimation with his majesty. Well, what will you have more? This matter was so handled that the Cardinal was commanded to prepare himself to this journey, the which he was fain to take upon him; but whether it was with his good will or no, I am not well able to tell you. But this I knew, that he made a short abode after the determinate[6] resolution thereof, but caused all things to be prepared onward toward his journey, and everyone of his servants were appointed that should attend upon him in the same.

When all things was fully concluded and for this noble ambasset provided and furnished, then was no let[7] but advance forwards in the name of good. My Lord Cardinal had with him such of the lords and bishops and other worthy persons as were not privy of the conspiracy.

Then marched he forward out of his own house at Westminster,[8] passing through all London, over London Bridge. having before him of gentlemen a great number, three in a rank, in black velvet livery coats, and the most part of them with great chains of gold about their necks, and all his yeomen, with noblemen and gentlemen's servants, following him in French tawny[9] livery coats; having embroidered upon their backs and breasts of the same coats these letters, T and C,[1] under the Cardinal's hat. His sumpter[2] mules, which were twenty in number and more, with his carts and other carriages

3. accomplish.   4. risk, dare.   5. vilify.   6. final.   7. delay.
8. Wolsey left London on July 3, 1527 and returned to the King at Richmond on Se. pember 30.   9. i.e. cloth of a tawny color.
1. standing for "Thomas Cardinal (Wolsey)."   2. pack.

of his train, were passed on before, conducted and guarded
with a great number of bows and spears. He rode like a Cardinal, very sumptuously on a mule, trapped with³ crimson
velvet upon velvet, and his stirrups of copper and gilt, and his
spare mule following him with like apparel. And before him he
had his two great crosses of silver, two great pillars of silver, the
Great Seal of England, his Cardinal's hat, and a gentleman
that carried his valance, otherwise called a cloak bag, which
was made altogether of fine scarlet cloth, embroidered over
and over with cloth of gold very richly, having in it a cloak
of fine scarlet. Thus passed he through London and all the
way of his journey, having his harbingers passing before to
provide lodgings for his train.

The first journey he made to Dartford in Kent unto Sir
Richard Wiltshire's house, which is two miles beyond Dartford, where all his train were lodged that night and in the
country thereabout. The next day he rode to Rochester and
lodged in the Bishop's palace there and the rest of his train in
the city and in Stroud on this side the bridge. The third
day he rode from thence to Feversham and there was lodged
in the abbey and his train in the town and some in the country
thereabouts. The fourth day he rode to Canterbury, where he
was encountered with the worshipfullest⁴ of the town and
country and lodged in the Abbey of Christ's Church in the
prior's lodging, and all his train in the city; where he continued three or four days, in which time there was the great
Jubilee and a fair in honor of the feast of Saint Thomas, their
patron. In which day of the said feast within the Abbey there
was made a solemn procession and my Lord Cardinal [went]
presently in the same, apparelled in his legantine ornaments
with his Cardinal's hat on his head; who commanded the
monks and all their choir to sing the litany after this sort,
Sancta Maria, ora pro Papa nostro Clemente and so perused
the litany through, my Lord Cardinal kneeling at the choir
door at a form⁵ covered with carpets and cushions, the monks
and all the choir standing all that while in the midst of the

3. *trapped with:* adorned with trappings of.   4. highest ranking.
5. kneeling bench.

body of the church. At which time I saw the Cardinal weep very tenderly; which was, as we supposed, for heaviness[6] that the Pope was at that present in such calamity and great danger of the Lance Knights.[7]

The next day I was sent with letters from my Lord Cardinal unto Calais by empost,[8] in so much as I was that same night in Calais. And at my landing I found standing upon the pier without Lantern Gate all the council of the town, to whom I delivered and dispatched my message and letters or[9] ever I entered the town. Whereas I lay two days after or my lord came thither; who arrived in the haven there two day after my coming about eight of the clock in the morning, where he was received in procession with all the worshipfullest persons of the town in most solemnest wise. And in the Lantern Gate was set for him a form with carpets and cushions, whereat he kneeled and made his prayers before his entry any further in the town; and there he was censed[1] with two great censers of silver and sprinkled with holy water. That done, he arose up and passed on with all that assembly before him, singing unto Saint Mary's Church, where he, standing at the high altar, turning himself to the people, gave them his benediction and clean remission.[2] And then they conducted him from thence unto an house called the Checker, where he lay and kept his house as long as he abode in the town (going immediately to his naked bed[3] because he was somewhat troubled with sickness in his passage upon the seas that night). Unto this place of the Checker resorted to him Monsieur du Biez, Captain of Boulogne, with a number of gallant gentlemen, who dined with him. And after some consultation with the Cardinal he, with the rest of the gentlemen, departed again to Boulogne. Thus the Cardinal was daily visited with one or other of the French nobility.

Then when all his train and carriages were landed at Calais and everything prepared in a readiness for his journey, he

6. sorrow.   7. German mercenaries in the imperial army.
8. *by empost:* as a special courier.   9. before.   1. offered incense.
2. *clean remission:* i.e. a plenary indulgence.
3. *naked bed:* i.e. removing his normal wearing apparel.

called before him all his noblemen and gentlemen into his privy chamber; where, they being assembled, [he] said unto them in this wise in effect: "I have," quod he, "called you hither to this intent, to declare unto you that I, considering the diligence that ye minister unto me and the good will that I bear you again for the same, intending to remember your diligent service hereafter in place where ye shall receive condign[4] thanks and rewards; and also I would show you further what authority I have received directly from the King's highness. And to instruct you somewhat of the nature of the Frenchmen, and then to inform you what reverence ye shall use unto me for the high honor of the King's majesty, and also how ye shall entertain the Frenchmen whensoever ye shall meet at any time: first, ye shall understand that the King's majesty, upon certain weighty considerations, hath for the more[5] advancement of his royal dignity assigned me in this journey to be his lieutenant-general. And what reverence belongeth to the same I will tell you. That for my part I must, by virtue of my commission of lieutenantship, assume and take upon me in all honor and degrees to have all such service and reverence as to his highness's presence is meet and due, and nothing thereof to be neglected or omitted by me that to his royal estate is appurtenant.[6] And for my part ye shall see me that I will not omit one jot thereof. Therefore, because ye shall not be ignorant in that behalf, is one of the especial causes of this your assembly, willing and command[ing] you as ye intend my favor,[7] not to forget the same in time and place, but every of you do observe this information and instruction as ye will at my return avoid the King's indignation, but to obtain his highness's thanks, the which I will further for you as ye shall deserve.

"Now to the point of the Frenchmen's nature. Ye shall understand that their disposition is such that they will be at the first meeting as familiar with you as[8] they had been acquainted with you long before and commune with you in the French tongue as though ye understood every word they

4. worthy.   5. greater.   6. *is appurtenant:* belongs.
7. *my favor:* to be favored by me.   8. as if.

spoke. Therefore in like manner; and be ye as familiar with them again as they be with you. If they speak to you in the French tongue, speak you to them in the English tongue; for if you understand not them, they shall no more understand you." And my lord speaking merrily to one of the gentlemen there (being a Welshman), said, "Rice," quod he, "speak thou Welsh to him, and I am well assured that thy Welsh shall be more diffuse[9] to him than his French shall be to thee." And then quod he again to us all, "let all your entertainment and behavior be according to all gentleness and humanity that it may be reported after your departure from thence that ye be gentlemen of right good havior[1] and of much gentleness, and that ye be men that knoweth your duty to your sovereign lord and to your master, allowing much[2] your great reverence. Thus shall ye not only obtain to yourselves great commendation and praise for the same, but also advance the honor of your prince and country. Now go your ways admonished of all these points and prepare yourselves against tomorrow, for then we intend (God willing) to set forward." And thus we being by him instructed and informed departed to our lodgings, making all things in a readiness against the next day to advance forth with my lord.

The next morrow being Mary Magdalen's day all things being furnished, my Lord Cardinal rode out of Calais with such a number of black velvet coats as hath not been seen with an ambassador. All the spears[3] of Calais, Guines, and Hammes were there attending upon him in this journey, in black velvet coats; many great and massy chains of gold were worn there.

Thus passed he forth with three gentlemen in a rank, which occupied the length of three quarters of a mile or more, having all his accustomed and glorious furniture carried before him even as I before have rehearsed, except the Broad Seal,[4] the which was left with Doctor Taylor in Calais, then Master of the Rolls, until his return. Passing thus on his way and

9. obscure.   1. behavior.   2. *allowing much:* accepting as true.
3. gentlemen-at-arms.
4. The Great Seal was not to leave the English domain. Yet in 1521 Wolsey had not hesitated to take it with him to Bruges.

being scant a mile of his journey, it began to rain so vehemently that I have not seen the like for the time,[5] that endured[6] until we came to Boulogne. And or[7] we came to Sandingfield the Cardinal of Lorraine, a goodly young gentleman, encountered my lord and received him with great reverence and joy. And so passed forth together until they came to Sandingfield, which is a place of religion[8] standing between the French, English, and the Emperor's dominions, being neuter,[9] holding of neither of them. And being come thither, met with him there Le Countie Brian, Captain of Picardy, with a great number of men of arms, as Stradiots and Arbanois,[1] with other standing in array in a great piece[2] of oats, all in harness[3] upon light horses, passing with my lord as it were in a wing all his journey through Picardy; for my lord somewhat doubted the Emperor, lest he would lay an ambush to betray him; for which cause the French King commanded them to await upon my lord for the assurance of his person out of the danger of his enemies.

Thus rode he accompanied until he came to the town of Boulogne, where he was encountered within a mile thereof with the worshipfullest citizens of the town, having among them a learned man that made to him an oration in Latin; unto the which my lord made answer semblably[4] in Latin. And that done Monsieur du Biez, Captain of Boulogne, with the retinue there of gentlemen met him on horseback; which conveyed him into the town with all this assembly, until he came to the abbey gate, where he lighted and went directly into the church and made his prayers before the image of Our Lady, to whom he made his offering. And that done he gave there his blessing to the people with certain days of pardon. Then went he into the abbey where he was lodged and his train were lodged in the high and base[5] towns.

The next morning after he heard Mass he rode unto Montreuil sur la mer, where he was encountered in like case[6] as he was the day before with the worshipfullest of the town, all in

5. *for the time:* at that time of year.   6. lasted.   7. before.
8. *of religion:* inhabited by religious orders.   9. neutral.
1. *Stradiots and Arbanois:* light-armed cavalry.   2. field.   3. armor.
4. fittingly.   5. low.   6. *like case:* a similar manner.

one livery, having one learned that made an oration before
him in Latin, whom he answered in like manner in Latin. And
as he entered into the town there was a canopy of silk embroidered with the letters and hat that was on their servants'
coats, borne over him with the most[7] persons of estimation
within the town. And when he was alighted his footmen seized
the same as a fee due to their office. Now was there made
divers pageants for joy of his coming, who was called there and
in all other places within the realm of France as he travelled,
Le Cardinal Pacifique; and in Latin, *Cardinalis Pacificus;*[8] who
was accompanied all that night with divers worthy gentlemen
of the country thereabout.

The next day he rode towards Abbeville, where he was encountered with divers gentlemen of the town and country, and
so conveyed unto the town, where he was most honorably received with pageants of divers kinds, wittily and costly invented,[9] standing in every corner of the streets as he rode
through the town; having a like canopy borne over him, being
of more richer sort than the other at Montreuil, or at Boulogne
was. They brought him to his lodging, which was as it seemed
a very fair house, newly built with brick. At which house
King Louis married my Lady Mary, King Harry the Eighth's
sister, which was after married to the Duke of Suffolk,
Charles Brandon.[1] And being within, it was in manner of a
gallery;[2] yet notwithstanding it was very necessary.[3] In this
house my lord remained either eight or ten days; to whom
resorted daily divers of the Council of France, feasting them
and other noblemen and gentlemen that accompanied the
council both at dinners and suppers.

Then when the time came that he should depart from thence,
he rode to a castle beyond the water of Somme, called Picquigny Castle, adjoining unto the said water, standing upon a
great rock or hill, within the which was a goodly college of

7. greatest.   8. i.e. the "peace-making cardinal."
9. *wittily . . . invented:* cleverly and expensively devised.
1. Mary and Louis XII were married on October 9, 1514. Louis died
on January 1, 1515 and Mary and Suffolk were married the following
spring.   2. *in . . . gallery:* shaped like a gallery, i.e. long and narrow.
3. commodious.

priests; the situation whereof was most like unto the Castle of Windsor in England. And there he was received with a solemn procession conveying[4] him first into the church and after unto his lodging within the castle. At this castle King Edward the Fourth met with the French King[5] upon the bridge that goeth over the water of Somme, as ye may read in the chronicles of England.

When my lord was settled within his lodging, it was reported unto me that the French King should come that day into Amiens, which was within six English miles of Picquigny Castle. And being desirous to see his first coming into the town, asked license, and took with me one or two gentlemen of my lord's, and rode incontinent[6] thither, as well to provide me of a necessary lodging as to see the King. And when we came thither, being but strangers,[7] took up our inn (for the time) at the sign of the Angel directly against[8] the west door of the cathedral church de Notre Dame Sainte Marie. And after we had dined there, and tarrying until three or four of clock expecting[9] the King's coming, in came Madame Regent (the King's mother)[1] riding in a very rich chariot; and in the same with her was her daughter, the Queen of Navarre,[2] furnished with an hundred ladies or gentlewomen or more following, riding upon white palfreys, over and besides divers other ladies and gentlewomen that rode some in rich chariots, and some in horse litters; who lighted at the west door with all this train, accompanied with many other noblemen and gentlemen besides her guard, which was not small in number.

Then within two hours after, the King came into the town with a great shot of guns and divers pageants made for the nonce[3] at the King's *bien venue;*[4] having about his person both before him and behind him, beside the wonderful number of noblemen and gentlemen, three great guards diversely ap-

4. escorting.
5. The meeting of Edward IV and Louis XI occurred on August 29, 1475, when the Treaty of Picquigny was signed.
6. immediately.   7. foreigners.   8. opposite.   9. awaiting.
1. Louise of Savoy (1476–1531).
2. Marguerite d'Orleans, who had married Henri d'Albret, King of Navarre, on January 3, 1526.   3. occasion.   4. welcome.

parelled. The first was of Souches[5] and Burgundians with guns
and halfhacks.[6] The second was of Frenchmen, some with
bows and arrows and some with bills.[7] The third guard was
pour le corps,[8] which was of tall Scots, much more comelier
persons than all the rest. The French guard and the Scots had
all one livery, which were rich coats of fine white cloth, with a
guard [9] of silver bullions[1] embroidered an handful broad.[2] The
King came riding upon a goodly jennet[3] and lighted at the west
door of the said church, and so [was] conveyed into the
church up to the high altar where he made his prayers upon
his knees; and then conveyed into the bishop's palace where
he was lodged and also his mother.

The next morning I rode again to Picquigny to attend upon
my lord, at which time my lord was ready to take his mule
towards Amiens. And passing on his journey thitherward he
was encountered from place to place with divers noble and
worthy personages, making to him divers orations in Latin, to
whom he made answer again *extempore;* at whose excellent
learning and pregnant wit they wondered [4] very much.

Then was word brought my lord that the King was coming
to encounter him; with that, he, having none other shift,[5] was
compelled to alight in an old chapel that stood by the highway
and there newly apparelled him into more richer apparel. And
then mounted upon a new mule very richly trapped with a
footcloth and trapper of crimson velvet upon velvet, purled [6]
with gold and fringed about with a deep fringe of gold, very
costly, his stirrups of silver and gilt, the bosses and checks of
his bridle of the same. And by that time that he was mounted
again after this most gorgeous sort, the King was come very
near, within less than a quarter of a mile English, mustering
upon an hillside, his guard standing in array along the same, expecting my lord's coming. To whom my lord made as much
haste as conveniently it became him, until he came within a
pair of butt lengths,[7] and there he stayed a while. The King,

5. Swiss.   6. small-sized hackbuts.   7. long staves terminating in a
short, hooked blade.   8. *pour le corps:* i.e. a bodyguard.   9. trimming.
1. ornamental fringes.   2. *handful broad:* full hand's breadth.
3. Spanish horse.   4. marvelled.   5. resource.   6. edged.
7. *a pair . . . lengths:* length of an archery range.

perceiving that, stood still and having two worthy gentlemen, young and lusty, being both brethren and brethren to the Duke of Lorraine and to the Cardinal of Lorraine; whereof one of them was called Monsieur de Guise, and the other Monsieur Vaudemont; they were both apparelled like the King in purple velvet lined with cloth of silver and their coats cut.[8] The King caused Monsieur Vaudemont to issue from him and to ride unto my lord to know the cause of his tracting;[9] who rode upon a fair courser, taking his race[1] in a full gallop even until he came unto my lord; and there caused his horse to come aloft once or twice so nigh my lord's mule that he[2] was in doubt[3] of his horse. And with that he lighted from his courser and doing his message to my lord with humble reverence; which done, he mounted again and caused his horse to do the same at his departing as he did before, and so repaired again to the King.

And after his answer made, the King advanced forward. That seeing, my lord did the like and in the midway they met, embracing each other on horseback with most amiable countenance, entertaining each other right nobly. Then drew into the place all noblemen and gentlemen on both sides with wonderful cheer made one to another as they had been of an old acquaintance. The press[4] was such and thick that divers had their legs hurt with horses. Then the King's officers cried, "Marche, marche devant, allez devant," [5] and the King and my Lord Cardinal (on his right hand) rode together to Amiens, every English gentleman accompanied with another of France. The train of French and English endured [6] two long miles, that is to say, from the place of their encounter unto Amiens; where they were very nobly received with shot of guns and costly pageants until the King had brought my lord to his lodging and there departed asunder for that night, the King being lodged in the bishop's palace.

The next day after dinner my lord with a great train of noblemen and gentlemen of England rode unto the King's court, at which time the King kept his bed, being somewhat

8. slashed (in the fashionable manner).   9. delaying.   1. run, course.
2. i.e. Wolsey.   3. fear.   4. throng.   5. "forward march."
6. stretched out for.

diseased.[7] Yet notwithstanding my lord came into his bed-chamber, where sat on the one side of his bed his mother, Madame Regent, and on the other side the Cardinal of Lorraine with divers other noblemen of France. And after a short communication and drinking of a cup of wine with the King's mother, my lord departed again to his lodging, accompanied with divers gentlemen and noblemen of France who supped with him. Thus continued the King and my lord in Amiens the space of two weeks and more, consulting and feasting each other divers times.

And in the feast of the Assumption of Our Lady my lord rose betimes[8] and went to the Cathedral Church de Notre Dame, and there before my Lady Regent and the Queen of Navarre in Our Lady Chapel he said his service and Mass; and after Mass he himself ministered the sacrament unto both my Lady Regent and to the Queen of Navarre. And that done the King resorted unto the church and was conveyed into a rich traverse[9] at the high altar's end; and directly against[1] him on the other side of the altar sat my Lord Cardinal in another rich traverse three gresses[2] higher than the King's. And at the altar before them both a bishop sang high Mass and at the fraction[3] of the host the same bishop divided the sacrament between the King and the Cardinal for the performance of the peace concluded between them; which Mass was sung solemnly by the King's chapel, having among them cornets and sackbuts.[4] And after Mass was done the trumpeters blew in the roodloft until the King was passed inward to his lodging out of the church. And at his coming into the bishop's palace, where he intended to dine with my Lord Cardinal, there sat within a cloister about two hundred persons diseased with the king's evil[5] (upon their knees). And the King or[6] ever he went to dinner perused[7] every of them with rubbing and blessing them with his bare hands, being bareheaded all the while; after whom followed his almoner distributing of money unto the persons diseased. And that done he said certain prayers over them and

7. ill. Francis I had chafed his leg while hunting.   8. early.
9. compartment enclosed by a screen.   1. opposite.   2. steps.
3. breaking.   4. early form of the slide trombone.
5. *king's evil*: scrofula.   6. before.   7. handled one by one.

then washed his hands and so came up into his chamber to dinner, where as my lord dined with him.

Then it was determined that the King and my lord should remove out of Amiens, and so they did to a town or city called Compiègne, which was more than twenty English miles from thence; unto which town I was sent to prepare my lord's lodging. And so as I rode on my journey, being upon a Friday, my horse chanced to cast a shoe in a little village where stood a fair castle. And as it chanced there dwelt a smith to whom I commanded my servant to carry my horse to shoe; and standing by him while my horse was a-shoeing, there came to me one of the servants of the castle, perceiving me to be the Cardinal's servant and an Englishman, who required me to go with him into the castle to my lord his master, whom he thought would be very glad of my coming and company. To whose request I granted because that I was always desirous to see and be acquainted with strangers, in especial with men in honor and authority. So I went with him, who conducted me unto the castle. And being entered in the first ward, the watchmen of that ward, being very honest tall men, came and saluted me most reverently. And knowing the cause of my coming, desired me to stay a little while until they had advertized my lord their master of my being there. And so I did.

And incontinent the lord of the castle came out to me, who was called Monsieur Crecqui, a nobleman born and very nigh of blood to King Louis, the last King that reigned before this King Francis. And at his first coming he embraced me, saying that I was right heartily welcome, and thanked me that I so gently would visit him and his castle, saying furthermore that he was preparing to encounter the King and my lord to desire them most humbly the next day to take[8] his castle in the way, if he could so entreat them. And true it is that he was ready to ride in a coat of velvet with a pair of velvet arming shoes[9] on his feet and a pair of gilt spurs on his heels. Then he took me by the hand and most gently led me into his castle through another ward. And being once entered into the base[1] court of the castle, I saw all his family and household servants stand-

8. stop over at.   9. *arming shoes:* shoes worn with armor.   1. lower.

ing in goodly order in black coats and gowns, like mourners; who led me into the hall, which was hanged with hand-guns as thick as one could hang by another upon the walls. And in the hall stood also an hawk's perk,[2] whereon stood three or four fair goshawks. Then went we into the parlor, which was hanged with fine old arras; and being there but a while, communing together of my Lord of Suffolk, how he was there to have besieged the same,[3] his servants brought to him bread and wine of divers sorts, whereof he caused me to drink. "And after," quod he, "I will show you the strength of my house, how hard it would have been for my Lord of Suffolk to have won it." Then led he me upon the walls, which was very strong, more than fifteen foot thick, and as well garnished[4] with battery pieces of ordnance[5] ready charged to shoot off against the King and my lord's coming.

When he had showed me all the walls and bulwarks about the castle, he descended from the walls and came down into a fair inner court where his jennet stood for to mount upon, with twelve other jennets, the most fairest beasts that ever I saw. And in especial his own, which was a mare jennet. He showed me that he might have had for her four hundred crowns. But upon the other twelve jennets were mounted twelve goodly young gentlemen called pages of honor, all bareheaded in coats of cloth of gold and black velvet cloaked, and on their legs boots of red Spanish leather and spurs parcel-gilt.[6] Then he took his leave of me, commanding his steward and other his gentlemen to attend upon me and conduct me unto my lady his wife to dinner. And that done he mounted upon his jennet and took his journey forth out of his castle. And then the steward with the rest of the gentlemen led me up into a tower in the gatehouse where then my lady their mistress lay for the time that the King and my lord should tarry there; I being in a fair great dining chamber, where the table was covered to dinner, and there I, attending my lady's coming.

And after she came thither out of her own chamber she re-

2. perch.
3. i.e. during the 1523 invasion of France when Brandon led the English forces.   4. equipped.   5. *battery . . . ordnance:* large cannon.
6. partially gilded.

ceived me most gently like an noble estate,[7] having a train of twelve gentlewomen. And when she with her train came all out, she said to me, "For as much," quod she, "as ye be an Englishman, whose customent[8] is in your country to kiss all ladies and gentlewomen without offence, and although it be not so here in this realm, yet will I be so bold to kiss you and so shall all my maidens." By means whereof I kissed my lady and all her women. Then went she to her dinner, being as nobly served as I have seen any of her estate here in England, having all the dinner time with me pleasant communication, which was of the usage and behavior of our gentlewomen and gentlemen of England, and commended much the behavior of them right excellently; for she was with the King at Ardres,[9] when the great encounter and meeting was between the French King and the King our sovereign lord; at which time she was both for her person and goodly havior[1] appointed to company with[2] the ladies of England. And to be short, after dinner, pausing a little, I took my leave of her and so departed and rode on my journey.

I passed so forth on my journey by reason of my tracting of [3] time in Castle de Crecqui, that I was constrained that night to lie in a town by the way called Montdidier, the suburbs whereof my Lord of Suffolk had lately burned. And in the next morning I took my journey and came to Compiègne upon the Saturday, then being there the market day. And at my first coming I took my inn in the midst of the market place, and being there set at dinner in a fair chamber that had a fair window looking into the street, I heard a great rumor[4] and clattering of bills. With that I looked out into the street and there I espied where the officers of the town brought a prisoner to execution, whose head they strake[5] off with a sword. And when I demanded [6] the cause of his offence, it was answered me that it was for killing of a red deer in the forest thereby, the punishment whereof is but death. Incontinent[7] they had

7. either "as if I were a nobleman" or "in a manner befitting her own social rank."   8. custom.
9. i.e. at the Field of the Cloth of Gold in June 1520.   1. behavior.
2. *company with:* accompany.   3. *tracting of:* prolonging the.
4. noise.   5. struck.   6. asked.   7. immediately.

set up the poor man's head upon a pole in the market place between the stag's horns, and his quarters in four parts of the forest.

Then went I about to prepare my lord's lodging and to see it furnished, which was there in the great castle of the town, whereof to my lord was assigned the one half and the other half was reserved for the King. And in like wise there was a long gallery divided between them, wherein was made in the midst thereof a strong wall with a door and window. And there the King and my lord would many times meet at the same window and secretly talk togethers and divers times they would go the one to the other at the said door.

Now was there lodged also Madame Regent, the King's mother, and all her train of ladies and gentlewomen. Unto which place the Chancellor of France[8] came (a very witty man) with all the King's grave counsellors, who took great pains daily in consultation. In so much as I heard my Lord Cardinal fall out with the Chancellor, laying unto his charge that he went about to hinder the league which my said Lord Cardinal had before his coming concluded between the King our sovereign lord and the French King his master. In so much that my lord stomached[9] the matter very stoutly[1] and told him that it should not lie in his power to dissolve the amiable fidelity between them. And if his master the King, being there present, forsake his promise and follow his counsel, he should not fail after his return into England to feel the smart, and what a thing it is to break promise with the King of England, whereof he should be well assured. And therewithal he arose and went into his own lodging, wondersly[2] offended. So that his stout countenance and bold words made them all in doubt how to pacify his displeasure and revoke him[3] again to the council, who was then departed in a fury. There was sending, there was coming, there was also entreating, and there was great submission made to him to reduce[4] him to his former friendly communication; who would in no wise relent until Madame Regent came herself, who handled the matter so discreetly and

8. Antoine Duprat (1463–1535).   9. resented.   1. haughtily.
2. extremely.   3. *revoke him:* call him back.   4. restore.

wittily that she reconciled him to his former communication. And by that means he brought there matters to pass that before he could not attain nor cause the council to grant; which was more for fear than for any affection to the matter. He had the heads of all the council so under his girdle that he might rule them all there as well as he might the council of England.

The next morning after this conflict, he rose early in the morning about four of the clock, sitting down to write letters into England unto the King, commanding one of his chaplains to prepare him to Mass, in so much that his said chaplain stood revested [5] until four of the clock at afternoon. All which season my lord never rose once to piss, ne yet to eat any meat but continually wrote his letters with his own hands, having all that time his nightcap and keverchief [6] on his head. And about four of the clock at afternoon, he made an end of writing, commanding one Christopher Gunner, the King's servant, to prepare him without delay to ride empost[7] into England with his letters, whom he dispatched away or ever he drank. And that done, he went to Mass, and said his other divine service with his chaplain, as he was accustomed to do; and then went straight into a garden; and after he had walked the space of an hour or more, and there said his evensong, he went to dinner and supper all at once. And making a small repast, he went to his bed to take his rest for that night.

The next night following he caused a great supper to be provided for Madame Regent and the Queen of Navarre and other great estates of ladies and noble women. There was also Madame Renée,[8] one of the daughters of King Louis, whose sister King Francis had married (lately dead). These sisters were by their mother inheritrices[9] of the Duchy of Britanny, and for as much as the King had married one of the sisters, by whom he had the moiety[1] of the said duchy, and to attain the other moiety, and to be lord of the whole, he kept the said Lady Renée without marriage, intending that she, having none issue, that the whole duchy might descend to him or to his succession after her death for want of issue of her body.

5. in his vestments.   6. covering for the head.   7. in haste.
8. Renée, daughter of Louis XII. Francis I had married her sister Claude (d. 1524).   9. heiresses.   1. half.

But now let us return again to the supper or rather a solemn banquet, where all these noble persons were highly feasted. And in the midst of their triumph, the French King with the King of Navarre[2] came suddenly in upon them unknown, who took their places at the nether[3] end of the table. There was not only plenty of fine meats, but also much mirth and solace, as well in communication as in instruments of music set forth with my lord's minstrels, who played there so cunningly and dulce[4] all that night that the King took therein great pleasure, in so much that he desired my lord to lend them unto him the next night. And after supper and banquet finished, the ladies and gentlewomen went to dancing, among whom one Madame Fountaine, a maid, had the prize. And thus passed they the night in pleasant mirth and joy.

The next day the King took my lord's ministrels and rode unto a nobleman's house, where was some goodly image that he had avowed a pilgrimage unto, to perform his devotion. When he came there he danced and other with him the most part of that night. My lord's ministrels played there so excellently all that night that the shalm[5] (whether it were with extreme labor of blowing or with poisoning—as some judged—because they were more commended and accepted with the King than his own, I cannot tell), but he that played the shalm (an excellent man in that art) died within a day or twain after.

Then the King returned again unto Compiègne, and caused a wild boar to be lodged for him in the forest there; whither my lord rode with the King to the hunting of the wild swine within a toil;[6] where the Lady Regent stood in chariots or wagons, looking over the toil, on the outside thereof, accompanied with many ladies and damsels, among whom my lord stood by the Lady Regent to regard and behold the pastime and manner of hunting. There was within the toil divers goodly gentlemen with the King, ready garnished[7] to this high enterprise and dangerous hunting of the perilous wild swine, the King being in his doublet and hosen only, without

2. Henri d'Albret (1503–1555).
3. lower.   4. *cunningly and dulce:* expertly and sweetly.
5. an oboe-like instrument.   6. net into which game is driven.
7. equipped.

any other garments, all of sheep's color cloth. His hosen from the knee upward was altogether thrommed [8] with silk very thick of the same color: having in a slip[9] a fair brace of great white greyhounds, armed, as the manner is to arm their greyhounds, from the violence of the boar's tusks. And all the rest of the King's gentlemen, being appointed to hunt this boar, were likewise in their doublets and hosen, holding each of them in their hands a very sharp boar's spear.

The King being thus furnished, commanded the hunts[1] to uncouch[2] the boar, and that every other person should go to a standing,[3] among whom were divers gentlemen and yeomen of England. And incontinent[4] the boar issued out of his den, chased with an hound into the plain. And being there, [he] stalled [5] a while, gazing upon the people; and incontinent, being forced by the hound, he espied a little bush standing upon a bank over a ditch, under the which lay two gentlemen of France. And thither fled the boar to defend him, thrusting his head snuffing into the same bush where these two gentlemen lay, who fled with such speed as men do from the danger of death. Then was the boar by violence and pursuit of the hound and hunts driven from thence, and ran straight to one of my lord's footmen, a very comely person and an hardy, who held in his hand an English javelin, with the which he was fain to defend himself from the fierce assault of the boar, who foined [6] at him continually with his great tusks; whereby he was compelled at the last to pitch his javelin in the ground between him and the boar, the which the boar breke[7] with his force of foining. And with that the yeoman drew his sword and stood at defence; and with that the hunts came to the rescue and put him once again to flight.

With that he fled and ran to another young gentleman of England called Master Ratcliff, son and heir to the Lord Fitzwalter, and after Earl of Sussex,[8] who by chance had borrowed of a French gentleman a fine boar spear very sharp; upon whom the boar, being sore chafed, began to assault very ea-

8. fringed.   9. leash.   1. huntsmen.   2. release.   3. hunter's station.
4. immediately.   5. came to a stand.   6. lunged.   7. broke.
8. Henry Ratcliff (1506?–1557), Earl of Sussex in 1542.

gerly. And the young gentleman deliverly[9] avoided his strokes and in turning about he stroke the boar with such violence with the same spear (that he had borrowed) upon the houghs that he cut the sinews of both his legs at one stroke, that the boar was constrained to sit down upon his haunches and defend himself, for he could go no more. This gentleman, perceiving his most[1] advantage, thrust his spear into the boar under the shoulder up to the heart. And thus he slew the great boar. Wherefore among the noblemen of France it was reputed to be one of the noblest enterprises that a man might do, as though he had slain a man of arms. And thus our Master Ratcliff bare then away the prize of that feat of hunting this dangerous and royal pastime in killing of the wild boar, whose tusks the Frenchmen doth most commonly doubt[2] above all other dangers, as it seemed to us Englishmen then being present.

In this time of my Lord's being in France, over and besides his noble entertainment with the King and nobles, he sustained divers displeasures of the French slaves,[3] that devised a certain book, which was set forth in divers articles upon the causes of my lord's being there: which should be as they surmised that my lord was come thither to conclude two marriages, the one between the King our sovereign lord and Madame Renée, of whom I spake heretofore, and the other between the Princess then of England (now being Queen of this realm), my Lady Mary, the King's daughter,[4] and the French King's second son, the Duke of Orleans, who is at this present King of France,[5] with divers other conclusions and agreements touching the same. Of these books many were imprinted and conveyed into England, unknown to my lord, being then in France, to the great slander of the realm of England and of my Lord Cardinal. But whether they were devised of policy[6] to pacify the muttering of the people which had divers communications and imaginations of my lord's being there, or whether it were devised of some malicious person as the disposition of the common people are accustomed to do upon such secret consultations, I

9. agilely.   1. greatest.   2. fear.   3. Frenchmen (contemptuously).
4. Queen Mary Tudor.   5. Henry II (d. 1559).
6. *of policy*: as a matter of political expedience.

know not. But whatsoever the occasion or cause was the author hath set forth such books, this I am well assured, that after my lord was thereof advertized,[7] and had perused one of the same books, he was not a little offended, and assembled all the privy council of France together, to whom he spake his mind thus; saying that it was not only a suspicion in them but also a great rebuke and a defamation to the King's honor to see and know any such seditious untruth openly divulged and set forth by any malicious and subtle traitor of this realm; saying furthermore that if the like had been attempted within the realm of England he doubted not but to see it punished according to the traitorous demeanor[8] and deserts. Notwithstanding I saw but small redress.

So this was one of the displeasures that the Frenchmen showed him for all his pains and travail that he took for qualifying[9] of their King's ransom. Also another displeasure was this. There was no place where he was lodged after he entered the territory of France, but that he was robbed in his privy chamber either of one thing or other. And at Compiègne he lost his standish[1] of silver and gilt. And there it was espied and the party taken, which was but a little boy of twelve or thirteen year of age, a ruffian's page of Paris, which haunted my lord's lodging without any suspicion until he was taken lying under my lord's privy stairs; upon which occasion he was apprehended and examined and incontinent confessed all things that was missed, which he stole, and brought to his master the ruffian, who received the same and procured him so to do. After the spial [2] of this boy, my lord revealed the same unto the council, by means whereof the ruffian, the boy's master, was apprehended and set on the pillory in the midst of the market place—a goodly recompense for such an heinous offence. Also another displeasure was [that] some lewd [3] person (whosoever it was) had engraved in the great chamber window where my lord lay, upon the leaning stone[4] there, a Cardinal's hat with a pair of gallows over it in derision of my

---

7. informed.   8. behavior.   9. mitigating.   1. ink pot.   2. discovery.
3. ignorant.   4. *leaning stone:* stone forming the inner sill.

lord; with divers other unkind demeanors,[5] the which I leave
here to write, they be matters so slanderous.

Thus passing divers days in consultation, expecting the return of Christopher Gunner, which was sent into England with
letters unto the King as it is rehearsed heretofore, by empost,
who at last returned again with other letters; upon receipt
whereof my Lord Cardinal made haste to return into England.

In the morning that my lord should depart and remove,
being then at Mass in his closet, he consecrated the Chancellor
of France a Cardinal and put upon him the habit due to that
order. And then took his journey into Englandward, making
such necessary expedition[6] that he came to Guines, where he
was nobly received of my Lord Sands, captain there, with all
the retinue thereof. And from thence he rode to Calais, where
he tarried the shipping of his stuff, horses, and train. And in the
meantime he established there a mart to be kept for all nations
(but how long [it] endured, and in what sort it was used, I
know not), for I never heard of any great good that it did, or
of any worthy assembly there of merchants or merchandise,
that was brought thither for the furniture[7] of so weighty a
matter.

These things finished, and others for the weal [8] of the town,
he took shipping and arrived at Dover; from whence he rode
to the King (being then in his progress at Sir Harry Wyatt's[9]
house in Kent), supposed among us his servants that he should
be joyfully received at his homecoming as well of the King
as of all other noblemen—but we were deceived in our expectation. Notwithstanding he went immediately after his coming to
the King, with whom he had long talk and continued there in
the court two or three days, and then returned to his house at
Westminster, where he remained until Michaelmas Term,
which was within a fortnight after, and using his room[1] of
chancellorship as he was wont to do.

At which time he caused an assembly to be made in the Star
Chamber of all the noblemen, judges, and justices of the peace

5. *unkind demeanors:* ungrateful actions.
6. *necessary expedition:* convenient speed.   7. implementation.
8. well being.   9. d. 1537, the father of the poet, Sir Thomas Wyatt.
1. office.

of every shire that was at that present in Westminster Hall. And there [he] made to them a long oration, declaring unto them the cause of his ambasset into France and of his proceedings there. Among the which he said that he had concluded such an amity and friendship as never was heard of in this realm in our time before, as well between the Emperor and us as between the French King and our sovereign lord, concluding a perpetual peace, which shall be confirmed in writing, alternately sealed with the broad seals of both the realms graved in fine gold; affirming furthermore that the King should receive yearly his tribute (by that name) for the Duchy of Normandy, with all other costs which he hath sustained in the wars. And where there was a restraint made in France of the French Queen's dower (whom the Duke of Suffolk had married) for divers years during the wars, it is fully concluded that she shall not only receive the same yearly again, but also the arrearages, being unpaid during the restraint.

All which things should be perfected at the coming of the great ambasset out of France, in the which shall be a great number of noblemen and gentlemen for the conclusion of the same, as hath not been seen repair hither out of one realm in an ambasset. This peace thus concluded, there shall be such an amity between gentlemen of each realm, and intercourse of merchants with merchandise, that it shall seem to all men the territories to be but one monarchy. Gentlemen may travel quietly from one country to another for their recreation and pastime; and merchants, being arrived in each country, shall be assured to travel about their affairs in peace and tranquillity, so that this realm shall joy and prosper forever. Wherefore it shall be well done for all true Englishmen to advance and set forth this perpetual peace, both in countenance and gesture, with such entertainment as it may be a just occasion unto the Frenchmen to accept the same in good part, and also to use you with the semblable,[2] and make of the same a noble report in their countries.

"Now, good my lords and gentlemen, I most entirely require you in the King's behalf that ye will show yourselves herein

---

2. *with the semblable:* in like manner.

very loving and obedient subjects, wherein the King will much rejoice your towardness and give to every man his princely thanks for such liberality and gentleness as ye or any of you shall minister unto them." And here he ended his persuasion, and so departed into the dining chamber there, and dined among the lords of the council.

This great ambasset, long looked for, was now come over, which were in number above four score persons of the most noblest and worthiest gentlemen in all the court of France, who were right honorably received from place to place after their arrival, and so conveyed through London unto the bishop's palace in Paul's churchyard, where they were lodged. To whom divers noblemen resorted and gave them divers goodly presents; and in especial the Mayor and City of London, as wine, sugar, wax, capons, wild fowl, beeves, muttons, and other necessaries in great abundance for the expenses of their house. Then the next Sunday after their resort to London they repaired to the court at Greenwich, and [were] there by the King's majesty most highly received and entertained. They had a special commission to create and stall [3] the King's majesty in the royal order of France; for which purposely they brought with them a collar of fine gold of the order with a Michael [4] hanging thereat and robes to the same appurtenant,[5] the which was wonderous costly and comely, of purple velvet richly embroidered. I saw the King in all this apparel and habit passing through the chamber of presence unto his closet; and [he] offered [6] in the same habit at Mass beneath in the chapel. And to gratify the French King with like honor [he] sent incontinent unto the French King the like order of England by a nobleman (the Earl of Wiltshire), purposely for that intent, to create him one of the same order of England, accompanied with Garter the Herald, with all robes garter and other habiliments[7] to the same belonging, as costly in every degree as the other was of the French King's;—the which was done before the return of the great ambasset.

And for the performance of this noble and perpetual peace,

3. install.   4. medal representing St. Michael.   5. belonging.
6. assisted.   7. accouterments.

it was concluded and determined that a solemn Mass should be sung in the Cathedral Church of Paul's by the Cardinal. Against which time there was prepared a gallery, made from the west door of the Church of Paul's unto the choir door, railed on every side, upon the which stood vessels full of perfumes burning. Then the King and my Lord Cardinal and all the French with all other noblemen and gentlemen were conveyed upon this gallery unto the high altar into their traverses.[8] Then my Lord Cardinal prepared himself to Mass, associated with[9] twenty-four miters of bishops and abbots attending upon him and to serve him in such ceremonies as to him (by virtue of his legantine prerogative) was due.

And after the last Agnus,[1] the King rose out of his traverse and kneeled upon a cushion and carpet at the high altar; and the Grand Master of France, the chief ambassador that represented the King his master's person, kneeled by the King's majesty, between whom my lord divided the sacrament as a firm oath and assurance of this perpetual peace. That done, the King resorted again unto his traverse and the Grand Master in like wise to his. This Mass finished (which was sung with the King's chapel and the choir of Paul's), my Lord Cardinal took the instrument of this perpetual peace and amity and read the same openly before the King and the assembly both of English and French; to the which the King subscribed with his own hand and the Grand Master for the French King in like wise, the which was sealed with seals of fine gold, engraven and delivered to each other as their firm[2] deeds. And all this done and finished, they departed.

The King rode home to the Cardinal's house at Westminster to dinner, with whom dined all the Frenchmen, passing all day after in consultation in weighty matters touching the conclusion of this peace and amity. That done, the King went again by water to Greenwich; at whose departing it was determined by the King's devise that the French gentlemen should resort unto Richmond to hunt there in every of the parks; and from thence to Hampton Court, and there in like wise to hunt; and

8. screened compartments.   9. *associated with*: assisted by.
1. *Agnus Dei*: the part of the Mass immediately preceding the Communion.   2. sure, certain.

there my Lord Cardinal to make for them a supper and lodge them there that night; and from thence they should ride to Windsor, and there to hunt; and after their return to London they should resort to the court, whereas the King would banquet them. And this perfectly determined, the King and the French departed.

Then was there no more to do but to make provision at Hampton Court for this assembly. Against the day appointed my lord called for his principal officers of his house, as his steward, controller, and the clerks of his kitchen, whom he commanded to prepare for this banquet at Hampton Court; and neither to spare for expenses or travail to make them such triumphant cheer as they may not only wonder at it here, but also make a glorious report in their country to the King's honor and of this realm. His pleasure once known, to accomplish his commandment they sent forth all their cators,[3] purveyors,[4] and other persons to prepare of the finest viands that they could get either for money or friendship among my lord's friends. Also they sent for all the expertest cooks besides my lord's that they could get in all England, where they might be gotten, to serve to garnish this feast. The purveyors brought and sent in such plenty of costly provision as ye would wonder at the same. The cooks wrought both night and day in divers subtleties and many crafty devices, where lacked neither gold, silver, ne any other costly thing meet for their purpose. The yeomen and grooms of the wardrobes were busied in hanging of the chambers with costly hangings and furnishing the same with beds of silk and other furniture apt for the same in every degree.

Then my Lord Cardinal sent me, being gentleman usher, with two other of my fellows, to Hampton Court to foresee all things touching our rooms[5] to be nobly garnished[6] accordingly. Our pains were not small or light, but travailing daily from chamber to chamber. Then the carpenters, the joiners, the masons, the painters, and all other artificers necessary to glorify

3. caterers. 4. purchasers.
5. *touching our rooms:* pertaining to our duties.
6. *nobly garnished:* carried out in a manner befitting the nobility.

the house and feast were set a work. There was carriage and recarriage of plate, stuff, and other rich implements, so that there was nothing lacking or to be imagined or devised for the purpose. There was also fourteen score beds provided and furnished with all manner of furniture to them belonging, too long particularly here to rehearse. But to all wise men it sufficeth to imagine, that knoweth what belongeth to the furniture of such a triumphant feast or banquet.

The day was come that to the Frenchmen was assigned, and they ready assembled at Hampton Court, something before the hour of their appointment. Wherefore the officers caused them to ride to Hanworth, a place and park of the King's within two or three miles, there to hunt and spend the time until night. At which time they returned again to Hampton Court, and every of them conveyed to his chamber severally, having in them great fires and wine ready to refresh them, remaining there until their supper was ready and the chambers where they should sup were ordered in due form. The first waiting chamber was hanged with fine arras, and so was all the rest, one better than another, furnished with tall yeomen. There was set tables round about the chamber banquet-wise, all covered with fine cloths of diaper.[7] A cupboard with plate of parcel-gilt,[8] having also in the same chamber to give the more light, four plates of silver set with lights upon them, a great fire in the chimney.

The next chamber, being the chamber of presence [was] hanged with very rich arras; wherein was a gorgeous and a precious cloth of estate hanged up, replenished [9] with many goodly gentlemen ready to serve. The boards[1] were set as the other boards were in the other chamber before, save that the high table was set and removed beneath the cloth of estate towards the midst of the chamber, covered with fine linen cloths of damask work, sweetly perfumed. There was a cupboard made for the time, in length of the breadth of the nether end of the same chamber, of six desks[2] high, full of gilt plate, very sumptuous and of the most newest fashions; and

7. a rich linen.   8. partially gilded.   9. fully stocked.   1. tables.
2. shelves.

upon the nethermost desk garnished all with plate of clean[3] gold having two great candlesticks of silver and gilt, most curiously wrought, the workmanship whereof, with the silver, cost three hundred marks,[4] and lights of wax as big as torches burning upon the same. This cupboard was barred in round about that no man might come nigh it; for there was none of the same plate occupied[5] or stirred during this feast, for there was sufficient besides. The plates that hung on the walls to give lights in the chamber were of silver and gilt, with lights burning in them and a great fire in the chimney, and all other things necessary for the furniture of so noble a feast.

Now was all things in a readiness and supper time at hand. My lord's officers caused the trumpets to blow to warn to supper, and the said officers went right discreetly in due order and conducted these noble personages from their chambers unto the chamber of presence where they should sup. And they, being there, caused them to sit down. Their service was brought up in such order and abundance, both costly and full of subtleties, with such a pleasant noise of divers instruments of music, that the Frenchmen (as it seemed) were rapt into an heavenly paradise.

Ye must understand that my lord was not there ne yet come. But they, being merry and pleasant with their fare, devising and wondering upon the subtleties before the second course, my Lord Cardinal came in among them, booted and spurred— all suddenly—and bade them proface.[6] At whose coming they would have risen and give place with much joy; whom my lord commanded to sit still and keep their rooms.[7] And straightway, being not shifted of his riding apparel, [he] called for a chair and sat himself down in the midst of the table, laughing and being as merry as ever I saw him in all my life.

Anon came up the second course with so many dishes, subtleties, and curious devices, which were above an hundred in number, of so goodly proportion and costly that I suppose the Frenchmen never saw the like. The wonder was no less than it was worthy in deed. There were castles with images in

3. pure.   4. the mark was worth 13s. 4d.   5. used.
6. a formula of welcome: "here's to you."   7. positions.

the same; Paul's Church and steeple in proportion for the quantity as well counterfeited[8] as the painter should have painted it upon a cloth or wall. There were beasts, birds, fowls of divers kinds, and personages, most lively made and counterfeit in dishes; some fighting (as it were) with swords, some with guns and crossbows, some vaulting and leaping, some dancing with ladies, some in complete harness jousting with spears, and with many more devices than I am able with my wit to describe. Among all one I noted: there was a chessboard, subtly made of spiced plate[9] with men to the same; and for the good proportion, because that Frenchmen be very expert in that play, my lord gave the same to a gentleman of France, commanding that a case should be made for the same in all haste to preserve it from perishing in the conveyance thereof into his country.

Then my lord took a bowl of gold, which was esteemed at the value of five hundred marks, and filled with hypocras[1] (whereof there was plenty), putting off his cap, said: "I drink to the King my sovereign lord and master, and the King, your master," and therewith drank a good draught. And when he had done, he desired the Grand Master to pledge him cup and all, the which cup he gave him; and so caused all the other lords and gentlemen in other cups to pledge these two royal princes. Then went cups merrily about, that many of the Frenchmen were fain to be led to their beds. Then went my lord, leaving them sitting still, into his privy chamber to shift him;[2] and making a very short supper, or rather a small repast, returned again among them into the chamber of presence, using them so nobly, with so loving and familiar countenance and entertainment that they could not commend him too much.

And whilst they were in communication and other pastimes, all their liveries[3] were served to their chambers. Every chamber had a basin and an ewer of silver and some clean gilt and some parcel gilt; and some two great pots of silver in like manner, and one pot at the least with wine and beer, a bowl or goblet, and a silver pot to drink beer; a silver candlestick or

8. imitated, modelled.   9. sweetmeats.   1. spiced wine.
2. *shift him:* change his clothes.   3. provisions.

two, both with white lights and yellow lights of three sizes of wax; and a staff torch,[4] a fine manchet[5] and a cheat loaf[6] of bread. Thus was every chamber furnished throughout the house, and yet the two cupboards in the two banqueting chambers not once touched. Then, being past midnight, as time served they were conveyed to their lodgings to take their rest for that night. In the morning of the next day (not early) they rose and heard Mass and dined with my lord, and so departed toward Windsor and there hunted, delighting much of the castle and college and in the Order of the Garter. They being departed from Hampton Court, my lord returned again to Westminster because it was in the midst of the term.

It is not to be doubted but that the King was privy of all this worthy feast, who intended far to exceed the same—whom I leave until the return of the Frenchmen—who gave a special commandment to all his officers to devise a far sumptuouser banquet for these strangers,[7] otherwise than they had at Hampton Court, which was not neglected, but most speedily put in execution with great diligence.

After the return of these strangers from Windsor, which place with the goodly order thereof they much commended, the day approached that they were invited to the court at Greenwich; where first they dined, and after long consultation of the sagest with our counsellors, dancing of the rest, and other pastimes, the time of supper came on. Then was the banqueting chamber in the Tiltyard furnished for the entertainment of these estrangers,[7] to the which place they were conveyed by the noblest persons being then in the court, where they both supped and banqueted. But to describe the dishes, the subtleties, the many strange devices and order in the same, I do both lack wit in my gross old head and cunning in my bowels to declare the wonderful and curious imaginations in the same invented and devised. Yet this ye shall understand, that although it was at Hampton Court marvelous sumptuous, yet did this banquet far exceed the same as fine gold doth silver in weight and value. And for my part I must needs con-

4. tall, thick candle.   5. the finest wheaten bread.
6. a loaf of the second quality.   7. foreigners.

fess (which saw them both) that I never saw the like or read in any story or chronicle of any such feast. In the midst of this banquet there was turning[8] at the barriers, even in the chamber, with lusty gentlemen in gorgeous complete harness on foot. Then was there the like on horseback, and after all this there was the most goodliest disguising or interlude made in Latin and French, whose apparel was of such exceeding riches that it passeth my capacity to expound.[9]

This done, then came in such a number of fair ladies and gentlewomen that bare any bruit or fame of beauty in all this realm, in the most richest apparel, and devised in divers goodly fashions that all the cunningest[1] tailors could devise to shape or cut to set forth their beauty, gesture, and the goodly proportion of their bodies—who seemed to all men more angelic than earthly, made of flesh and bone. Surely to me, simple soul, it seemed inestimable to be described, and so I think it was to other of a more higher judgment;—with whom these gentlemen of France danced until another masque came in of noble gentlemen, who danced and masked with these fair ladies and gentlewomen, every man as his fancy served them. This done, and the maskers departed, there came in another masque of ladies so gorgeously apparelled in costly garments that I dare not presume to take upon me to make thereof any declaration, lest I should rather deface than beautify them—therefore I leave it untouched. These ladies maskeresses took each of them a French gentleman to dance and mask with them. Ye shall understand that these lady maskers spake good French, which delighted much these gentlemen to hear these ladies speak to them in their own tongue.

Thus was this night occupied and consumed from five of the clock until two or three after midnight, at which time it was convenient for all estates to draw to their rest. And thus every man departed, whither as they had most relief. Then, as nothing, either health, wealth, or pleasure, can always endure, so ended this triumphant banquet, the which in the next morning seemed to all the beholders but as a fantastical dream.

After all this solemn cheer, at a day appointed, they pre-

8. tourneying, jousting.   9. describe.   1. most expert.

pared them to return with bag and baggage. Then, as to the office[2] of all honorable persons doth appertain, they resorted in good order to the court to take their leave of the King and other noblemen then being there; to whom the King committed his princely commendations to the King their master, and thanked them of their pains and travail, and after long communication with the most honorable of that ambasset, he bade them adieu, who was assigned by the council to repair unto my Lord Cardinal for to receive the King's most noble reward. Wherefore they repaired to my lord, and taking of their leave, they received every man the King's reward after this sort: every honorable person in estimation had most commonly plate to the value of three or four hundred pounds, and some more and some less, besides other great gifts received at the King's hands before, as rich gowns, horses, or goodly geldings of great value and goodness; and some had weighty chains of fine gold with divers other gifts which I cannot now call to my remembrance. But this I know, that the least of them all had a sum of crowns of gold—the worst page among them had twenty crowns for his part. And thus they, nobly rewarded, departed. And my lord, after humble commendations had to the French King, he bade them adieu. And the next day they conveyed all their stuff and furniture unto the sea's side, accompanied with lusty young gentlemen of England; but what praise or commendations they made in their country at their return, in good faith I cannot tell you, for I never heard anything thereof.

Then began other matters to brew and take place that occupied all men's heads with divers imaginations, whose stomachs were therewith fulfilled without any perfect disgestion.[3] The long hid and secret love between the King and Mistress Anne Boleyn began to break out into every man's ears. The matter was then by the King disclosed to my Lord Cardinal, whose persuasion to the contrary made to the King upon his knees could not effect.[4] The King was so amorously affectionate that will bare place[5] and high discretion [was] banished for the

2. duty.   3. digestion.   4. accomplish anything.
5. *bare place:* held sway.

time. My lord, provoked[6] by the King to declare his wise opinion in this matter for the furtherance of his desired affect,[7] who thought it not meet for him alone to wade too far to give his hasty judgment or advice in so weighty a matter, desired of the King license to ask the counsel of men of ancient study and of famous learning both in the laws divine and civil. That obtained, he, by his legantine authority, sent out his commission unto all the bishops of this realm, and for other that was exactly[8] either learned in any of the said laws, or else had in any estimation for their prudent counsel and judgment in princely affairs of long experience.

Then assembled these prelates before my Lord Cardinal at his place in Westminster with many other famous and notable clerks[9] of both the universities, Oxford and Cambridge, and also out of divers colleges and cathedral churches of this realm, renommed [1] and allowed [2] learned and of witty discretion in the determination of doubtful questions. Then was the matter of the King's case debated, reasoned, and argued, consulting from day to day and time to time, that it was to men learned a goodly hearing. But in conclusion it seemed me by[3] the departure of the ancient fathers of the laws, that they departed with one judgment contrary to the expectation of the principal parties. I heard the opinion of some of the most famous persons among that sort report that the King's case was so[4] obscure and doubtful for any learned man to discuss; the points therein were so dark to be credited that it was very hard to have any true understanding or intelligence. And therefore they departed without any resolution or judgment.

Then in this assembly of bishops it was thought most expedient that the King should first send out his commissioners into all the universities of Christendom, as well here in England as into foreign countries and regions, to have among them his grace's case argued substantially, and to bring with them from thence the very[5] definition of their opinions in the same under the seals of every several university. Thus was their determination for this time. And thereupon agreed, that commissioners

6. called upon.   7. passion.   8. expertly.   9. clerical scholars.
1. renowned.   2. acknowledged.   3. at.   4. too.   5. true.

were incontinent appointed and sent forth about this matter
into several universities, as some to Oxford, some to Cambridge, some to Louvain, some to Paris, some to Orleans, some
to Bologna, and some to Padua, and some to other. Although
these commissioners had the travail, yet was the charges the
King's, the which was no small sums of money. And all went
out of the King's coffers into foreign regions. For as I heard
it reported of credible persons (as it seemed indeed), that
besides the great charges of the commissioners, there was
inestimable sums of money given to the famous clerks to
choke them,[6] and in especial to such as had the governance
and custody of their university seals. In so much as they agreed
not only in opinions, but also obtained of them the universities'
seals, the which attained, they returned home again furnished
for their purpose. At whose return there was no small joy made
of the principal parties, in so much as the commissioners were
not only ever in great estimation, but also most liberally
advanced and rewarded far beyond their worthy deserts. Notwithstanding they prospered, and the matter went still forward,
having then, as they thought, a sure foundation to ground
them[7] upon.

    These proceedings being once declared to my Lord Cardinal,
[he] sent again for all the bishops, whom he made privy of
the expedition of the commissioners; and for the very proof
thereof he showed them the opinions of the several universities
in writing under their universities' seals. These matters being
thus brought to pass, they went once again to consultation how
these matters should be ordered to the purpose. It was then
thought good, and concluded by the advice of them all, that
the King should (to avoid all ambiguities) send unto the Pope
a legation with the instrument[8] declaring the opinions of the
universities under their seals. To the which it was thought
good that all these prelates in this assembly should join with
the King in this legation, making intercession and suit to the
Pope for advice and judgment in this great and weighty matter.
And if the Pope would not directly consent to the same request,
that then the ambassadors should further require of him a

6. *choke them*: shut them up.   7. themselves.   8. document.

commission to be directed under lead[9] to establish a court judicial in England (*hac vice tantum*),[1] directed to my Lord Cardinal and unto the Cardinal Campeggio,[2] which was then Bishop of Bath, although he were a stranger[3]—which the King gave him at such time as he was the Pope's ambassitory[4] here in England—to hear and determine according to the just judgments of their conscience. The which, after long and great suit, they obtained of the Pope his commission. This done and achieved, they made return into England, making report unto the King of their expedition, trusting that his grace's pleasure and purpose should now perfectly be brought to pass, considering the estate[5] of the judges, who were the Cardinals of England and of Campeggio, being both his highness's subjects in effect.

Long was the desire and greater was the hope on all sides, expecting the coming of the legation and commission from Rome—yet at length it came. And after the arrival of the legate Campeggio (with this solemn commission) in England, he, being sore vexed with the gout, was constrained by force thereof to make a long journey or ever he came to London;[6] who should have been most solemnly received at Blackheath, and so with great triumph conveyed to London; but his glory was such that he would in no wise be entertained with any such pomp or vainglory, who suddenly came by water in a wherry[7] to his own house without Temple Bar, called then Bath Place, which was furnished for him with all manner of stuff and implements of my lord's provision; where he continued and lodged during his abode here in England.

Then after some deliberation, his commission understood, read, and perceived, it was by the council determined that the King and the Queen his wife should be lodged at Bridewell. And that in the Black Friars a certain place should be appointed whereas the King and the Queen might most conveniently

9. a leaden seal.   1. for this occasion only.
2. Lorenzo Campeggio (1472–1539), who had been in England as legate in 1518 and had received the Bishopric of Salisbury (not Bath) in 1524. Pope Clement VII granted the commission on June 8, 1528.
3. foreigner.   4. ambassador.   5. social position.
6. Campeggio reached London on October 9.   7. small boat.

repair to the court there to be erected and kept for the disputation and determination of the King's case, whereas these two legates sat in judgment as notable judges, before whom the King and the Queen were duly cited and summoned to appear. Which was the strangest and newest sight and device that ever was read or heard in any history or chronicle in any region—that a King and a Queen to be convented[8] and constrained by process compellatory[9] to appear in any court as common persons, within their own realm or dominion, to abide the judgment and decrees of their own subjects, having the diadem and prerogative thereof!

Is it not a world to consider the desire of wilful princes when they fully be bent and inclined to fulfil their voluptuous appetites, against the which no reasonable persuasions will suffice; little or nothing weighing or regarding the dangerous sequels that doth ensue as well to themselves as to their realm and subjects? And above all things there is no one thing that causeth them to be more wilful than carnal desire and voluptuous affection of foolish love. The experience is plain in this case, both manifest and evident, for what surmised inventions hath been invented, what laws hath been enacted, what noble and ancient monasteries overthrown and defaced, what diversities of religious opinions hath risen, what executions hath been committed, how many famous and notable clerks hath suffered death, what charitable foundations were perverted from the relief of the poor unto profane uses, and what alterations of good and wholesome ancient laws and customs hath been tossed[1] by will and wilful desire of the prince, almost to the subversion and desolation of this noble realm. All men may understand what hath chanced to this region; the proof[2] thereof hath taught all us Englishmen a common experience, the more is the pity, and to all good men very lamentable to be considered. If eyes be not blind men may see, if ears be not stopped they may hear, and if pity be not exiled they may lament the sequel of this pernicious and inordinate carnal love, the plague whereof is not ceased (although this love lasted

8. *to be convented*: should be summoned.   9. compulsory.
1. bandied about.   2. experience.

but a while), which our Lord quench and take from us His indignation, *Quia peccavimus cum patribus nostris et injuste egimus, etc.*[3]

Ye shall understand, as I said before, that there was a court erected in the Black Friars in London, where these two Cardinals sat for judges. Now will I set you out the manner and order of the court there. First there was a court placed with tables, benches, and bars, like a consistory,[4] a place judicial for the judges to sit on. There was also a cloth of estate under the which sat the King; and the Queen sat some distance beneath the King; under the judges' feet sat the officers of the court. The chief scribe there was then Doctor Stephens[5] (which was after Bishop of Winchester); the apparitor[6] was one Cook[7] (most commonly called Cook of Winchester). Then sat there within the said court, directly before the King and judges, the Archbishop of Canterbury (Doctor Warham) and all the other bishops. Then at both the ends, with a bar made for them, the counsels on both sides. The doctors for the King was Doctor Sampson,[8] which was after Bishop of Chichester, and Doctor Bell,[9] which after was Bishop of Worcester, with divers other. The proctors on the King's part was Doctor Peter,[1] which was after made the King's chief secretary, and Doctor Tregonell,[2] and divers other.

Now on the other side stood the counsel for the Queen, Doctor Fisher,[3] Bishop of Rochester, and Doctor Standish,[4] sometime a grey friar,[5] and then Bishop of Saint Asaph in Wales, two notable clerks in divinity, and in especial the Bishop of Rochester, a very godly man and a devout person, who after suffered death at Tower Hill, the which was greatly lamented through all the foreign universities of Christendom.

3. Psalms 106:6.   4. a bishop's court for ecclesiastical causes.
5. Stephen Gardiner (d. 1555), Bishop of Winchester in 1531.
6. officer of ecclesiastical court.
7. John Cook, a notary public of Wolsey's Winchester diocese.
8. Richard Sampson (d. 1554), Bishop of Chichester in 1536.
9. John Bell (d. 1556), Bishop of Worcester in 1537.
1. Peter Vannes (d. 1562). He was actually in Rome at this time.
2. Sir John Tregonell (d. 1565), an admiralty lawyer in Henry's service.
3. John Fisher, Bishop of Rochester since 1504; executed by Henry in 1535.   4. Henry Standish (d. 1535), Bishop of St. Asaph since 1518.
5. i.e. a Franciscan.

There was also another ancient doctor called, as I do remember, Doctor Ridley,[6] a very small person in stature, but surely a great and an excellent clerk in divinity.

The court being thus furnished and ordered,[7] the judges commanded the crier to command silence. Then was the judges' commission, which they had of the Pope, published and read openly before all the audience there assembled. That done, the crier called the King by the name of "King Harry of England come into the court etc." With that the King answered and said "Here, my lords." Then he called also the Queen by the name of "Catherine Queen of England come into the court etc."; who made no answer to the same, but rose up incontinent[8] out of her chair whereas she sat and, because she could not come directly to the King, for the distance which severed them, she took pain to go about unto the King, kneeling down at his feet in the sight of all the court and assembly, to whom she said in effect, in broken English, as followeth:

"Sir," quod she, "I beseech you for all the loves that hath been between us and for the love of God, let me have justice and right; take of me some pity and compassion, for I am a poor woman and a stranger, born out of your dominion. I have here no assured friends, and much less indifferent[9] counsel. I flee to you as to the head of justice within this realm. Alas, sir, wherein have I offended you, or what occasion of displeasure have I deserved against your will or pleasure? Intending, as I perceive, to put me from you, I take God and all the world to witness that I have been to you a true, humble, and obedient wife, ever confirmable[1] to your will and pleasure, that never said or did anything to the contrary thereof, being always well pleased and contented with all things wherein ye had any delight or dalliance;[2] whether it were in little or much, I never grudged in word or countenance, or showed a visage or spark of discontentation.[3] I loved all those whom ye loved only for your sake, whether I had cause or no, and whether they were my friends or my enemies. This twenty years I have been your

6. Robert Ridley (d. 1536).   7. The court opened on June 18, 1529.
8. at once.   9. impartial.   1. conformable, obedient.
2. amorous amusement.   3. discontent.

true wife (or more), and by me ye have had divers children, although it hath pleased God to call them out of this world, which hath been no default in me.

"And when ye had me at the first (I take God to be my judge) I was a true maid without touch of man; and whether it be true or no, I put it to your conscience. If there be any just cause by the law that ye can allege against me, either of dishonesty[4] or any other impediment, to banish and put me from you, I am well content to depart to my great shame and dishonor. And if there be none, then here I most lowly[5] beseech you let me remain in my former estate[6] and to receive justice at your princely hands. The King your father was in the time of his reign of such estimation through the world for his excellent wisdom that he was accompted[7] and called of all men 'the second Solomon'; and my father Ferdinand,[8] King of Spain, who was esteemed to be one of the wittiest[9] princes that reigned in Spain many years before—who were both wise and excellent Kings in wisdom and princely behavior. It is not therefore to be doubted but that they elected and gathered as wise counsellors about them as to their high discretions was thought meet. Also, as me seemeth, there was in those days as wise, as well learned men, and men of as good judgment as be at this present in both realms, who thought then the marriage between you and me good and lawful. Therefore it is a wonder to me what new inventions are now invented against me, that never intended but honesty. And cause me to stand to the order and judgment of this new court, wherein ye may do much wrong if ye intend any cruelty; for ye may condemn me for lack of sufficient answer, having no indifferent counsel, but such as be assigned me, with whose wisdom and learning I am not acquainted. Ye must consider that they cannot be indifferent counsellors for my part which be your subjects and taken out of your own council before, wherein they be made privy,[1] and dare not for your displeasure disobey your will and intent, being once made privy thereto.

4. lewdness.　　5. humbly.　　6. situation.　　7. reckoned.
8. Ferdinand of Aragon (d. 1516).　　9. most intelligent.
1. *made privy:* fully informed (of your wishes).

Therefore I most humbly require you in the way of charity
and for the love of God (who is the just judge) to spare the
extremity of this new court, until I may be advertized[2] what
way and order my friends in Spain will advise me to take. And
if ye will not extend to me so much indifferent favor, your
pleasure then be fulfilled, and to God I commit my case."

And even with that she rose up, making low curtsy to the
King, and so departed from thence. [They] supposed that she
would have resorted again to her former place, but she took
her direct way out of the house, leaning (as she was wont
always to do) upon the arm of her general receiver,[3] called
Master Griffith. And the King being advertized of her departure, commanded the crier to call her again, who called her by
the name of "Catherine Queen of England, come into the
court etc." With that quod Griffith, "Madam, ye be called
again." "On, on," quod she, "it makes no matter, for it is no
indifferent court for me. Therefore I will not tarry, go on
your ways." And thus she departed out of that court without
any further answer at that time or at any other, nor would
never appear in any court after.

The King, perceiving that she was departed in such sort,
calling to his grace's memory all her lament[able] words that
she had pronounced before him and all the audience, said thus
in effect: "For as much," quod he, "as the Queen is gone,
I will in her absence declare unto you all my lords here presently assembled [that]she hath been to me as true, obedient,
and as confirmable[4] a wife as I could in my fancy wish or
desire. She hath all the virtuous qualities that ought to be in a
woman of her dignity or in any other of baser estate.[5] Surely
she is also a noble woman born, if nothing were in her but
only her conditions will well declare the same." [6]

With that quod my Lord Cardinal, "Sir, I most humbly
beseech your highness to declare me before all this audience
whether I have been the chief inventor or first mover of this

2. informed.   3. treasurer, who here acts as her master of ceremonies.
4. conformable, acquiescent.   5. *baser estate:* lower rank in society.
6. *but only . . . same:* i.e. her manner and bearing would, by themselves, indicate her nobility.

matter unto your majesty, for I am greatly suspected of all men herein." "My Lord Cardinal," quod the King, "I can well excuse you herein. Marry indeed, ye have been rather against me in attempting or setting forth thereof. And to put you all out of doubt, I will declare unto you the especial cause that moved me hereunto. It was a certain scripulosity[7] that pricked my conscience upon divers words that were spoken at a certain time by the Bishop of Bayonne, the French King's ambassador, who had lien[8] here long upon the debating for the conclusion of a marriage to be concluded between the Princess our daughter Mary[9] and the young Duke of Orleans,[1] the French King's second son.

"And upon the resolution and determination thereof he desired respite to advertize the King his master thereof, whether our daughter Mary should be legitimate in respect of the marriage which was sometime between the Queen here and my brother late Prince Arthur.[2] These words were so conceived within my scrupulous conscience that it bred a doubtful prick within my breast, which doubt pricked, vexed, and troubled so my mind, and so disquieted me, that I was in great doubt[3] of God's indignation; which, as seemed me, appeared right well, much the rather for that he hath not sent me any issue male; for all such issue males as I have received of the Queen died incontinent[4] after they were born, so that I doubt[5] the punishment of God in that behalf. Thus being troubled in waves of a scrupulous conscience, and partly in despair of any issue male by her, it drave[6] me at last to consider the estate of this realm, and the danger it stood in for lack of issue male to succeed me in this imperial dignity. I thought it good therefore in the relief of the weighty burden of scrupulous conscience, and the quiet estate of this noble realm, to attempt the law therein, and whether I might take another wife in case that my first copulation with this gentlewoman were not

---

7. scrupulousness.   8. dwelt.   9. later Queen Mary Tudor.
1. Henry, Duke of Orleans (1518–1559), later King of France. The marriage negotiations were conducted in 1527 by Gabriel de Grammont, Bishop of Tarbes, not by the Bishop of Bayonne.
2. Catherine and Arthur were married in November 1501. He died five months later.   3. fear.   4. immediately.   5. fear.   6. drove, forced.

lawful; which I intend not for any carnal concupiscence, ne for any displeasure or mislike of the Queen's person or age, with whom I could be as well content to continue during my life, if our marriage may stand with God's laws, as with any woman alive. In which point consisteth all this doubt that we go now about to try by the learned wisdom and judgments of you our prelates and pastors of this realm here assembled for that purpose, to whose conscience and judgment I have committed the charge, according to the which (God willing) we will be right well contented to submit ourself, to obey the same for my part.

"Wherein after I once perceived my conscience wounded with the doubtful case herein, I moved first this matter in confession to you, my Lord of Lincoln,[7] my ghostly father.[8] And for as much as then yourself were in some doubt to give me counsel, moved me to ask further counsel of all you, my lords, wherein I moved you first my Lord of Canterbury,[9] asking your license, for as much as you were our metropolitan,[1] to put this matter in question. And so I did of all you, my lords, to the which ye have all granted by writing under all your seals, the which I have here to be showed."

"That is truth if it please your highness," quod the Bishop of Canterbury, "I doubt not but all my brethren here present will affirm the same." "No, sir, not I," quod the Bishop of Rochester,[2] "ye have not my consent thereto." "No hath," quod the King, "look here upon this, is not this your hand and seal?" And showed him the instrument[3] with seals. "No, forsooth, sir," quod the Bishop of Rochester, "it is not my hand nor seal." To that quod the King to my Lord of Canterbury, "Sir, how say ye? Is it not his hand and seal?" "Yes, sir," quod he. "That is not so," quod the Bishop of Rochester, "for indeed you were in hand with me[4] to have both my hand and seal, as other of my lords hath already done, but then I said to you that I would never consent to no such act for it were much against my conscience, nor my hand and seal should never be

7. John Longland (1473–1547), Bishop of Lincoln since 1521.
8. confessor.   9. Archbishop Warham.
1. head of an ecclesiastical province.   2. John Fisher.   3. document.
4. *in . . . me:* endeavoring to persuade me.

seen at any such instrument (God willing) with much more matter touching the same communication between us." "You say truth," quod the Bishop of Canterbury, "such words ye had unto me, but at the last ye were fully persuaded that I should for you subscribe your name and put to[5] a seal myself, and ye would allow the same." "All which words and matter," quod the Bishop of Rochester, "under your correction, my lord, and supportation[6] of this noble audience, there is nothing more untrue." "Well, well," quod the King, "it shall make no matter. We will not stand with you in argument herein, for you are but one man." And with that the court was adjourned until the next day of their session.

The next court day the Cardinals sat there again. At which time the counsels on both sides were there present. The King's counsel alleged the marriage not good from the beginning because of the carnal knowledge committed between Prince Arthur, her first husband, the King's brother, and her. This matter being very sore touched[7] and maintained by the King's counsel, and the contrary defended by such as took upon them to be on that other part with the good Queen; and to prove the same carnal copulation they alleged many colored[8] reasons and similitudes of truth. It was answered again negatively on the other side, by which it seemed that all their former allegations to be[9] very doubtful to be tried, so that it was said that no man could know the truth. "Yes," quod the Bishop of Rochester, "*Ego nosco veritatem.*"[1] "How know ye the truth?" quod my Lord Cardinal. "Forsooth," quod he, "*Ego sum professor veritatis,*[2] I know that God is truth itself, nor He never spake but truth; which said '*Quod deus coniunxit, homo non separet.*'[3] And for as much as this marriage was made and joined by God to a good intent, I say that I know the truth, the which cannot be broken or loosed by the power of man upon no one feigned occasion."

"So much doth all faithful men know," quod my Lord Car-

---

5. *put to:* affix.   6. with the permission.
7. *sore touched:* heavily emphasized.   8. feigned.   9. *to be:* were.
1. *Ego . . . veritatem:* I know the truth.
2. *Ego . . . veritatis:* I am a professor of truth.   3. Matthew 19: 6.

dinal, "as well as you. Yet this reason is not sufficient in this case; for the King's counsel doth allege divers presumptions to prove the marriage not good at the beginning. *Ergo*, say they, it was not joined by God at the beginning and therefore it is not lawful; for God ordaineth nor joineth nothing without a just order. Therefore it is not to be doubted but that their presumptions must be true, as it plainly appears; and nothing can be more true in case their allegations cannot be avoided. Therefore to say that the matrimony was joined of God, ye must prove it further than by that text which ye have alleged for your matter; for ye must first avoid their presumptions." Then quod one Doctor Ridley, "it is a shame and a great dishonor to this[4] honorable persons that any such presumptions should be alleged in this open court, which be to all good and honest men most detestable to be rehearsed." "What," quod my Lord Cardinal, *"Domine Doctor, magis reverenter."* [5] "No, no, my lord," quod he, "there belongeth no reverence to be given to this[6] abominable presumptions, for an unreverent[7] tale would be unreverently answered." And there they left and proceeded no further at that time.

Thus this court passed from session to session and day to day, in so much that a certain day the King sent for my lord at the breaking up one day of the court to come to him into Bridewell. And to accomplish his commandment he went unto him, and being there with him in communication in his grace's privy chamber from eleven unto twelve of the clock and past at noon, my lord came out and departed from the King and took his barge at the Black Friars stairs and so went to his house at Westminster. The Bishop of Carlisle,[8] being with him in his barge, said unto him, wiping the sweat from his face, "Sir," quod he, "it is a very hot day." "Yea," quod my Lord Cardinal, "if ye had been as well chafed as I have been within this hour, ye would say it were very hot."

And as soon as he came home to his house at Westminster,

---

4. these.   5. *Domine . . . reverenter:* My dear doctor, more reverently.
6. these.   7. irreverent.
8. John Kite (d. 1537), Bishop of Carlisle since 1521.

he went incontinent to his naked bed,[9] where he had not lien[1] fully the space of two hours, but that my Lord of Wiltshire[2] came to speak with him of a message from the King. My lord, having understanding of his coming, caused him to be brought unto his bedside. And he, being there, showed that the King's pleasure was that he should incontinent (accompanied with the other Cardinal) repair unto the Queen at Bridewell into her chamber, to persuade her by their wisdoms, advising her to surrender the whole matter into the King's hands by her own will and consent; which should be much better to her honor than to stand to the trial of the law and to be condemned, which should be much to her slander and defamation. To fulfill the King's pleasure, quod my lord, he was ready and would prepare him to go thither out of hand[3] saying further to my Lord of Wiltshire, "ye and other of my lords of the council which be near unto the King are not a little to blame and misadvised to put any such fantasies into his head, whereby ye are the causers of great trouble to all this realm. And at length get you but small thanks either of God or of the world," with many other vehement words and sentences that was like to ensue of this matter;[4] which words caused my Lord of Wiltshire to water his eyes, kneeling all this while by my lord's bedside, and in conclusion departed.

And then my lord rose up and made him ready, taking his barge, and went straight to Bath Place to the other Cardinal, and so went together unto Bridewell, directly to the Queen's lodging. And they, being in her chamber of presence, showed to the gentleman usher that they came to speak with the Queen's grace. The gentleman usher advertized the Queen thereof. Incontinent[5] with that she came out of her privy chamber with a skein of white thread about her neck into the chamber of presence, where the Cardinals were giving of attendance upon her coming. At whose coming quod she, "Alack, my lords, I am sorry to cause you to attend upon me. What is your pleasure with me?" "If it please you," quod my

9. *naked bed:* i.e. removing his normal wearing apparel.   1. lain.
2. Sir Thomas Boleyn, father of Anne.   3. at once.
4. *that . . . matter:* concerning what was bound to follow from this matter.   5. at once.

Lord Cardinal, "to go into your chamber, we will show you the cause of our coming." "My lord," quod she, "if ye have anything to say, speak it openly before all these folks, for I fear nothing that ye can say or allege against me, but that I would all the world should both hear and see it. Therefore I pray you speak your mind openly." Then began my lord to speak to her in Latin. "Nay, good my lord," quod she, "speak to me in English, I beseech you, although I understand Latin." "Forsooth then," quod my lord, "Madam, if it please your grace, we come both to know your mind, how ye be disposed to do in this matter between the King and you, and also to declare secretly our opinions and our counsel, unto which we have intended of very zeal and obedience that we bear to your grace."

"My lords, I thank you then," quod she, "of your good wills. But to make answer to your request I cannot so suddenly, for I was set among my maidens at work, thinking full little of any such matter, wherein there needeth a longer deliberation and a better head than mine to make answer to so noble wise men as ye be. I had need of good counsel in this case, which toucheth me so near, and for any counsel or friendship that I can find in England are nothing to my purpose or profit. Think you, I pray you, my lords, will any Englishman counsel or be friendly unto me against the King's pleasure, they being his subjects? Nay forsooth, my lords! And for my counsel in whom I do intend to put my trust be not here, they be in Spain in my native country. Alas, my lords, I am a poor woman, lacking both wit and understanding sufficiently to answer such approved[6] wise men as ye be both in so weighty a matter. I pray you to extend your good and indifferent[7] minds in your authority unto me, for I am a simple woman, destitute and barren of friendship and counsel here in a foreign region. And as for your counsel, I will not refuse but be glad to hear."

And with that she took my lord by the hand and led him into her privy chamber with the other Cardinal, where they were in long communication. We in the other chamber might

6. experienced.   7. impartial.

sometime hear the Queen speak very loud, but what it was we could not understand. Their communication ended, the Cardinals departed and went directly to the King, making to him relation of their talk with the Queen. And after resorted home to their houses to supper.

Thus went this strange case forward from court day to court day, until it came to judgment, so that every man expected the judgment to be given upon the case at the next court day.[8] At which day the King came thither and sat within a gallery against[9] the door of the same that looked unto the judges, where they sat, whom he might see and hear speak, to hear what judgment they would give in his suit. At which time all their proceedings were first openly read in Latin. And that done, the King's learned counsel at the bar called fast for judgment.

With that quod the Cardinal Campeggio, "I will give no judgment herein until I have made relation unto the Pope of all our proceedings, whose counsel and commandment in this high case I will observe. The case is too high, and notable known[1] through all the world, for us to give any hasty judgment, considering the highness of the persons and the doubtful allegations. And also whose commissioners we be, under whose authority we sit here, it were therefore reason that we should make our chief head a counsel in the same before we proceed into judgment definitive. I come not so far to please any man for fear, meed,[2] or favor, be he King or any other potentate. I have no such respect to the persons that I will offend my conscience. I will not for favor or displeasure of any high estate[3] or mighty prince do that thing that should be against the law of God. I am an old man, both sick and impotent, looking daily for death. What should it then avail me to put my soul in the danger of God's displeasure to my utter damnation for the favor of any prince or high estate in this world? My coming and being here is only to see justice ministered according to my conscience, as I thought thereby the matter good or bad.

8. July 23, 1529.   9. opposite.   1. *notable known:* i.e. too well known.
2. reward.   3. high-ranking nobleman.

"And for as much as I do understand and having persever-ance[4] by the allegations and negations[5] in this matter laid for both the parties, that the truth in this case is very doubtful to be known, and also that the party defendant will make no answer thereunto, doth rather appeal from us, supposing that we be not indifferent,[6] considering the King's high dignity and authority within this his own realm, which he hath over his own subjects; and we being his subjects and having our livings and dignities in the same, she thinketh that we cannot minister true and indifferent justice for fear of his displeasure. There-fore, to avoid all these ambiguities and obscure doubts, I intend not to damn my soul for no prince or potentate alive. I would therefore (God willing) wade no further in this matter unless I have the just opinion and judgment with the assent of the Pope and such other of his counsel as hath more expe-rience and better learning in such doubtful laws than I have. Wherefore I will adjourn this court for this time, according to the order of the court in Rome[7] from whence this court and jurisdiction is derived. And if we should go further than our commission doth warrant us, it were folly, and vain, and much to our slander and blames, and might be for the same accompted[8] breakers of the orders of the higher court, from whence we have (as I said) our original authorities." With that the court was dissolved and no more plea holden.

With that stepped forth the Duke of Suffolk from the King, and by his commandment spake these words with a stout and hault[9] countenance, "It was never," quod he, "merry in Eng-land whilst we had Cardinals among us." Which words were set forth with such a vehement countenance that all men marvelled what he intended. To whom no man made answer. The duke again spake those words in great despite.

To the which words my Lord Cardinal, perceiving his vehemency, soberly made answer and said, "Sir, of all men

4. *having perseverance:* am aware.   5. denials.   6. impartial.
7. *according . . . Rome:* i.e. according to the custom in Rome, where the Curia did not sit from the end of July until October. The Cardinals' decision was made before Clement VII's order revoking the case to Rome had reached England.   8. reckoned.
9. *stout and hault:* proud and arrogant.

within this realm ye have least cause to dispraise or be offended with Cardinals; for if I, simple Cardinal, had not been, ye should have had at this present no head upon your shoulders wherein ye should have a tongue to make any such report in despite of us who intended you no manner of displeasure, nor we have given you any occasion with such despite to be revenged with your hault words. I would ye knew it, my lord, that I and my brother here intended the King and his realm as much honor, wealth, and quietness as ye or any other, of what estate or degree so ever he be within this realm, and would as gladly accomplish his lawful desire as the poorest subject he hath. But, my lord, I pray, show me what would ye do if ye were the King's commissioner in a foreign region, having a weighty matter to treat upon and the conclusion being doubtful thereof, would ye not advertize the King's majesty or ever ye went through with the same? Yes, yes, my lord, I doubt not. Therefore I would ye should banish your hasty malice and despite out of your heart, and consider that we be but commissioners for a time, and can, ne may not, by virtue of our commission proceed to judgment without the knowledge and consent of the chief head of our authority, and having his consent to the same—which is the Pope. Therefore we do no less ne otherwise than our warrant will bear[1] us; and if any man will be offended with us therefore, he is an unwise man. Wherefore, my lord, hold your peace, and pacify yourself, and frame your tongue like a man of honor and of wisdom, and not to speak so quickly or so reproachfully by[2] your friends; for ye know best what friendship ye have received at my hands, the which yet I never revealed to no person alive before now, neither to my glory ne to your dishonor." And therewith the Duke gave over the matter without any words to reply, and so departed and followed after the King, which was gone into Bridewell at the beginning of the Duke's first words.

This matter continued long thus, and my Lord Cardinal was in displeasure with the King for that the matter in his suit took no better success, the fault whereof was ascribed much to my

1. allow. 2. of.

lord; notwithstanding my lord excused him always by his commission, which gave him no further authority to proceed in judgment without knowledge of the Pope, who reserved the same to himself.

At the last they were advertized by their post that the Pope would take deliberation in respite of judgment until his courts were opened, which should not be afore Bartholomew-tide next.[3] The King considering the time to be very long or the matter should be determined, thought it good to send a new ambasset to the Pope to persuade him to show such honorable favor unto his grace that the matter might be sooner ended than it was likely to be, or else at the next court in Rome to rule the matter over according to the King's request. To this ambasset was appointed Doctor Stephens, then Secretary, that after was made Bishop of Winchester; who went thither and there tarried until the latter end of summer, as ye shall hear after.

The King commanded the Queen to be removed out of the court and sent unto another place. And his highness rode in his progress with Mistress Anne Boleyn in his company all the grease season.[4]

It was so that the Cardinal Campeggio made suit to be discharged that he might return again to Rome. And it chanced that the Secretary, which was the King's ambassador to the Pope, was returned from Rome; whereupon it was determined that the Cardinal Campeggio should resort to the King at Grafton in Northamptonshire and that my Lord Cardinal should accompany him thither, where Campeggio should take his leave of the King. And so they took their journey thitherward from the More and came to Grafton upon the Sunday[5] in the morning; before whose coming there rose in the court divers opinions that the King would not speak with my Lord Cardinal, and thereupon were laid many great wagers.

These two prelates being come to the gates of the court, where they alighted from their horses, supposing that they

3. August 24.
4. the season when the harts were fat and fit for killing (August–October).   5. September 19.

should have been received by the head officers of the house as they were wont to be; yet for as much as Cardinal Campeggio was but a stranger in effect, the said officers received them and conveyed him to a lodging within the court, which was prepared for him only. And after my lord had brought him thus to his lodging, he left him there and departed, supposing to have gone directly likewise to his chamber, as he was accustomed to do. And by the way as he was going, it was told him that he had no lodging appointed for him in the court. And being therewith astonied,[6] Sir Harry Norris,[7] groom of the stole with the King, came unto him (but whether it was by the King's commandment or no I know not) and most humbly offered him his chamber for the time, until another might somewhere be provided for him. "For, sir, I assure you," quod he, "here is very little room in this house, scantly[8] sufficient for the King; therefore I beseech your grace to accept mine for the season." Whom my lord thanked for his gentle offer, and went straight to his chamber, whereas my lord shifted[9] his riding apparel; and being thus in this chamber, divers noble persons and gentlemen, being his loving friends, came to visit him and to welcome him to the court; by whom my head was advertized[1] of all things touching the King's displeasure towards him, which did him no small pleasure and caused him to be the more readily provided of sufficient excuses for his defense.

Then was my lord advertized by Master Norris that he should prepare himself to give attendance in the chamber of presence against the King's coming thither, who was disposed there to talk with him and with the other Cardinal; who came to my lord's chamber and they together went into the said chamber of presence, where the lords of the council stood in a row in order along the chamber. My lord putting off his cap to every of them most gently, and so did they no less to him, at which time the chamber was so furnished with noblemen,

6. amazed.
7. Sir Henry Norris, later executed with Anne Boleyn in 1536.
8. hardly.   9. changed.   1. informed.

gentlemen, and other worthy persons that only expected[2] the meeting and the countenance of the King and him, and what entertainment the King made him.

Then immediately after came the King into the chamber, and standing there under the cloth of estate, my lord kneeled down before him, who took my lord by the hand, and so he did the other Cardinal. Then he took my lord up by both arms and caused him to stand up, whom the King received with as amiable a cheer as ever he did and called him aside and led him by the hand to a great window, where he talked with him and caused him to be covered.

Then to behold the countenance of those that had made their wagers to the contrary, it would have made you to smile; and thus were they all deceived, as well worthy for their presumption. The King was in long and earnest communication with him, in so much as I heard the King say, "How can that be? Is not this your own hand?" And plucked out from his bosom a letter or writing and showed him the same. And as I perceived that it was answered so by my lord that the King had no more to say in that matter, but said to him, "My lord, go to your dinner, and all my lords here will keep you company. And after dinner I will resort to you again, and then we will commune further with you in this matter." And so departed. The King dined that same day with Mistress Anne Boleyn in her chamber (who kept there an estate more like a Queen than a simple maid).

Then was a table set up in the chamber of presence for my lord and other lords of the council, where they all dined together. And sitting thus at dinner communing of divers matters, quod my lord, "it were well done if the King would send his chaplains and bishops to their cures[3] and benefices." "Yea, marry," quod my Lord of Norfolk,[4] "ye say very well. And so it were for you too." "I could be contented therewith very well," quod my lord, "if it were the King's pleasure to

2. *that only expected:* i.e. whose only reason for being there was their anticipation of etc.
3. parishes or dioceses.
4. Thomas Howard II, third Duke of Norfolk (1473–1554), the uncle of Anne Boleyn.

grant me license with his favor to go to my benefice of Winchester." "Nay," quod my Lord of Norfolk, "to your benefice of York, where consisteth your greatest honor and charge." "Even as it shall please the King," quod my lord, and so fell into other communication. For the lords were very loth to have him planted so nigh the King as to be at Winchester. Immediately after dinner they fell in secret talk until the waiters had dined.

And as I heard it reported by them that waited upon the King at dinner, that Mistress Anne Boleyn was much offended with the King, as far as she durst, that he so gently entertained my lord, saying, as she sat with the King at dinner in communication of [5] him, "Sir," quod she, "is it not a marvelous thing to consider what debt and danger the Cardinal hath brought you in with all your subjects?" "How so, sweetheart?" quod the King. "Forsooth, sir," quod she, "there is not a man within all your realm worth five pounds but he hath indebted you unto him by his means" (meaning by a loan that the King had but late of his subjects). "Well, well," quod the King, "as for that there is in him no blame, for I know that matter better than you or any other." "Nay, sir," quod she, "besides all that what things hath he wrought within this realm to your great slander and dishonor. There is never a nobleman within this realm that if he had done but half so much as he hath done but he were well worthy to lose his head. If my Lord of Norfolk, my Lord of Suffolk, my lord my father, or any other noble person within your realm had done much less than he, but they should have lost their heads or this." "Why then I perceive," quod the King, "ye are not the Cardinal's friend." "Forsooth, sir," then quod she, "I have no cause nor any other man that loveth your grace. No more have your grace if ye consider well his doings." At this time the waiters had taken up the table and so they ended their communication.

Now ye may perceive the old malice beginneth to break out and newly to kindle the brand that after proved to[6] a great fire, which was much procured by his secret enemies (touched something before)[7] as of herself. After all this com-

5. *communication of*: conversation with.   6. *proved to*: turned out to be.
7. *touched . . . before*: whom I have already mentioned.

munication the dinner thus ended, the King rose up and went incontinent into the chamber of presence, whereas my lord and other of the lords were attending his coming. To whom he called my lord into the great window and talked with him there a while very secretly. And at the last the King took my lord by the hand and led him into his privy chamber, sitting there in consultation with him all alone, without any other of the lords of the council, until it was night; the which blanked [8] his enemies very sore,[9] and made them to stir the coals, being in doubt what this matter would grow unto, having now none other refuge to trust to but to Mistress Anne, in whom was all their whole and firm trust and affiance,[1] without whom they doubted [2] all their enterprise but frustrate and void.

Now was I fain, being warned that my lord had no lodging in the court, to ride into the country to provide for my lord a lodging. So that I provided a lodging for him at an house of Master Empson's[3] called Euston, three miles from Grafton, whither my lord came by torchlight, it was so late or the King and he departed. At whose departing the King commanded him to resort again early in the morning to the intent they might finish their talk which they had then begun and not concluded. After their departing my lord came to the said house at Euston to his lodging, where he had to supper with him divers of his friends of the court.

And sitting at supper, in came to him Doctor Stephens the Secretary, late ambassador unto Rome, but to what intent he came I know not. Howbeit my lord took it that he came both to dissemble[4] a certain obedience and love towards him or else to espy his behavior and to hear his communication at supper. Notwithstanding my lord bade him welcome and commanded him to sit down at the table to supper. With whom my lord had this communication with him under this manner: "Master Secretary," quod my lord, "ye be welcome home out of Italy. When came ye from Rome?" "Forsooth," quod he, "I came home almost a month ago." "And where," quod my lord, "hath ye been ever since?" "Forsooth," quod

8. nonplussed.   9. grievously.   1. faith.   2. feared.
3. Thomas Empson, the son of Sir Richard.   4. simulate, pretend.

he, "following the court this progress." "Then have ye hunted and had good game and pastime." "Forsooth, sir," quod he, "and so I have, I thank the King's majesty." "What good greyhounds have ye?" quod my lord. "I have some, sir," quod he. And thus in hunting and like disports passed they all their communication at supper. And after supper my lord and he talked secretly together until it was midnight or[5] they departed.

The next morning my lord rose early and rode straight to the court; at whose coming the King was ready to ride, willing my lord to resort to the council with the lords in his absence, and said he could not tarry with him, commanding him to return with Cardinal Campeggio, who had taken his leave of the King. Whereupon my lord was constrained to take his leave also of the King, with whom the King departed amiably in the sight of all men. The King's sudden departing in the morning was by the special labor of Mistress Anne, who rode with him only to lead him about, because he should not[6] return until the Cardinals were gone; the which departed after dinner, returning again towards the More. The King rode that morning to view a ground for a new park, which is called at this day Hartwell Park, where Mistress Anne had made provision for the King's dinner, fearing his return or the Cardinals were gone.

Then rode my lord and the other Cardinal after dinner on their way homeward. And so came to the Monastery of Saint Albans, whereof he himself was commendatory,[7] and there lay one whole day. And the next day they rode to the More, and from thence the Cardinal Campeggio took his journey towards Rome with the King's reward (what it was I am uncertain). Nevertheless after his departure the King was informed that he carried with him great treasures of my lord's, conveyed in great tuns,[8] notable sums of gold and silver to Rome, whither they surmised my lord would secretly convey himself out of this realm. In so much that a post[9] was sent speedily after the Cardinal to search him; whom they overtook

5. before.   6. *because . . . not:* so that he might not.
7. *was commendatory:* i.e. held in lieu of a permanent incumbent.
8. large barrels.   9. messenger on horseback.

at Calais, where he was stayed until search was made. There was not so much money found as he received of the King's reward, and so he was dismissed and went his way.

After Cardinal Campeggio was thus departed and gone, Michaelmas Term[1] drew near, against the which[2] my lord returned unto his house at Westminster; and when the term began he went to the hall in such like sort and gesture[3] as he was wont most commonly to do, and sat in the Chancery, being Chancellor. After which day he never sat there more. The next day he tarried at home, expecting the coming of the two Dukes of Suffolk and Norfolk, which came not that day. But the next day they came unto him, to whom they declared how the King's pleasure was that he should surrender and deliver up the Great Seal into their hands, and to depart simply[4] unto Esher, an house (situate nigh[5] Hampton Court) belonging to the Bishop of Winchester. My lord understanding their message, demanded of them what commission they have to give him any such commandment. Who answered him again that they were sufficient commissioners in that behalf, having the King's commandment by his mouth so to do.

"Yet," quod he, "that is not sufficient for me without a further commandment of the King's pleasure; for the Great Seal of England was delivered me by the King's own person to enjoy during my life with the ministration of the office and high room of Chancellorship of England; for my surety whereof I have the King's letters patents to show." Which matter was greatly debated between the Dukes and him with many stout[6] words between them; whose words and checks[7] he took in patience for the time, in so much that the Dukes were fain to depart again without their purpose at that present,[8] and returned again unto Windsor to the King. And what report they made I cannot tell; howbeit the next day they came again from the King, bringing with them the King's letters. After the receipt[9] and reading of the same by my lord, which

1. Term began on October 9 in 1529.
2. *against the which:* in preparation for which.
3. *sort and gesture:* manner and behavior.
4. in an unostentatious manner.   5. *situate nigh:* located near.
6. haughty.   7. rebukes.   8. present moment.   9. reception.

was done with much reverence, he delivered unto them the Great Seal, contented to obey the King's high commandment. And seeing that the King's pleasure was to take his house with the contents, [he] was well pleased simply to depart to Esher, taking nothing but only some provision for his house.

And after long talk between the Dukes and him, they departed with the Great Seal of England to Windsor unto the King. Then went my lord and called all officers in every office in his house before him to take accompt[1] of all such stuff as they had in charge. And in his gallery there was set divers tables, whereupon a great number of rich stuff of silk in whole pieces of all colors, as velvet, satin, damask, caffa,[2] taffeta, grograine,[3] sarcinet,[4] and of other not in my remembrance. Also there lay a thousand pieces of fine holland cloth,[5] whereof, as I heard him say afterward, there was five hundred pieces thereof conveyed[6] both from the King and him.

Furthermore there was also the walls of the gallery hanged with cloths of gold and tissue[7] of divers makings, and cloth of silver in likewise on both the sides, and rich cloths of baudkin[8] of divers colors. There hung also the richest suits of copes[9] of his own provision, which he caused to be made for his colleges of Oxford and Ipswich,[1] that ever I saw in England. Then had he in two chambers adjoining to the gallery, the one called the gilt chamber and the other called most commonly the council chamber, wherein were set in each two broad and long tables upon trestles, whereupon was set such a number of plate of all sorts as were almost incredible. In the gilt chamber was set out upon the tables nothing but all gilt plate, and upon a cupboard standing under a window was garnished[2] all wholly with plate of clean[3] gold, whereof some was set with pearl and rich stones. And in the council chamber was set all white plate and parcel-gilt.[4] And under the tables in both the chambers were set baskets with old plate, which was not

1. inventory.   2. a rich silk.   3. a coarse fabric.
4. a fine silk material.   5. a costly linen.   6. i.e. stolen.
7. a sheer fabric, usually silk.   8. a rich embroidered stuff.
9. ecclesiastical vestments.
1. Both taken over by the king. The latter was dissolved and the former eventually refounded as Christ Church.   2. covered.   3. pure.
4. partially gilded.

esteemed but for broken plate and old, not worthy to be occupied;[5] and books containing the value and weight of every parcel laid by them ready to be seen. And so was also books set by all manner of stuff, containing the contents of everything. Thus everything being brought in good order and furnished, he gave the charge of the delivery thereof (unto the King) to every officer within his office of such stuff as they had before in charge by indenture of every parcel; for the order of his house was such as that every officer was charged by indenture with all such parcels as belonged to their office.

Then all thing being ordered as it is before rehearsed, my lord prepared him to depart by water. And before his departing he commanded Sir William Gascoigne,[6] his treasurer, to see those things before remembered[7] delivered safely to the King at his repair. That done, the said Sir William said unto my lord, "Sir, I am sorry for your grace, for I understand ye shall go straightway to the Tower." "Is this the good comfort and counsel," quod my lord, "that ye can give your master in adversity? It hath been always your natural inclination to be very light of credit[8] and much more lighter in reporting of false news. I would ye should know, Sir William and all other such blasphemers, that it[9] is nothing more false than that. For I never (thanks be to God) deserved by no ways[1] to come there under any arrest, although it hath pleased the King to take my house ready furnished for his pleasure at this time. I would all the world knew, and so I confess, to have nothing, either riches, honor, or dignity, that hath not grown of him and by him; therefore it is my very duty to surrender the same to him again as his very own with all my heart, or else I were an unkind servant. Therefore go your ways and give good attendance unto your charge that nothing be embezzled."

And therewithal he made him ready to depart with all his gentlemen and yeomen, which was no small number. And took his barge at his privy stairs, and so went by water unto Putney, where all his horses waited his coming. And at the taking of his barge there was no less than a thousand boats

5. used.   6. The grandfather of the Elizabethan poet, George Gascoigne,
7. mentioned.   8. *very . . . credit:* too quick to give credit, gullible.
9. there.   1. *by no ways:* in any way whatsoever.

full of men and women of the City of London waffeting[2] up
and down in Thames, expecting my lord's departing, supposing
that he should have gone directly from thence to the Tower;
whereat they rejoiced, and I dare be bold to say that the most
part never received damage at his hands.

O wavering and newfangled multitude! Is it not a wonder
to consider the inconstant mutability of this uncertain world!
The common people always desiring alterations and newelties[3]
of things for the strangeness of the case, which after turneth
them to small profit and commodity. For if the sequel of this
matter be well considered and digested, ye shall understand
that they had small cause to triumph at his fall. What hath
succeeded,[4] all wise men doth know and the common sort
of them hath felt. Therefore to grudge or wonder at it surely
were but folly; to study a redress, I see not how it can be
holpen,[5] for the inclination and the natural disposition of
Englishmen is and hath always been to desire alteration of officers which hath been thoroughly fed with long continuance
in their rooms[6] with sufficient riches and possessions. And they
being put out, then cometh another hungry and a lean officer
in his place that biteth nearer the bone than the old. So the
people be ever pilled and polled[7] with hungry dogs through
their own desire of change of new officers. Nature hath so
wrought in the people that it will not be redressed. Wherefore
I cannot see but always men in authority be disdained with
the common sort of men; and such most of all that justly min-
istereth equity to all men indifferently.[8] For where they please
someone which receiveth the benefit of the law at his hands
according to justice, there doth they in likewise displease
the contrary party, who supposeth to sustain great wrong,
where they have equity and right. Thus all good justicers[9]
be always in contempt with some for executing of indifferency.[1] And yet such ministers must be, for if there should
be no ministers of justice, the world should run full of error
and abomination and no good order kept ne quietness among

2. sailing.   3. novelties.   4. followed.   5. helped.   6. offices.
7. *pilled and polled:* ruined by depradations or extortions.
8. impartially.   9. ministers of justice.
1. *executing of indifferency:* acting impartially.

the people. There is no good man but he will commend such justicers as dealeth uprightly in their rooms and rejoice at their continuance and not at their fall. And whether this be true or no, I put me to the judgment of all discreet persons. Now let us leave and begin again where we left.

When he was with all his train arrived and landed at Putney, he took his mule and every man his horse. And setting forth not past the length of a pair of garden butts,[2] he espied a man come riding empost[3] down the hill in Putney town, demanding[4] of his footmen who they thought it should be. And they answered again and said that they supposed it should be Sir Harry Norris. And by and by he came to my lord and saluted him and said that the King's majesty had him commended to his grace, and willed him in any wise to be of good cheer, for he was as much in his highness's favor as ever he was and so shall be. And in token thereof he delivered him a ring of gold with a rich stone, which ring he knew very well for it was always the privy[5] token between the King and him when so ever the King would have any special matter dispatched at his hands. And said furthermore that the King commanded him to be of good cheer and take no thought for he should not lack. "And although the King hath dealt with you unkindly as ye suppose, he saith that it is for no displeasure that he beareth you, but only to satisfy more the minds of some (which he knoweth be not your friends) than for any indignation. And also ye know right well that he is able to recompense you with twice as much as your goods amounteth unto. And all this he bade me that I should show you. Therefore, sir, take patience. And for my part I trust to see you in better estate than ever ye were."

But when he heard Master Norris rehearse all the good and comfortable words of the King, he quickly lighted from his mule, all alone, as though he had been the youngest person among us. And incontinent kneeled down in the dirt upon both his knees, holding up his hands for joy. Master Norris, perceiving him so quickly from his mule upon the ground,

2. *length . . . butts:* distance between two archery butts.
3. in post haste.   4. asking.   5. secret.

mused and was astonied[6] therewith. And therewith he alighted also and kneeled by him, embracing him in his arms, and asked him how he did, calling upon him to credit his message. "Master Norris," quod he, "when I consider your comfortable and joyful news, I can do no less than to rejoice; for the sudden joy surmounted my memory, having no respect neither to the place or time, but thought it my very bounden duty to render thanks to God my maker and to the King my sovereign lord and master, who hath sent me such comfort in the very place where I received the same."

And talking with Master Norris upon his knees in the mire, he would have pulled off his under cap of velvet, but he could not undo the knot under his chin. Wherefore with violence he rent the laces and pulled it from his head and so kneeled bareheaded. And that done, he covered again his head and arose, and would have mounted his mule, but he could not mount again with such agility as he lighted before, where his footmen had as much ado to set him in his saddle as they could have. Then rode he forth up the hill in the town, talking with Master Norris. And when he came upon Putney Heath Master Norris took his leave and would have departed. Then quod my lord unto him, "Gentle Norris, if I were lord of a realm the one half thereof were insufficient a reward to give you for your pains and good comfortable news. But, good Master Norris, consider with me that I have nothing left me but my clothes on my back. Therefore I desire you to take this small reward of my hands" (the which was a little chain of gold made like a bottle chain)[7] with a cross of gold hanging thereat, wherein was a piece of the holy cross (which he wore continually about his neck next his skin). And said furthermore, "I assure you, Master Norris, that when I was in prosperity, although it seem but small in value, yet I would not gladly have departed[8] with it for the value of a thousand pounds. Therefore I beseech you take it in gree[9] and wear it about your neck for my sake. And as often as ye shall happen to look upon it, have me in remembrance unto the King's majesty as oppor-

6 amazed.   7. apparently a chain to attach a cork to a bottle.
8. parted.   9. *in gree:* with good will.

tunity shall serve you; unto whose highness and clemency I
desire you to have me most lowly[1] commended, for whose
charitable disposition towards me I can do nothing but only
minister my prayer unto God for the preservation of his royal
estate, long to reign in honor, health, and quiet life. I am his
obedient subject, vassal, and poor chaplain, and so do intend
(God willing) to be during my life, accompting[2] that of my
self I am of no estimation nor of no substance, but only by him
and of him, whom I love better than myself, and hath justly
and truly served to the best of my gross[3] wit."

And with that he took Master Norris by the hand and bade
him farewell. And being not gone but a small distance, he returned and called Master Norris again. And when he was returned, he said unto him, "I am sorry," quod he, "that I have
no condign[4] token to send to the King; but if ye would at
this my request present the King with this poor fool, I trust
his highness would accept him well. Surely for a nobleman's
pleasure he is worth a thousand pounds." So Master Norris
took the fool with him, with whom my lord was fain to send
six of tall yeomen with him to conduct and convey the fool to
the court; for the poor fool took on and fired[5] so in such a
rage when he saw that he must needs depart from my lord. Yet
notwithstanding they conveyed him with Master Norris to the
court, where the King received him most gladly.

After the departure of Master Norris with his token to the
King, my lord rode straight to Esher, an house appertaining
unto the Bishoprick of Winchester, situate within the County
of Surrey, not far from Hampton Court; where my lord and
his family[6] continued the space of three or four weeks without
beds, sheets, tablecloths, cups, and dishes to eat our meat or to
lie in. Howbeit there was good provision of all kind of victuals
and of drink both beer and wine, whereof there was sufficient
and plenty. My lord was of necessity compelled to borrow of
the Bishop of Carlisle and of Sir Thomas Arundel both dishes
to eat his meat in and plate to drink in and also linen cloths to

1. humbly.   2. reckoning.   3. dense, thick.   4. appropriate, suitable.
5. became angry.   6. household.

occupy.[7] And thus continued he in this strange estate until the feast of All-Hallowtide[8] was past.

It chanced me upon All-Hallow Day in the morning to come there into the great chamber to give mine attendance, where I found Master Cromwell[9] leaning in the great window with a primer in his hand, saying of Our Lady matins[1] (which had been since a very strange sight). He prayed not more earnestly than the tears distilled[2] from his eyes. Whom I bade good morrow, and with that I perceived the tears upon his cheeks. To whom I said, "Why, Master Cromwell, what meaneth all this your sorrow? Is my lord in any danger for whom ye lament thus? Or is it for any loss that ye have sustained by any misadventure?" "Nay, nay," quod he, "it is my unhappy adventure,[3] which am like to lose all that I have travailed for all the days of my life for doing of my master true and diligent service." "Why, sir," quod I, "I trust ye be too wise to commit anything by my lord's commandment otherwise than ye ought to do of right, whereof ye have any cause to doubt[4] of loss of your goods."

"Well, well," quod he, "I cannot tell; but all things, I see before mine eyes, is as it is taken.[5] And this I understand right well, that I am in disdain with most men for my master['s] sake—and surely without just cause. Howbeit an ill[6] name once gotten will not lightly be put away. I never had any promotion by my lord to the increase of my living.[7] And thus much will I say to you, that I do intend (God willing) this afternoon when my lord hath dined to ride to London and so to the court, where I will either make or mar or[8] I come again. I will put myself in the press[9] to see what any man is able to lay to my charge of untruth or misdemeanor."[1] "Marry, sir," quod I, "in so doing in my conceit[2] ye shall do very well and wisely,

7. make use of (as bedding and table cloths).   8. November 1.
9. Thomas Cromwell (1485?–1540), later to enjoy great power in the service of Henry VIII.
1. *Our Lady matins:* morning prayers to the Blessed Virgin.   2. gushed.
3. fortune.   4. be afraid.
5. *all things . . . taken:* i.e. the value of any action depends upon the interpretation which people place upon it.
6. evil.   7. income.   8. before.   9. crowd.   1. evil behavior.
2. *in my conceit:* to my mind.

beseeching God to be your guide and send you good luck, even as I would myself." And with that I was called into the closet[3] to see and prepare all thing ready for my lord, who intended that day to say Mass there himself; and so I did.

And then my lord came thither with his chaplain, one Doctor Marshall, saying first his matins, and heard two Masses on his knees. And then after he was confessed, he himself said Mass. And when he had finished Mass and all his divine service, [he] returned into his chamber, where he dined among divers of his doctors,[4] where as Master Cromwell dined also. And sitting at dinner it chanced that my lord commended the true and faithful service of his gentlemen and yeomen; whereupon Master Cromwell took an occasion to say to my lord that in conscience he ought to consider their truth and loyal service that they did him in this his present necessity, which never forsaketh him in all his trouble.

"It shall be well done therefore," said he, "for your grace to call them before you, all these your most worthy gentlemen and right honest yeomen, and let them understand that ye right well consider their patience, truth, and faithfulness. And then give them your commendation with good words and thanks, which shall be to them great courage to sustain your mishap in patient misery and to spend their life and substance in your service."

"Alas, Thomas," quod my lord unto him, "ye know I have nothing to give them. And words without deeds be not often well taken. For if I had as I have had of late, I would depart with them[5] so frankly[6] as they should be well content; but nothing hath no savor; and I am ashamed and also sorry that I am not able to requite their faithful service. And although I have cause to rejoice considering the fidelity that I perceive in the number of my servants who will not depart from me in my miserable estate, but be as diligent, obedient, and serviceable about me as they were in my great triumphant glory, yet do I lament again the want of substance to distribute among them."

"Why, sir," quod Master Cromwell, "have ye not here a

3. private chamber.   4. clerics with advanced university degrees.
5. *depart with them:* divide it with them.   6. freely.

number of chaplains to whom ye have departed very liberally
with spiritual promotions, in so much as some may dispend by
your grace's preferment a thousand marks[7] by the year and
some five hundred marks and some more and some less? Ye
have no one chaplain within all your house or belonging unto
you but he may dispend at the least well, by your procurement
or preferment, three hundred marks yearly, who had all the
profits and advantages at your hands and these your servants
none at all. And yet hath your poor servants taken much more
pain for you in one day than all your idle chaplains hath done
in a year. Therefore if they will not freely and frankly consider your liberality and depart[8] with you of the same goods
gotten in your service now in your great indigence and necessity, it is pity that they live. And all the world will have them
in indignation and hatred for their abominable ingratitude to
their master and lord."

"I think no less, Thomas," quod my lord, "wherefore cause
all my servants to be called and to assemble without in my
great chamber after dinner, and see them stand in order, and
I will declare unto them my mind according to your advice."
After that the board's end was taken up, Master Cromwell
came to me and said, "Heard ye not what my lord said even
now?" "Yes, sir," quod I, "that I did." "Well then," quod he,
"assemble all my lord's servants up into the great chamber."
And so I did. And when they were all there assembled, I assigned all the gentlemen to stand on the right side of the chamber and the yeomen on the left side. And at the last my lord
came thither, apparelled in a white rochet[9] upon a violet gown
of cloth like a bishop, who went straight into the great window.

Standing there a while, and his chaplains about him, beholding the number of his servants divided in two parts, [he]
could not speak unto them for tenderness of his heart, the flood
of tears that distilled [1] from his eyes declared no less; the which
perceived by his servants caused the fountains of water to
gush out of their faithful hearts down their cheeks in such
abundance as it would cause a cruel heart to lament. At the

7. the mark was worth 13s. 4d.   8. divide.
9. linen vestment worn by bishops.   1. flowed.

last, after he had turned his face to the wall and wiped his eyes with his handkerchief, he spake to them after this sort in effect: "Most faithful gentlemen and true-hearted yeomen, I do not only lament your personal presence about me, but I do lament my negligent ingratitude towards you all on my be-half, in whom hath been a great default that in my prosperity hath not done for you as I might have done either in word or deed, which was then in my power to do. But then I knew not my jewels and special treasures that I had of you, my faithful servants, in my house; but now approved [2] experience hath taught me, and with the eyes of my discretion (which before were hid) do perceive full well the same. There was never thing that repenteth me more that ever I did than doth the remembrance of my oblivious negligence and ungentleness, that I have not promoted or preferred you to condign rooms[3] and preferments according to your demerits.[4] Howbeit it is not unknown unto you all that I was not so well furnished of tem-poral advancements as I was of spiritual preferments. And if I should have promoted you to any of the King's offices and rooms, then should I have incurred the indignation of the King's servants, who would not much let[5] to report in every place behind my back that there could no office or room of the King's gift escape the Cardinal and his servants. And thus should I incur the obloquy and slander before all the whole world. But now it is come to this pass that it hath pleased the King to take all that ever I have into his possession, so that I have nothing left me but my bare clothes upon my back, the which be but simple in comparison to those that ye have seen me have or[6] this. Howbeit if they may do you any good or pleasure I would not stick[7] to divide them among you, yea, and the skin off my back if it might countervail [8] anything in value among you.

"But, good gentlemen and yeomen, my trusty and faithful servants, of whom no prince hath the like in my opinion, I most heartily require you to take with me some patience a little

2. tried, tested.   3. *condign rooms:* fitting appointments.   4. deserts.
5. hesitate.   6. before.   7. hesitate.   8. make an equivalent return for.

while; for I doubt not but that the King, considering the offence suggested against me by my mortal enemies to be of
small effect,[9] will shortly, I doubt not, restore me again to my
livings so that I shall be more able to divide some part thereof
yearly among you, whereof ye shall be well assured. For the
surplusage[1] of my revenues, whatsoever shall remain at the
determination of my accompts,[2] shall be (God willing) distributed among you. For I will never hereafter esteem the
goods and riches of this uncertain world but as a vain thing,
more than shall be sufficient for the maintenance of mine
estate and dignity that God hath or shall call me unto in
this world during my life. And if the King do not thus shortly
restore me, then will I see you bestowed according to your
own requests, and write for you either to the King or to any
other noble person within this realm to retain you into service; for I doubt not but that the King or any nobleman or
worthy gentleman of this realm will credit my letter in your
commendation. Therefore in the meantime mine advice is that
ye repair home to your wives (such as hath any), and such
among you as hath none to take this time to visit your parents
and friends in the country. There is none of you all but once
in a year would require license to visit your wives and other of
your friends; take this time, I pray you, in respect thereof. And
at your return I will not refuse you if I should beg with you.
I consider that the service of my house hath been such and of
such a sort that ye be not meet or apt to serve no man under
the degree of a King. Therefore I would wish you to serve
no man but the King, who I am sure will not reject you.
Therefore I desire you to take your pleasures for a month and
then ye may come again unto me. And I trust by that time the
King['s] majesty will extend his clemency upon me."

"Sir," quod Master Cromwell, "there is divers of these your
yeomen that would be glad to see their friends but they lack
money. Therefore here is divers of your chaplains who hath
received at your hands great benefices and high dignities. Let
them therefore now show themselves unto you as they are

9. *small effect:* little importance.   1. excess, surplus.
2. *determination . . . accompts:* settling of my accounts.

bound by all humanity to do. I think their honesty and charity is not so slender and void of grace that they would not see you lack where they may help to refresh you. And for my part, although I have not received of your grace's gift any one penny towards the increase of my yearly living, yet will I depart with you this towards the dispatch of your servants"— and delivered him five pounds in gold. "And now let us see what your chaplains will do. I think they will depart with you much more than I have done, who be more able to give you a pound than I one penny. Go to,[3] masters," quod he to the chaplains, in so much as some gave him ten pounds, some ten marks, some one hundred shillings, and so some more and some less as at that time their powers did extend. Whereby my lord received among them as much money of their liberality as he gave to each of his yeomen a quarter's wages and board wages for a month. And they departed down into the hall, where some determined to go to their friends, and some said that they would not depart from my lord until they might see him in better estate.

My lord returned into his chamber, lamenting the departure from his servants, making his moan unto Master Cromwell, who comforted him the best he could, and desired my lord to give him leave to go to London, where he would either make or mar or he came again (which was always his common saying). Then after long communication with my lord in secret he departed and took his horse and rode to London, at whose departing I was by; whom he bade farewell and said, "ye shall hear shortly of me, and if I speed well, I will not fail to be here again within these two days." And so I took my leave of him. And he rode forth on his journey. Sir Rafe Sadler[4] (now knight) was then his clerk and rode with him.

After that my lord had supped that night (being All-Hallow Day at night), and all men gone to bed, it chanced so about midnight that one of the porters came unto my chamber door and there knocked. And waking of me, [I] perceived who it was [and] asked him what he would have that time of the

3. *Go to:* get started, go ahead.
4. Sir Ralph Sadler (1507–1587), knighted in 1540.

night. "Sir," quod the porter, "there is a great number of horsemen at the gate that would come in, saying to me that it is Sir John Russell, and so it appears to me by his voice. What is your pleasure that I shall do?" "Marry," quod I, "go down again and make a great fire in your lodge, against I come, to dry them"—for it rained all that night the sorest[5] that it did all that year before. Then I rose and put on my nightgown, and came to the gates and asked who was there. With that Master Russell spake, whom I knew by his voice. And then I caused the porters to open the gates and let them all in, who were wet to the skin, desiring Master Russell to go into the lodge to the fire, and he showed me that he was come from the King unto my lord in message, with whom he required me to speak. "Sir," quod I, "I trust your news be good?" "Yea, I promise you on my fidelity," quod he, "and so, I pray you, show him I have brought him such news that will please him right well." "Then will I go," quod I, "and wake him and cause him to rise."

I went incontinent to my lord's chamber door and waked my lord, who asked me what I would have. "Sir," said I, "to show you that Sir John Russell is come from the King, who is desirous to speak with you." And then he called up one of his grooms to let me in. And being within I told him what a journey Master Russell had that night. "I pray God," quod he, "all be for the best." "Yes, sir," quod I, "he showed me and so bade me tell you that he had brought you such news as ye will greatly rejoice thereat." "Well then," quod he, "God be praised and welcome be his grace. Go ye and fetch him unto me, and by that time I will be ready to talk with him."

Then I returned from him to the lodge and brought Master Russell from thence to my lord, who had cast on his nightgown. And when Master Russell was come into his presence, he most humbly reverenced him upon his knee, [to] whom my lord bowed down and took him up and bade him welcome. "Sir," quod he, "the King commendeth him unto you"; and delivered him a great ring of gold with a turquoise for a token. "And willed you to be of good cheer, who loveth you as well as ever he did, and is not a little disquieted for your trouble,

5. heaviest.

whose mind is full of your remembrance. In so much as his grace before he sat to supper called me unto him, and commanded me to take this journey secretly to visit you to your comfort the best of my power. And, sir, if it please your grace, I have had this night the sorest[6] journey for so little a way that ever I had to my remembrance."

My lord thanked him for his pains and good news, and demanded [7] of him if he had supped. And he said "Nay." "Well then," quod my lord to me, "cause the cooks to provide some meat for him, and cause a chamber with a good fire to be made ready for him that he may take his rest a while upon a bed." All which commandment I fulfilled. And in the meantime my lord and Master Russell were in very secret communication. And in fine[8] Master Russell went to his chamber, taking his leave of my lord for all night, and said he would not tarry but a while, for he would (God willing) be at the court at Greenwich again before day, for he would not for anything that it were known his being with my lord that night. And so being in his chamber, having a small repast, [he] rested him a while upon a bed whilst his servants supped and dried themselves by the fire. And then incontinent he rode away with speed to the court. And shortly after his being there my lord was restored again unto plenty of household stuff, vessel,[9] and plate, and of all things necessary some part, so that he was indifferently[1] furnished much better than he was of late. And yet not so abundantly as the King's pleasure was; the default whereof was in the officers and in such as had the oversight[2] of the delivery thereof. And yet my lord rejoiced in that little in comparison to that he had before.

Now let us return again to Master Cromwell to see how he hath sped since his departure last from my lord. The case stood so that there should begin shortly after All-Hallowtide the Parliament; and [he], being within London, devised with himself to be one of the burgesses of the Parliament, and chanced to meet with one Sir Thomas Rush, knight (a special friend of his), whose son was appointed to be one of the

6. most difficult.   7. asked.   8. *in fine:* in conclusion.   9. utensils.
1. tolerably well.   2. management.

burgesses of that Parliament, of whom he obtained his room,[3] and by that means put his foot into the Parliament House. Then within two or three days after his entry into the Parliament, he came unto my lord to Esher with a much pleasanter countenance than he had at his departure. And meeting with me before he came to my lord, said unto me that he had once adventured to put in his foot, where he trusted shortly to be better regarded or all were done. And when he was come to my lord, they talked together in secret manner. And that done he rode out of hand [4] again that night to London, because he would not be absent from the Parliament the next morning. There could nothing be spoken against my lord in the Parliament House but he would answer it incontinent,[4] or else take day[5] until the next day, against[6] which time he would resort to my lord to know what answer he should make in his behalf. In so much that there was no matter alleged against my lord but that he was ever ready furnished with a sufficient answer; so that at length for his honest behavior in his master's case he grew into such estimation in every man's opinion that he was esteemed to be the most faithfullest servant to his master of all other, wherein he was of all men greatly commended.

Then was there brought a bill of articles into the Parliament House to have my lord condemned of treason; against which bill Master Cromwell inveighed so discreetly, with such witty persuasions and deep reasons, that the same bill could take there no effect. Then were his enemies compelled to indict him in a *praemunire*,[7] and all was done only to the intent to entitle the King to all his goods and possessions, the which he had gathered together and purchased for his colleges in Oxford and Ipswich, and for the maintenance of the same, which was then a-building in most sumptuous wise. Wherein when he was demanded [8] by the judges, which were sent him purposely to examine him, what answer he would make to the same, he said: "The King's highness knoweth right well whether I have

3. seat.   4. immediately.   5. *take day:* i.e. delay it.   6. in preparation for.
7. The statute of 16 Richard II, c. 5 provided for writs of *praemunire* under which the defendant's estate could be confiscated. The *praemunire* against Wolsey was issued on October 9, 1529.   8. asked.

offended his majesty and his laws or no in using of my prerogative legantine,[9] for the which ye have me indicted. Notwithstanding I have the King's license in my coffers under his
hand and broad seal for exercising and using the authority
thereof in the largest wise within his highness's dominions, the
which remaineth now in the hands of my enemies. Therefore
because I will not stand in question or trial with the King in
his own case, I am content here of mine own frank[1] will and
mind in your presence to confess the offence in the indictment,
and put me wholly in the mercy and grace of the King, having
no doubts in his godly disposition and charitable conscience,
whom I know hath an high discretion to consider the truth
and my humble submission and obedience. And although I
might justly stand in the trial with him therein, yet I am content to submit myself to his clemency. And thus much ye may
say to him in my behalf, that I am entirely his obediencer[2] and
do intend (God willing) to obey and fulfil all his princely
pleasure in everything that he will command me to do; whose
will and pleasure I never yet disobeyed or repugned,[3] but was
always contented and glad to accomplish his desire and commandment before God, whom I ought most rathest[4] to have
obeyed, the which negligence now greatly repenteth me.[5]
Notwithstanding I most heartily require you to have me most
humbly to his royal majesty commended, for whom I do and
will pray for the preservation of his royal person, long to reign
in honor, prosperity and quietness, and to have the victory
over his mortal and cankered enemies." And they took their
leave of him and departed.

Shortly after the King sent the Duke of Norfolk unto him in
message (but what it was I am not certain). But my lord being
advertized [6] that the Duke was coming even at hand,[7] he
caused all his gentlemen to wait upon him down through the
hall into the base[8] court to receive the Duke at the entry of the
gates, and commanded all his yeomen to stand still in the hall
in order. And he and his gentlemen went to the gates, where he

9. as papal legate.   1. free.   2. obedient subject.   3. opposed.
4. *most rathest:* most of all.
5. *greatly . . . me:* i.e. I am very sorry for it.   6. informed.
7. *even at hand:* and was already at hand.   8. lower.

encountered with my Lord of Norfolk, whom he received bareheaded; who embraced each other, and so led him by the arm through the hall into his chamber. And as the Duke passed through the hall at the upper end thereof he turned again his visage down the hall, regarding the number of the tall yeomen that stood in order there, and said, "Sirs," quod he, "your diligent and faithful servance[9] unto my lord here (your master) in this time of his calamity hath purchased for yourself of all noble men much honesty.[1] In so much as the King commanded me to say to you in his grace's name that for your true and loving service that ye have done to your master, his highness will see you all furnished at all times with service according to your demerits."

With that my Lord Cardinal put off his cap and said to my Lord of Norfolk, "Sir," quod he, "these men be all approved[2] men, wherefore it were pity they should want either service or livings. And being sorry that I am not able to do for them as my heart doth wish, [I] do therefore require[3] you my good lord to be good lord unto them and extend your good word for them when ye shall see opportunity at any time hereafter, and that ye will prefer their diligent and faithful service to the King." "Doubt ye not thereof," quod my Lord of Norfolk, "but I will do for them the best of my power; and when I shall see cause I will be an earnest suitor for them to the King, and some of you I will retain myself in service for your honesty's sake. And as ye have begun, so continue and remain here still with my lord until ye hear more of the King's pleasure. God's blessing and mine be with you."

And so went up into the great chamber to dinner, whom my Lord Cardinal thanked and said unto him, "yet my lord of all other noblemen I have most cause to thank you, for your noble heart and gentle nature which ye have showed me behind my back, as my servant Thomas Cromwell hath made report unto me. But even as ye are a nobleman indeed, so have ye showed yourself no less to all men in calamity, and in especial to me; and even as ye have abated[4] my glory and high estate and

9. service.   1. good reputation.   2. experienced, tried and true.
3. request.   4. brought down.

brought it full low, so have ye extended your honorable favor most charitably unto me being prostrate before ye. Forsooth, sir, ye do right well deserve to bear in your arms the noble and gentle lion, whose natural inclination is that when he hath vanquished any beast and seeth him yielded, lying prostrate before him at his foot, then will he show most clemency unto his vanquished and do him no more harm, ne suffer any other devouring beast to damage[5] him. Whose nature and quality ye do ensue;[6] therefore these verses may be ascribed to your lordship, which be these:

> *Parcere prostratis, scit nobilis ira leonis;*
> *Tu quoque fac simile, quisquis regnabis in orbem.*[7]

With that the water was brought them to wash before dinner, to the which my lord called my Lord of Norfolk to wash with him; but he refused of courtesy and desired to have him excused, and said that it became him not to presume to wash with him any more now than it did before in his glory. "Yes, forsooth," quod my Lord Cardinal, "for my authority and dignity legantine[8] is gone, wherein consisted all my high honor." "A straw," quod my Lord of Norfolk, "for your legacy. I never esteemed your honor the more or higher for that. But I regarded your honor for that ye were Archbishop of York and a Cardinal, whose estate[9] of honor surmounteth[1] any Duke now being within this realm. And so will I honor you, and acknowledge the same, and bear you reverence accordingly. Therefore I beseech you content yourself, for I will not presume to wash with you; and therefore I pray you hold me excused." Then was my Lord Cardinal constrained to wash alone; and my Lord of Norfolk all alone also when he had done. And when he had done my Lord Cardinal would fain have had my Lord of Norfolk to sit down in the chair in the inner side of the table, but surely he refused the same

---

5. harm.   6. follow.
7. The exact source of Wolsey's distich has not been located. It may be translated as follows: "The wrathful, noble lion knows how to spare those who are prostate before him; go and do likewise, you who will rule over the earth." Norfolk's coat of arms depicted a lion.
8. as papal legate.   9. degree.   1. surpasseth.

also with much humbleness. Then was there set another chair for my Lord of Norfolk over against[2] my Lord Cardinal on the outside of the table, the which was by my Lord of Norfolk based [3] something beneath my lord. And during the dinner all their communication was of the diligent service of the gentlemen which remained with my lord there, attending upon him there at dinner, and how much the King and all other noblemen doth esteem them with worthy commendations for so doing; and at this time how little they be esteemed in the court that are come to the King's service and forsaken their master in his necessity, whereof some he blamed by name. And with this communication the dinner being ended, they rose from the table and went together into my lord's bed-chamber, where they continued in consultation a certain season.

And being there, it chanced Master Shelley[4] the judge to come thither, sent from the King; whereof relation was made to my lord, which caused the Duke and him to break up their communication. And the Duke desired to go into some chamber to repose him for a season. And as he was coming out of my lord's chamber, he met with Master Shelley, to whom Master Shelley made relation of the cause of his coming, and desired the Duke to tarry and assist him in doing of his message; whom he denied and said, "I have nothing to do with your message, wherein I will not meddle." And so departed into a chamber where he took his rest for an hour or two. And in the meantime my lord issued out of his chamber and came to Master Shelley to know his message. Who declared unto him, after due salutation, that the King's pleasure was to have his house at Westminster (then called York Place), belonging to his Bishoprick of York, intending to make of that house a palace royal and to possess the same according to the laws of this his grace's realm. "His highness hath therefore sent for all the judges and for all his learned counsel to know their opinions in the assurance thereof; in whose determinations it was fully resolved that your grace should recognize before a judge the right thereof to be in the King and his successors.

2. opposite.   3. placed.   4. Sir William Shelley (1480–1549).

And so his highness shall be assured thereof. Wherefore it hath pleased his majesty to appoint me by his commandment to come hither to take of you this recognizance, who hath in you such affiance,[5] that ye will not refuse so to do accordingly. Therefore I shall desire your grace to know your good will therein."

"Master Shelley," quod my lord, "I know that the King of his own nature is of a royal stomach[6] and yet not willing more than justice shall lead him unto by the law. And therefore I counsel you and all other fathers of the law and learned men of his counsel to put no more into his head than the law may stand with good conscience; for when ye tell him 'this is the law' it were well done ye should tell him also that 'although this be the law, yet this is conscience.' For law without conscience is not good to be given unto a King in counsel to use for a lawful right, but always to have a respect to conscience before the rigor of the common law, for *'laus est facere quod decet, non quod licet.'* [7] The King ought of his royal dignity and prerogative to mitigate the rigor of the law where conscience hath the most force. Therefore in his royal place of equal justice he hath constitute[8] a chancellor, an officer to execute justice with clemency where conscience is oppressed by the rigor of the law. And therefore the Court of Chancery hath been heretofore commonly called the Court of Conscience because it had jurisdiction to command the high ministers of the common law to spare execution and judgment where conscience had most effect. Therefore I say to you in this case, although you and other of your profession perceive by your learning that the King may by an order of your laws lawfully do that thing which ye demand of me—how say you, Master Shelley, may I do it with justice and conscience, to give that thing away from me and my successors which is none of mine? If this be law with conscience, show me your opinion, I pray you."

5. trust.   6. temper, spirit.
7. Wolsey quotes from Seneca's *Octavia,* a conversation between Nero and Seneca (who speaks these words) in which the proper exercise of political power is discussed: "It is praiseworthy to do what is fitting, not what is permitted."   8. appointed.

"Forsooth, my lord," quod he, "there is some conscience in this case; but having regard to the King's high power, and to be employed [9] to a better use and purpose, it may the better be suffered with conscience—who is sufficient to make recompense to the church of York with double the value." "That I know well," quod my lord, "but here is no such condition neither promised ne agreed, but only a bare and simple departure with[1] another's right forever. And if every bishop may do the like, then might every prelate give away the patrimony of their churches, which is none of theirs, and so in process of time leave nothing for their successors to maintain their dignities; which, all things considered, should be but small to the King's honor. Sir, I do not intend to stand in terms[2] with you in this matter, but let me see your commission." To whom Master Shelley showed him the same. And that seen and perceived by him, [he] said again, "Thus, Master Shelley," quod he, "ye shall make report to the King's highness that I am his obedient subject and faithful chaplain and beadman,[3] whose royal commandment and request I will in no wise disobey, but most gladly fulfil and accomplish his princely will and pleasure in all things and in especial in this matter in as much as ye, the fathers of the laws, say that I may lawfully do it. Therefore I charge your consciences and dischargeth mine. Howbeit I pray you show his majesty from me that I most humbly desire his highness to call to his most gracious remembrance that there is both heaven and hell." And therewith the clerk was called, who wrote my lord['s] recognizance, and after some secret talk Master Shelley departed. Then rose my Lord of Norfolk from his repose, and after some communication with my lord he departed.

Thus continued my lord at Esher, who received daily messages from the court, whereof some were not so good as some were bad, but yet much more evil than good. For his enemies, perceiving the great affection that the King bare always toward him, devised a mean[4] to disquiet and disturb his patience,

9. *to be employed:* considering that it (York Place) is to be employed.
1. *departure with:* expropriation of.
2. *stand in terms:* take part in controversy.
3. one who prays for another.   4. means, way.

thinking thereby to give him an occasion to fret and chafe, that death should rather ensue than increase of health or life, the which they most desired. They feared him more after his fall than they did before in his prosperity, doubting[5] much his readoption into authority by reason that the King's favor remained still towards him in such sort whereby they might rather be in danger of their estates[6] than in any assurance for their cruelty ministered by their malicious inventions surmised [7] and brought to pass against him.

Therefore they took this order among them in their matters, that daily they would send him something or do something against him wherein they thought that they might give him a cause of heaviness[8] or lamentation. As some day they would cause the King to send for four or five of his gentlemen from him to serve the King; and some other day they would lay matters newly invented against him. Another day they would take from him some of his promotions or of their promotions whom he preferred before. Then would they fetch from him some of his yeomen; in so much as the King took into service sixteen of them at once, and at one time put them into his guard. This order of life he led continually; that there was no one day but, or ever he went to bed, he had an occasion greatly to chafe or fret the heart out of his belly, but that he was a wise man and bare all their malice in patience.

At Christmas he fell sore[9] sick, that he was likely to die. Whereof the King, being advertized, was very sorry therefore, and sent Doctor Butts,[1] his grace's physician, unto him to see in what estate he was. Doctor Butts came unto him and, finding him very sick, lying in his bed, and perceiving the danger he was in, repaired again unto the King. Of whom the King demanded, saying, "how doth yonder man? Have you seen him?" "Yea, sir," quod he. "How do ye like him?" [2] quod the King. "Forsooth, sir," quod he, "if you would have him dead, I warrant your grace he will be dead within this four days if he receive no comfort from you shortly and Mistress

5. fearing.   6. conditions, situations.   7. entertained.   8. grief.
9. grievously.
1. Dr. William Butts (d. 1545), court physician since 1524.
2. *How . . . like him:* how does he appear to you?

Anne." "Marry," quod the King, "God forbid that he should die. I pray you, good Master Butts, go again unto him and do your cure upon him, for I would not lose him for twenty thousand pounds." "Then must your grace," quod Master Butts, "send him first some comfortable message as shortly as is possible." "Even so will I," quod the King, "by you. And therefore make speed to him again, and ye shall deliver him from me this ring for a token of our good will and favor towards him (in the which ring was engraved the King's visage within a ruby, as lively counterfeit[3] as was possible to be devised). This ring he knoweth very well for he gave me the same. And tell him that I am not offended with him in my heart nothing at all, and that he shall perceive (and God send him) life very shortly. Therefore bid him be of good cheer and pluck up his heart and take no despair. And I charge you come not from him until ye have brought him out of all danger of death."

And then he spake to Mistress Anne, saying, "Good sweetheart, I pray you, at this my instance[4] (as ye love us) to send the Cardinal a token with comfortable words. And in so doing ye shall do us a loving pleasure." She, being not minded to disobey the King's earnest request (whatsoever she intended in her heart towards the Cardinal), took incontinent her tablet[5] of gold hanging at her girdle and delivered it to Master Butts with very gentle and comfortable words in commendation to the Cardinal. And thus Master Butts departed and made speedy return to Esher to my Lord Cardinal; after whom the King sent Doctor Clement,[6] Doctor Wotton,[7] and Doctor Cromer[8] the Scot to consult[9] and assist Master Butts for my lord's health.

After that Master Butts had been with my lord and delivered the King's and Mistress Anne's tokens unto him, with the most comfortablest words he could devise on their behalf, whereat he rejoiced not a little, advancing him a little in his bed, and received these tokens most joyfully, thanking Master Butts for

3. *lively counterfeit:* portrayed in as lifelike a manner.
4. urgent entreaty.   5. writing tablet.   6. Dr. John Clement (d. 1572).
7. Dr. Edward Wotten (1492–1555).   8. Dr. Walter Cromer (d. 1547).
9. consult with.

his comfortable news and pains. Master Butts showed him furthermore that the King's pleasure was that he should minister unto him for his health; and for the most assured and brief ways to be had for the same hath sent Doctor Wotton, Doctor Clement, and Doctor Cromer to join with him in counsel and ministration. "Therefore, my lord," quod he, "it were well done that they should be called in to visit your person and estate;[1] wherein I would be glad to hear their opinions, trusting in almighty God that through his grace and assistance we shall ease you of your pains and rid you clean from your disease and infirmity." Wherewith my lord was well pleased and contented to hear their judgments; for indeed he trust[2] more to the Scottish doctor than he did to any of the other, because he was the very occasion that he inhabited here in England, and before he gave him partly his exhibition[3] in Paris. Then when they were come into his chamber and had talked with him, he took upon him to debate his disease learnedly among them, so that they might understand that he was seen[4] in that art. After they had taken order for ministration it was not long or they brought him out of all danger and fear of death. And within four days they set him on his feet and got him a good stomach to his meat. This done, and he in a good estate of amendment, they took their leave to depart, to whom my lord offered his reward; the which they refused, saying that the King gave them in special commandment to take nothing of him, for their pains and ministration, for at their return his highness said that he would reward them of his own costs. And thus with great thanks they departed from my lord, whom they left in good estate of recovery.

After this time my lord daily amended, and so continued still at Esher until Candlemas.[5] Against which feast the King caused to be sent him three or four cartloads of stuff, and most part thereof was locked in great standards[6] (except beds and kitchen stuff), wherein was both plate and rich hangings and chapel stuff. Then my lord, being thus furnished, was therewith well contented; although they whom the King assigned

1. condition.   2. trusted.   3. maintenance as a scholar.
4. knowledgeable.   5. February 2, 1530.   6. large chests.

did not deliver him so good ne so rich stuff as the King's pleasure was, yet was he joyous thereof and rendered most humble thanks to the King and to them that appointed the said stuff for him, saying to us his servants at the opening of the same stuff in the standards, the which we thought, and said, it might have been better if it had pleased them that appointed it. "Nay, sirs," quod my lord to us, "he that hath nothing is glad of somewhat though it be never so little. And although it be not in comparison half so much and good as we had before, yet we rejoice more of this little than we did before of the great abundance that we then had." And [he] thanked the King very much for the same, trusting after this to have much more. "Therefore let us all rejoice and be glad that God and the King hath so graciously remembered to restore us to some things to maintain our estate like a noble person."

Then commanded he Master Cromwell, being with him, to make suit to the King's majesty that he might remove thence to some other place, for he was weary of that house of Esher —for with continual use thereof the house waxed unsavory— supposing that if he might remove from thence he should much sooner recover his health. And also the council had put into the King's head that the new gallery at Esher (which my lord had late before his fall newly set up) should be very necessary[7] for the King to take down and set it up again at Westminster; which was done accordingly, and stands at this present day there. The taking away thereof before my lord's face was to him a corrosive,[8] which was invented by his enemies only to torment him, the which indeed discouraged him very sore to tarry[9] any longer there.

Now Master Cromwell thought it but vain and much folly to move any of the King's council to assist and prefer his suit to the King, among whom rested[1] the number of his mortal enemies, for they would either hinder his removing or else remove him farther from the King than to have holpen[2] him to any place nigh the King's common trade.[3] Wherefore he

7. convenient.   8. cause of annoyance.
9. *very . . . tarry:* very much from tarrying.   1. remained.   2. helped.
3. course, path.

refused any suit to them and made only suit to the King's own person, whose suit the King graciously heard and thought it very convenient[4] to be granted. And through the special motion of Master Cromwell the King was well contented that he should remove to Richmond, which place my lord had a little before repaired to his great cost and charge, for the King had made an exchange thereof with him for Hampton Court. All this his removing was done without the knowledge of the King's council, for if they might have had any intelligence thereof before then would they have persuaded the King to the contrary. But when they were advertized of the King's grant and pleasure, they dissimuled[5] their countenances in the King's presence, for they were greatly afraid of him, lest his nigh-being to the King [he] [6] might at length some one time resort to him and so call him home again, considering the great affection and love that the King daily shew[7] towards him. Wherefore they doubted[8] his rising again if they found not a mean to remove him shortly from the King.

In so much that they thought it convenient for their purpose to inform the King upon certain considerations which they invented, that it were very necessary that my lord should go down into the North, unto his benefice of York, where he should be a good stay[9] for the country. To the which the King, supposing that they had meant no less than good faith, granted and condescended to[1] their suggestion, which was farced[2] with so wonderful imagined considerations that the King, understanding nothing of their intent, was lightly[3] persuaded to the same. Whereupon the Duke of Norfolk commanded Master Cromwell, who had daily access unto him, to say to my lord that it is the King's pleasure that he should with speed go to his benefice, where lieth his cure,[4] and look to that according to his duty. Master Cromwell, at his next repair to my lord, declared unto him what my Lord of Norfolk said—who lay then at Richmond—how it was determined

4. fitting.   5. dissembled.
6. *lest* . . . [*he*]: i.e. for if he were close to the king, the king might, etc.   7. showed.   8. feared.   9. prop, support.
1. *condescended to:* acquiesced in.   2. stuffed.   3. easily.
4. spiritual obligations.

that he should go to his benefice. "Well then, Thomas," quod my lord, "seeing there is none other remedy, I do intend to go to my benefice of Winchester. And I pray you, Thomas, so show my Lord of Norfolk." "Contented, sir," quod Master Cromwell, and according to his commandment did so. To the which my Lord of Norfolk answered and said, "What will he do there? Nay," quod he, "let him go into his province of York, whereof he hath received his honor, and there lieth the spiritual burden and charge of his conscience, as he ought to do, and so show him."

The lords, who were not all his friends, having intelligence of his intent, thought to withdraw his appetite from Winchester [and] would in no wise permit him to plant himself so nigh the King; [they] moved therefore the King to give my lord but a pension out of Winchester and to distribute all the rest among the nobility and other of his worthy servants; and in likewise to do the same with the revenues of Saint Albans and of the revenues of his colleges in Oxford and Ipswich, the which the King took into his own hands; whereof Master Cromwell had the receipt and governance afore[5] by my lord's assignment. In consideration thereof it was thought most convenient that he should have so still. Notwithstanding out of the revenues of Winchester and Saint Albans the King gave to some one nobleman three hundred marks and to some one hundred pounds and to some more and to some less according to the King's royal pleasure. Now Master Cromwell executed his office. the which he had over the lands of the colleges, so justly and exactly that he was had in great estimation for his witty[6] behavior therein, and also for the true, faithful and diligent service extended towards my lord his master, that it came at length so to pass that those to whom the King's majesty had given any annuities or fees for term of life by patent[7] out of the forenamed revenues could not be good but during my lord's life, for as much as the King had no longer estate[8] or title therein, which came to him by reason of my lord's attendure[9] in the praemunire. And to make their estates good

5. before.   6. intelligent.   7. letters patent.   8. power.   9. attainder.

and sufficient according to their patents, it was thought necessary to have my lord's confirmation unto their grants. And
this to be brought about there was none other mean but to
make suit to Master Cromwell to attain their confirmation at
my lord's hands, whom they thought might best obtain the
same.

Then began both nobleman and other who had any patents
of the King out either of Winchester or Saint Albans to make
earnest suit to Master Cromwell for to solicit their causes to
my lord to get of him his confirmations. And for his pains
therein sustained, they promised every man not only worthily
to reward him, but also to show him such pleasures as should
at all times lie in their several powers, whereof they assured
him. Wherein Master Cromwell, perceiving an occasion and
a time given him to work for himself and to bring the thing
to pass which he long wished for, intended to work so in
these matters to serve their desires, that he might the sooner
bring his own enterprise to purpose.[1] Then at his next resort
to my lord he moved him privily in this matter to have his
counsel and his advice. And so by their witty heads it was
devised that they should work together by one line to bring
by their policies Master Cromwell in place and estate where he
might do himself good and my lord much profit.

Now began matters to work to bring Master Cromwell into
estimation in such sort as was afterward much to his increase
of dignity. And thus every man having an occasion to sue
for my lord's confirmation made now earnest travail to Master
Cromwell for these purposes, who refused none to make
promise that he would do his best in that case. And having
a great occasion of access to the King for the disposition of
divers lands whereof he had the order and governance, by
means whereof and by his witty demeanor he grew continually
into the King's favor, as ye shall hear after in this history.
But first let us resort to the great business about the assurance
of all these patents which the King hath given to divers noblemen and other of his servants, wherein Master Cromwell made

1. *to purpose:* into effect.

a countenance of[2] great suit to my lord for the same, that in process of time he served all their turns so that they had their purposes and he their good wills. Thus rose his name and friendly acceptance with all men. The fame of his honesty and wisdom sounded so in the King's ears that by reason of his access to the King he perceived to be in him no less wisdom than fame had made of him report, for as much as he had the governance and receipts of those lands which I showed you before. And the conference that he had with the King therein enforced[3] the King to repute him a very wise man and a meet instrument[4] to serve his grace, as it after came to pass.

Sir, now the lords thought long to remove him farther from the King and out of his common trade.[5] Wherefore (among other of the lords) my Lord of Norfolk said to Master Cromwell, "Sir," quod he, "me thinketh that the Cardinal your master maketh no haste northward. Show him that if he go not away shortly, I will, rather than he should tarry still, tear him with my teeth. Therefore I would advise him to prepare him away as shortly as he can, or else he shall be sent forward." These words Master Cromwell reported to my lord at his next repair to him, who then had a just occasion to resort to him for the dispatch of the noblemen's and others' patents. And here I will leave of this matter and show you of my lord's being at Richmond.

My lord, having license of the King to repair and remove to Richmond, wherefore my lord made haste to prepare him thitherward. And so he came and lodged within the great park there, which was a very pretty house and a neat, lacking no necessary[6] rooms that to so small a house was convenient and necessary; where was to the same a proper garden garnished[7] with divers pleasant walks and alleys. My lord continued in this lodge from the time that he came thither shortly after Candlemas, until it was Lent,[8] with a privy[9] number of serv-

2. *made . . . of:* i.e. acted as if he were making.   3. caused.
4. *meet instrument:* fit tool.   5. course, path.
6. comfortable.   7. embellished.   8. Lent began on March 2 in 1530.
9. small.

ants because of the smallness of the house; and the rest of his family went to board wages.[1]

I will tell you a certain tale by the way of communication.[2] Sir, as my lord was accustomed towards night to walk in the garden there to say his service, it was my chance then to wait upon him there. And standing still in an alley whilst he in another walked with his chaplain saying of his service. And as I stood I espied certain images of beasts counterfeit[3] in timber standing in a corner under the lodge wall, to the which I repaired to behold. Among whom I saw there a dun cow, whereon I mused most because it seemed me to be the most liveliest entailed[4] among all the rest. My lord being (as I said) walking on the other side of the garden, perceived me, came suddenly upon me at my back unwares,[5] said: "What have ye espied here that ye so attentively look upon?" "Forsooth, if it please your grace," quod I, "here I do behold these entailed images, the which I suppose were ordained[6] for to be set up within some place about the King's place. Howbeit, sir, among them all I have most considered the dun cow, the which, as it seemeth me, the workman hath most apertly[7] showed his cunning." [8]

"Yea, marry, sir," quod my lord, "upon this dun cow dependeth a certain prophecy, the which I will show you, for peradventure[9] ye never heard of it before. There is a saying," quod he, "that when this cow rideth the bull, then priest beware thy skull." Which prophecy neither my lord that declared it, ne I that heard it understood the effect of this prophecy, although that even then it was a-working to be brought to pass. For this cow the King gave[1] as one of his beasts appertaining of antiquity unto his Earldom of Richmond, which was his ancient inheritance. This prophecy was after expounded in this wise: this dun cow (because it was the King's beast) betokened the King; and the bull betokened

1. *went . . . wages:* had their room and board paid for them while they lodged elsewhere.
2. *by . . . communication:* as a matter of conversation.   3. reproduced.
4. *liveliest entailed:* carved in the most lifelike manner.
5. while I was unaware of his approach.   6. designed.   7. plainly.
8. skill.   9. perchance.   1. gave out, claimed.

Mistress Anne Boleyn (which was after Queen and the King's wife) because her father, Sir Thomas Boleyn, gave the same beast in his cognisance.[2] So that when the King had married her (the which was then unknown to my lord, or to any other at that time) then was this prophecy thought of all men to be fulfilled. For what a number of priests both religious and secular lost their heads for offending of such laws as was then made to bring this prophecy to effect, it is not unknown to all the world.

Therefore it was judged of all men that this prophecy was then fulfill[ed] when the King and she were joined in marriage. Now how dark and obscure riddles and prophecies be, you may behold in this same. For before it was brought to pass, there was not the wisest prophesier could perfectly discuss it, as it is now come to effect and purpose. Trust therefore (be mine advice) to no kind of dark riddles and prophecies, where ye may (as many hath been) be deceived and brought to destruction. And many times the imagination and travailous[3] business to avoid such dark and strange prophecies hath been the very occasion to bring the same the sooner to effect and perfection. Therefore let men beware to divine or assure themselves to expound any such prophecies, for who so doth shall first deceive themselves, and secondly bring many into error; the experience hath been lately experienced (the more pity). But if men will needs think themselves so wise to be assured of such blind prophecies, and will work their wills therein, either in avoiding or in fulfilling the same, God send him well to speed, for he may as well and much more sooner take damage[4] than to avoid the danger thereof. Let prophecies alone, a God's name![5] Apply your vocation,[6] and commit the exposition of such dark riddles and obscure prophecies to God that disposeth them as His divine pleasure shall see cause to alter and change all your enterprises and imaginations to nothing and deceive all your expectations and cause you to repent your great folly, the which when ye feel the

2. coat of arms.   3. laborsome.   4. *take damage:* be harmed.
5. *a God's name:* in the name of God.
6. *apply your vocation:* "mind your own business."

smart will yourself confess the same to be both great folly and much more madness to trust in any such fantasies. Let God therefore dispose them, who guerdoneth[7] and punisheth according to men's deserts and not to all men's judgments.

You have heard here before what words the Duke of Norfolk had to Master Cromwell touching my lord's going into the North to his benefice of York; at such time as Master Cromwell declared the same to my lord, to whom my lord answered in this wise, "Marry, Thomas," quod he, "then it is time to be going if my Lord of Norfolk take it so. Therefore I pray you go to the King and move his highness in my behalf and say that I would with all my heart go to my benefice in York but for want of money, desiring his grace to assist me with some money towards my journey. For ye may say that the last money that I received of his majesty hath been too little to pay my debts, compelled by his council so to do; therefore to constrain me to the payment thereof, and his highness having all my goods, hath been too much extremity, wherein I trust his grace will have a charitable respect.[8] Ye may say also to my Lord of Norfolk and other of the council that I would depart if I had money." "Sir," quod Master Cromwell, "I will do my best." And after other communication he departed again and went to London.

My lord then in the beginning of Lent removed out of the lodge into the Charterhouse of Richmond, where he lay in a lodging (which Doctor Colet,[9] sometime Dean of Paul's, had made for himself) until he removed northward, which was in the Passion Week after. And he had to the same house a secret gallery which went out of his chamber into the Charterhouse Church, whither he resorted every day to their service. And at afternoons he would sit in contemplation with one or other of the most ancient[1] fathers of that house in his cell, who among them and by their counsel persuaded [him] from the vainglory of this world, and gave him divers shirts of hair, the which he often wore afterward (whereof I am certain). And thus he persevered for the time of his abode there in godly contemplation.

7. rewardeth.   8. regard.   9. John Colet (1467?–1519).   1. oldest.

Now when Master Cromwell came to the court he chanced to move my Lord of Norfolk that my lord would gladly depart northward but for lack of money, wherein he desired his assistance to the King. Then went they both jointly to the King, to whom my Lord of Norfolk declared how my lord would gladly depart northward if he wanted not money to bring him thither. The King thereupon referred the assignment thereof to the council, whereupon they were in divers opinions. Some said he should have none, for he had sufficient but late delivered him. Some would he should have sufficient and enough, and some contrariwise would he should have but a small sum. And some thought it much against the council's honor, and much more against the King's high dignity, to see him want the maintenance of his estate which the King had given him in this realm; and also hath been in such estimation with the King and in great authority under him in this realm; it should be rathe[2] a great slander in foreign realms to the King and his whole council to see him want that lately had so much and now so little. "Therefore rather than he should lack," quod one among them, "that rather than he should lack, although he never did me good or any pleasure, yet would I lay my plate to gage[3] for him for a thousand pounds, rather than he should depart so simply as some would have him to do. Let us do to him as we would be done unto, considering his small offence and his inestimable substance,[4] that he only[5] hath departed with all[6] for the same, only for satisfying of the King's pleasure, rather than he would stand in defense with[7] the King in defending of his case, as he might justly have done, as all ye know. Let not malice cloak this matter whereby that pity and mercy may take no place. Ye have all your pleasures fulfilled which ye have long desired, and now suffer conscience to minister unto him some liberality. The day may come that some of us may be in the same case, ye have such alterations in persons as well assured as ye suppose yourselves to be, and to stand upon as sure a ground.

2. quickly.   3. *to gage:* as a pledge.
4. *inestimable substance:* huge wealth.   5. alone.
6. *departed with all:* given up completely.   7. against.

And what hangeth over our heads we know not. I can say no more, now do as ye list." [8]

Then after all this they began again to consult in this matter. And after long debating and reasoning about the same it was concluded that he should have by the way of prest[9] a thousand marks out of Winchester Bishoprick beforehand of his pension, which the King had granted him out of the same. For the King had resumed[1] the whole revenues of the Bishoprick of Winchester into his own hands; yet the King out of the same had granted divers great pensions unto divers noblemen and unto other of his council, so that I do suppose, all things accompted,[2] his part was the least. So that when this determination was fully concluded they declared the same to the King, who straightways commanded that one thousand marks to be delivered out of hand[3] to Master Cromwell, and so it was. The King, calling Master Cromwell to him secretly, bade him to resort to him again when he had received the said sum of money. And, according to the same commandment, he repaired again to the King, to whom the King said, "show my lord your master, although our council hath not assigned any sufficient sum of money to bear his charges, yet ye shall show him in my behalf that I will send him a thousand pounds of my benevolence. And tell him that he shall not lack, and bid him to be of good cheer."

Master Cromwell upon his knee most humbly thanked the King on my lord's behalf for his great benevolence and noble heart towards my lord, "whose comfortable words," quod he, "of your grace shall rejoice him[4] more than three times the value of your noble reward." And therewith departed from the King and came to my lord directly to Richmond. To whom he delivered the money and showed him all the argument in the council, which ye have heard before with the progress of the same; and of what money it was and whereof it was levied, which the council sent him, and of the money which the King sent him, and of his comfortable words; whereof my lord rejoiced not a little and [was] greatly com-

8. please.   9. payment in advance.   1. taken over.   2. considered.
3. immediately.   4. *rejoice him:* cause him to rejoice.

forted. And after the receipt of this money my lord consulted with Master Cromwell about his departure and of his journey with the order thereof.

Then my lord prepared all things with speed for his journey into the North, [and] sent to London for livery clothes for his servants that should ride with him thither. Some he refused— such as he thought were not meet to serve. And some again of their own mind desired him of his favor to tarry still here in the South, being very loth to enbandon[5] their native country, their parents, wives and children, wherewith he most gladly licensed[6] with his good will and favor, and rendered unto them his hearty thanks for their painful service and long tarriance with him in his troublesome decay and overthrow. So that now, all things being furnished towards this journey, which he took in the beginning of the Passion Week before Easter; and so rode to a place then the Abbot's of Westminster, called Hendon; and the next day he removed to a place called the Rye, where my Lady Parr[7] lay; the next day he rode to Royston and lodged in the monastery there; and the next he removed to Huntingdon and there lodged in the abbey; and from thence he removed to Peterborough and there lodged also within the abbey, being then Palm Sunday,[8] where he made his abode until the Thursday in Easter Week, with all his train; whereof the most part went to board wages[9] in the town, having twelve carts to carry his stuff of his own which came from his college in Oxford, where he had three score carts to carry such necessaries as belonged to his buildings there.

Upon Palm Sunday he went in procession with the monks, bearing his palm, setting forth God's service right honorably with such singing men as he then had remaining with him. And upon Maundy Thursday he made his maundy[1] in Our Lady's Chapel, having fifty-nine poormen whose feet he then

5. abandon.   6. gave them his permission.
7. Maud Parr (1495–1531), the mother of Catherine, Henry VIII's last wife.   8. April 10, 1530.
9. *went . . . wages:* had their room and board paid while living in town.
1. An old custom stemming from Christ's action (John 13: 5, 34). Each of the fifty-nine poormen represented a year of Wolsey's life.

washed, wiped and kissed. Each of these poormen had twelve
pence in money, three ells of canvas to make them shirts, a
pair of new shoes, a cast[2] of bread, three red herrings and
three white herrings, and the odd person had two shillings.
Upon Easter Day in the morning he rode to the resurrection,[3]
and that day he went in procession in his vesture cardinal[4]
with his hat and hood upon his head. And he himself sang
there the High Mass very devoutly and granted clean remission[5] to all the hearers, and there continued there all the holy
days.

My lord continuing at Peterborough after this manner, intending to remove from thence, sent me to Sir William Fitzwilliam,[6] a knight which dwelt within three or four miles of
Peterborough, to provide him there a lodging until Monday
next following on his journey northward. And being with him,
to whom I declared my lord's request, and he being thereof
very glad, rejoiced not a little that it would please my lord
to visit his house in his way, saying that he should be (the
King['s] majesty excepted) most heartiliest welcome to him
of any man alive. And that he should not need to discharge
the carriage of any of his stuff[7] for his own use during the
time of his being there, but have all things furnished ready
against his coming to occupy (his own bed excepted). Thus
upon my report made to my lord at my return, he rejoiced
of my message, commanding me therewith to give warning to
all his officers and servants to prepare themselves to remove
from Peterborough upon Thursday next. Then every man
made all things in such readiness as was convenient, paying in
the town for all things as they had taken of any person for
their own use, for which cause my lord caused a proclamation
to be made in the town that if any person or persons in the

2. large loaf.   3. the ceremonies connected with Easter.
4. *vesture cardinal:* robes as a Cardinal.
5. *clean remission:* full remission of the temporal punishment due to
sin.
6. Sir William Fitzwilliam (1460?–1534), one of the founders of the
Merchant Taylors guild, whom Wolsey had befriended in 1511. See
Cavendish's account below.
7. *discharge . . . stuff:* unload any of his own baggage.

town or country there were offended or grieved against any of my lord's servants that they should resort to my lord's officers, of whom they should have redress, and truly answered as the case justly required. So that all things being furnished, my lord took his journey from Peterborough upon the Thursday in Easter Week to Master Fitzwilliam, where he was joyously received and had right worthy and honorable entertainment at the only charges and expenses[8] of the said Master Fitzwilliam all his time being there.

The occasion that moved Master Fitzwilliam thus to rejoice of my lord's being in his house was that he sometime being a merchant of London and sheriff there, fell in debate with the City of London upon a grudge between the Aldermen of the Bench and him upon a new corporation that he would[9] erected there of a new mystery[1] called Merchant Tailors, contrary to the opinion of divers of the Bench of Aldermen of the City of London, which caused him to give and surrender his cloak, and departed from London and inhabited within the country. And against the malice of all the said aldermen and other rulers in the commonweal of the City, my lord defended him and retained him into service, whom he made first his treasurer of his house, and then after his high chamberlain, and in conclusion (for his wisdom, gravity, port and eloquence, being a gentleman of a comely stature) made him one of the King's council, and so continued all his life afterward. Therefore in consideration of all these gratitudes received at my lord's hands, as well in his trouble as in his preferment, was most gladdest (like a faithful friend of good remembrance) to requite him with semblable gratuity[2] and right joyous that he had any occasion to minister some pleasure, such as lay then in his power to do.

Thus my lord continued there until the Monday next, where lacked no good cheer of costly viands[3] both of wine and other goodly entertainment. So that upon the said Monday my lord departed from thence unto Stamford, where he lay

8. *at the . . . expenses:* i.e. at the expense of Master Fitzwilliam alone.
9. wished.   1. guild.   2. *semblable gratuity:* equal kindness.
3. provisions.

all that night. And the next day he removed from thence
unto Grantham and was lodged in a gentleman's house called
Master Hall; and the next day he rode to Newark, and lodged
in the castle all that night. The next day he rode to Southwell,
a place of my lord's within three or four miles of Newark,
where he intended to continue all that summer, as he did
after.

Here I must declare to you a notable tale of communication
which was done[4] at Master Fitzwilliam['s], before his departing from thence, between him and me, the which was this.
Sir, my lord being in the garden at Master Fitzwilliam['s],
walking and saying of his evensong with his chaplain, I being
there giving attendance upon him, his evensong finished,
commanded his chaplain that bare up the train of his gown
whilst he walked, to deliver me the same and he to go aside
when he had done. And after his chaplain was gone a good
distance out of any hearing, he said unto me in this wise:
"Ye have," quod he, "been late[5] at London." "Forsooth, my
lord," quod I, "not late, since that I was there to buy your
liveries for your servants." "And what news," quod he, "was
there then? Heard ye no communication there of me? I pray
you tell me."

Then, perceiving that I had a good occasion to talk my
mind plainly unto him, said: "Sir, if it please your grace, it
was my chance to be at a dinner in a certain place within the
City, where I, among divers other honest and worshipful
gentlemen, happed to sit, which were for the most part of my
old familiar acquaintance, wherefore they were the more
bolder to enter in communication with me. Understanding
that I was still your grace's servant, [they] asked me a question which I could not well assoil[6] them." "What was that?"
quod my lord. "Forsooth, sir," quod I, "first they asked me
how ye did and how ye accepted your adversity and trouble
and the loss of your goods, to the which I answered that ye
were in health (thanks be to God) and took all thing in good
part. And, sir, it seemed me[7] that they were all your indiffer-

4. *a notable . . . done:* a conversation which took place.   5. lately.
6. clear up for.   7. to me.

ent[8] friends, lamenting your decay and loss of your room[9] and goods, doubting[1] much that the sequel thereof could not be good in the commonwealth. For often changing of such officers which be fat fed into the hands of such as be lean and hungered for riches will sure travail by all means to get abundance and so the poor commons be pilled[2] and extorted for greedy lucre of riches and treasure. They said that ye were full fed and intended now much to the advancement of the King's honor and the commonwealth. Also they marvelled much that ye, being of so excellent a wit and high discretion, would so simply confess yourself guilty in the praemunire, wherein ye might full well have stand[3] in the trial of your case; for they understood by the report of some of the King's council learned that in your case, well considered, ye had great wrong. To the which I could make, as me thought, no sufficient answer, but said that I doubt not but that your so doing was upon some greater consideration than my wit could understand."

"Is this," quod he, "the opinion of wise men?" "Yea, forsooth, my lord," quod I, "and almost of all other men." "Well then," quod he, "I see that their wisdoms perceive not the ground of the matter that moved me so to do. For I considered that my enemies had brought the matter so to pass against me, and conveyed it so that they made it the King's case, and caused the King to take the matter into his own hands and quarrel, and after that he had upon occasion thereof seized all my goods and possession into his demesnes,[4] and then the quarrel to be his, he would rather than yield or take a foil[5] in the law, and thereby restore to me all my goods again, would sooner (by the procurement of my enemies and evil willers) imagine[6] my utter undoing and destruction—whereof the most ease therein had been for me perpetual imprisonment. And rather than I would jeopard[7] so far, or put my life in any such hazard, yet had I most levest[8] to yield and confess the matter,

8. unprejudiced.   9. office.   1. fearing.   2. despoiled.   3. stood.
4. *seized . . . demesnes:* i.e. made them his own property.
5. *take a foil:* suffer a defeat.   6. plot.   7. risk.
8. *most levest:* much rather.

committing the whole sum thereof as I did unto the King's clemency and mercy and live at large like a poor vicar, than to lie in prison with all the goods and honor that I had.

"And therefore it was most best way for me (all things considered) to do as I have done than to stand in trial with the King, for he would have been loth to have been noted a wrong-doer. And in my submission the King (I doubt not) had a great remorse of conscience, wherein he would rather pity me than malign me. And also there was a continual serpentine enemy about the King that would, I am well assured, if I had been found stiff-necked, [have] called continually upon the King in his ear (I mean the night crow)[9] with such a vehemency that I should (with the help of her assistance) have obtained sooner the King's indignation than his lawful favor; and his favor once lost (which I trust at this present I have) would never have been by me recovered. Therefore I thought it better for me to keep still his loving favor, with loss of my goods and dignities, than to win my goods and substance with the loss of his love and princely favor, which is but only death—*quia indignatio principis mors est.*[1] And this was the special ground and cause that I yielded myself guilty in the praemunire, which I perceive all men knew not. Wherein, since, I understand the King hath conceived a certain prick of conscience, who took secretly to himself the matter more grievous in his secret stomach[2] than all men knew; for he knew whether I did offend him therein so grievously as it was made[3] or no. To whose conscience I do commit my cause, truth, and equity." And thus we left the substance of all this communication, although we had much more talk. Yet is this sufficient to cause you to understand as well the cause of his confession in his offence, as also the cause of the loss of all his goods and treasure.

Now let us return where we left. My lord, being in the Castle of Newark, intending to ride to Southwell, which was four miles from thence, took now his journey thitherward

9. The allusion is to Anne Boleyn.
1. *quia . . . est:* "for the wrath of the king is death." Cf. Proverbs 16: 14. 2. heart. 3. made out to be.

against supper,[4] where he was fain for lack of reparation of the bishop's place, which appertained to the see of York, to be lodged in a prebendary's house against[5] the said place. And there kept house until Whitsuntide next, against which time he removed into the place newly amended and repaired, and there continued the most part of the summer, surely not without great resort of the most worshipfullest gentlemen of the country and divers other; of whom they were most gladly entertained and had of him the best cheer he could devise for them, whose gentle and familiar behavior with them caused him to be greatly beloved and esteemed through the whole country thereabouts.

He kept a noble house and plenty both of meat and drink for all comers, both for rich and poor, and much alms given at his gate. He used much charity and pity among his poor tenants and other, although the fame thereof was no pleasant sound in the ears of his enemies and of such as bare him no good will. Howbeit the common people will report as they find cause; for he was much more familiar among all persons than he was accustomed, and most gladdest when he had an occasion to do them good. He made many agreements and concords between gentleman and gentleman, and between some gentlemen and their wives that had been long asunder and in great trouble, and divers other agreements between other persons; making great assemblies for the same purpose and feasting of them, not sparing for any costs where he might make a peace and amity, which purchased him much love and friendship in the country.

It chanced that upon Corpus Christi Eve[6] after supper he commanded me to prepare all thing for him in a readiness against the next day for he intended to sing High Mass in the minster that day. And I, not forgetting his commandment, gave like warning to all his officers of his house and other of my fellows to foresee that all things appertaining to their rooms[7] were fully furnished to my lord's honor. This done,

4. *against supper:* so as to get there in time for supper.
5. across from.
6. June 15.   7. *appertaining . . . rooms:* regarding their offices.

I went to my bed, where I was scantly asleep and warm but that one of the porters came to my chamber door, calling upon me, and said there was two gentlemen at the gate that would gladly speak with my lord from the King. With that I arose up and went incontinent unto the gate with the porter, demanding what they were[8] that so fain would come in. They said unto me that there was Master Brereton,[9] one of the gentlemen of the King's privy chamber, and Master Wriothesley,[1] which were come from the King empost to speak with my lord. Then, having understanding what they were, [I] caused the porter to let them in. And after their entry they desired me to speak with my lord without delay, for they might not tarry. At whose request I repaired to my lord's chamber and waked him that was asleep. But when he heard me speak, he demanded of me what I would have. "Sir," quod I, "there be beneath in the porter's lodge Master Brereton, gentleman of the King's privy chamber, and Master Wriothesley, come from the King to speak with you. They will not tarry, therefore they beseech your grace to speak with you out of hand." [2] "Well, then," quod my lord, "bid them come up into my dining chamber, and I will prepare myself to come to them."

Then I resorted to them again and showed them that my lord desired them to come up unto him, and he will talk with them with a right good will. They thanked me and went with me unto my lord, and as soon as they perceived him, being in his night apparel, did to him humble reverence; whom my lord took by the hands, demanding of them how the King his sovereign lord did. "Sir," said they, "right well in health and merry, thanks be unto our Lord. Sir," quod they, "we must desire you to talk with you apart." "With a right good will," quod my lord, who drew them aside into a great window and there talked with them secretly. And after long talk they took out of a male[3] a certain coffer covered with green velvet and bound with bars of silver and gilt, with a lock of the same,

8. *demanding . . . were:* asking who they were.
9. William Brereton (d. 1536), afterwards executed as one of Anne's lovers.
1. Thomas Wriothesley (1505–1550), clerk of the signet and later Earl of Southampton.   2. *out of hand:* at once.   3. bag, pack.

having a key which was gilt, with the which they opened the
same chest; out of the which they took a certain instrument[4]
or writing containing more than one skin of parchment, having
many great seals hanging at it, whereunto they put more wax
for my lord's seal; the which my lord sealed with his own
seal and subscribed his name to the same. And that done they
would needs depart; and for as much as it was after midnight,
my lord desired them to tarry and take a bed. They thanked
him and said they might in no wise tarry, for they would with
all speed to the Earl of Shrewsbury's[5] directly without let[6]
because they would be there or[7] ever he stirred in the morning. And my lord, perceiving their hasty speed, caused them
to eat such cold meat as there was in store within the house
and to drink a cup or two of wine. And that done he gave
each of them four old sovereigns of gold, desiring them to
take it in gree,[8] saying that if he had been of greater ability,
their reward should have been better. And so taking their leave,
they departed.

And after they were departed, as I heard say, they were not
contented with their reward. Indeed, they were not none of
his indifferent[9] friends—which caused them to accept it so
disdainously. Howbeit, if they knew what little store of money
he had at that present, they would, I am sure (being but his
indifferent friends)—they would have given him hearty thanks.
But nothing is more lost or cast away than is such things
which is given to such ingrate[1] persons. My lord went again
to bed; and yet all his watch and disturbance that he had that
night notwithstanding, he sung High Mass the next day as he
appointed before. There was none in all his house that knew
of the coming or going of these two gentlemen, and yet there
lay within the said house many worshipful strangers.

After this sort and manner my lord continued at Southwell
until the latter end of grease time;[2] at which time he intended

4. document. This was the petition from the clergy and nobility to
Pope Clement VII, begging him to grant the King's wishes in the
divorce case.
5. George Talbot (1468–1538), the fourth Earl, who entertains Wolsey
later in the narrative at Sheffield Park.   6. stopping.   7. before.
8. *in gree:* in good part.   9. impartial.
1. ungrateful.   2. about September 1.

to remove to Scroby, which was another house of the Bishoprick of York. And against the day of his removing he caused
all his officers to prepare as well for provision to be made for
him there as also for carriage of his stuff and other matters
concerning his estate. His removing and intent was not so
secret but that it was known abroad in country, which was
lamentable to all his neighbors about Southwell. And as it was
lamentable unto them, so was it as much joy to his neighbors
about Scroby.

Against the day of his removing divers knights and other
gentlemen of worship in the country came to him to Southwell, intending to accompany and attend upon him in that
journey the next day and to conduct him through the forest
unto Scroby. But he, being of their purpose advertized, how
they did intend to have lodged a great stag or twain for him
by the way purposely to show him all pleasure and disport
they could devise, and having, as I said, thereof intelligence,
was very loth to receive any such honor and disport at their
hands, not knowing how the King would take it and being
well assured that his enemies would rejoice much to understand that he would take upon him any such presumption,
whereby they might find an occasion to inform the King how
sumptuous and pleasant he was, notwithstanding his adversity
and overthrow, and so to bring the King into a wrong opinion
of small hope in him of reconcilement, but rather that he
sought a mean to obtain[3] the favor of the country, to withstand the King's proceedings, with divers such imaginations,
wherein he might sooner catch displeasure than favor and
honor. And also he was loth to make the worshipful gentlemen privy to this his imagination, lest peradventure[4] that they
should conceive some toy or fancy in their heads by means
thereof and so to eschew their accustomed access and absent
themselves from him, which should be as much to his grief as
the other was to his comfort.

Therefore he devised this mean way (as hereafter followeth),
which should rather be taken for a laughing disport[5] than

3. *mean to obtain:* means of obtaining.   4. perchance.
5. bit of entertainment.

otherwise. First he called me unto him secretly at night, going to his rest, and commanded me in any wise most secretly that night to cause six or seven horses besides his mule for his own person to be made ready by the break of the day for him and for such persons as he appointed to ride with him to an abbey called Welbeck, where he intended to lodge by the way to Scroby, willing me to be also in a readiness to ride with him, and to call him so early that he might be on horseback after he had heard Mass by the breaking of day. Sir, what will you more? All things being accomplished according to his commandment, and the same finished and done, he with a small number before appointed, mounted upon his mule, setting forth by the breaking of the day towards Welbeck, which is about sixteen miles from thence; whither my lord and we came before six of the clock in the morning, and he went straight to his bed, leaving all the gentlemen strangers in their beds at Southwell, nothing privy[6] of my lord's secret departure, who expected[7] his uprising until it was eight of the clock. But after it was known to them and to all the rest there remaining behind him, then every man went to horseback, galloping after, supposing to overtake him; but he was at his rest in Welbeck or ever they rose out of their beds in Southwell. And so their chief hunting and coursing of the great stag was disappointed and dashed. But at their thither resort to my lord, sitting at dinner, the matter was jested and laughed out merrily, and all the matter well taken.

My lord the next day removed from thence, to whom resorted divers gentlemen of my Lord the Earl of Shrewsbury's servants to desire my lord in their master's name to hunt in a park of the Earl's called Worsopp Park, the which was within a mile of Welbeck, and the very best and next[8] way for my lord to travel through on his journey, where much plenty of game was laid in a readiness to show him pleasure. Howbeit he thanked my lord their master for his gentleness and them for their pains, saying that he was no meet man for any such pastime, being a man otherwise disposed. Such pastime and pleasure were meet for such noblemen as delight therein; never-

6. *nothing privy:* in no way aware.   7. awaited.   8. nearest.

theless he could do no less than to accompt[9] my Lord of
Shrewsbury to be much his friend, in whom he found such
gentleness and nobleness in his honorable offer; to whom he
rendered his most lowly thanks, but in no wise they could
entreat him to hunt. Although the worshipful gentlemen
being in his company provoked[1] him all that they could do
thereto, yet he would not consent, desiring them to be contented; saying that he came not into the country to frequent
or follow any such pleasures or pastimes, but only to attend
to a greater care that he had in hand, which was his duty,
study and pleasure. And with such reasons and persuasions he
pacified them for that time.

Howbeit yet as he rode through the park both my Lord of
Shrewsbury's servants and also the foresaid gentlemen moved
him once again, before whom the deer lay very fair for all
pleasant hunting and coursing, but it would not be. But [he]
made as much speed to ride through the park as he could;
and at the issue[2] out of the park he called the Earl's gentlemen
and the keepers unto him, desiring them to have him commended to my lord their master, thanking him for his most
honorable offer and good will, trusting shortly to visit him at
his own house; and gave the keepers forty shillings for their
pains and diligence, who conducted him through the park.

And so rode to another abbey called Rofford Abbey, and
after he rode to Blythe Abbey, where he lay all night. And the
next day to Scroby, where he continued until after Michaelmas, ministering many deeds of charity. Most commonly every
Sunday, if the weather did serve, he would travel unto some
parish church thereabout and there would say his divine service,
and either hear or say Mass himself, causing some one of his
chaplains to preach unto the people. And that done he would
dine in some honest house of that town, where should be
distributed to the poor a great alms, as well of meat and drink
as of money, to supply the want of sufficient meat, if the
number of the poor did so exceed of necessity. And thus with
other good deeds practising and exercising during his abode

9. reckon.   1. urged.   2. exit.

at Scroby, as making of love days[3] and agreements between party and party, being then at variance, he daily frequenting himself about such business and deeds of honest charity.

Then about the feast of Saint Michael[4] next ensuing my lord took his journey towards Cawood Castle, the which is within seven miles of York. And passing thither he lay two nights and a day at Saint Oswald's Abbey, where he himself confirmed children in the church from eight of clock in the morning until eleven of the clock at noon. And making a short dinner resorted again to the church at one of the clock, and there began again to confirm more children until four of the clock, where he was at the last constrained for weariness to sit down in a chair, the number of the children was such. That done, he said his evensong and then went to supper, and rested him there all that night. And the next morning he applied himself to depart towards Cawood; and or ever he departed he confirmed almost an hundred children more; and then rode on his journey. And by the way there were assembled at a stone cross standing upon a green, within a quarter of a mile of Ferrybridge, about the number of two hundred children to confirm; where he alighted and never removed his foot until he had confirmed them all. And then took his mule again and rode to Cawood, where he lay long after with much honor and love of the country, both of the worshipful and of the simple, exercising himself in good deeds of charity, and kept there an honorable and plentiful house for all comers; and also built and repaired the castle, which was then greatly decayed, having a great multitude of artificers and laborers, above the number of three hundred persons, daily in wages.

And lying there, he had intelligence by the gentlemen of the country that used to repair unto him that there was sprung a great variance[5] and deadly hate between Sir Richard Tempest and Master Brian Hastings, then but a squire, which was after made knight; between whom was like to ensue great murder unless some good mean might be found to redress the inconvenience[6] that was most likeliest to ensue. My lord being

<hr>

3. *love days:* days for the settlement of disputes.   4. September 29.
5. quarrel.   6. harm.

thereof advertized,[7] lamenting the case, made such means by his wisdom and letters with other persuasions that these two gentlemen were content to resort to my lord to Cawood, and there to abide his order, high and low. Then was there a day appointed of their assembly before my lord, at which day they came, not without great number on each party. Wherefore against which day my lord had required many worshipful gentlemen to be there present to assist him with their wisdoms to appease these two worthy gentlemen, being at deadly feud; and to see the King's peace kept, commanding no more of their number to enter into the castle with these two gentlemen than six persons of each of their menial servants, and all the rest to remain without in the town or where they listed [8] to repair. And my lord himself issuing out of the gates, calling the number of both parties before him, straintly[9] charging them most earnestly to observe and keep the King's peace, in the King's name, upon their perils, without either bragging or quarrelling either with other; and caused them to have both beer and wine sent them into the town; and then returned again into the castle, being about nine of the clock.

And because he would have these gentlemen to dine with him at his own table, [he] thought it good in avoiding of further inconvenience to appease their rancor before. Whereupon he called them into his chapel; and there, with the assistance of the other gentlemen, he fell into communication with[1] the matter, declaring unto them the dangers and mischiefs that through their wilfulness and folly were most likeliest to ensue, with divers other good exhortations. Notwithstanding, the parties laying and alleging many things for their defense, sometime adding each to other stout[2] and despiteful words of defiance, the which my lord and the other gentlemen had much a do to qualify, their malices was so great. Howbeit at length with long continuance, wise arguments, and deep persuasions made by my lord, they were agreed and finally accorded about four of the clock at after noon, and so made them friends. And, as it seemed, they both rejoiced and were right well contented therewith to the great comfort of all the other

7. informed.   8. pleased.   9. strictly.   1. regarding.   2. haughty.

worshipful gentlemen, causing them to shake hands and to go arm in arm to dinner; and so went to dinner, though it was very late to dine,[3] yet notwithstanding they dined together with the other gentlemen at my lord's table, where they drank lovingly each to other with countenance of great amity. After dinner my lord caused them to discharge their routs[4] and assembly that remained in the town and to retain with them no mo[5] servants than they were accustomed most commonly to ride with. And that done, these gentlemen, fulfilling his commandment, tarried at Cawood and lay there all night; whom my lord entertained in such sort that they accepted his noble heart in great worthiness, trusting to have of him a special jewel in their country, having him in great estimation and favor, as it appeared afterward by their behavior and demeanor towards him.

It is not to be doubted but that the worshipful persons, as doctors and prebendaries of the Close of York, would and did resort unto him according to their duties, as unto their father and patron of their spiritual dignities, being at his first coming into the country, their Church of York being within seven miles. Wherefore ye shall understand that Doctor Hickden, Dean of the Church of York, with the treasurer and divers other head officers of the same, repaired to my lord, welcoming him most joyously into the country, saying that it was to them no small comfort to see him among them as their chief head, which hath been so long absent from them, being all that while like fatherless children and comfortless, trusting shortly to see him among them in his own church. "It is," quod he, "the especial cause of all my travel into this country not only to be among you for a time, but also to spend my life with you as a very father and a mutual brother."

"Sir, then," quod they, "ye must understand that the ordinary rules of our church hath been of an ancient custom, whereof although ye be head and chief governor, yet be ye not so well acquainted with them as we be; therefore we shall, under the supportation of your grace,[6] declare some part

3. Dinner was normally at ten or eleven o'clock in the morning.
4. bands of retainers.   5. more.
6. *under . . . grace:* with your grace's permission.

thereof to you, as well of our ancient customs as of the laws and usage of the same. Therefore ye shall understand that where ye do intend to repair unto us, the old law and custom of our church hath been that the Archbishop, being our chief head and pastor as your grace now be, might ne ought not to come above the choir door nor have any stall in the choir until he by due order were there stalled;[7] for if ye should happen to die before your stallation, ye should not be buried above in the choir, but in the body of the same church beneath. Therefore we shall (*una voce*)[8] require[9] your grace in the name of all other our brethren, that you would vouchsafe to do herein as your noble predecessors and honorable fathers hath done; and that ye will not infringe or violate any of our laudable ordinances and constitutions of our church, to the observance and preservation whereof we be obliged by virtue of an oath at our first admittance, to see them observed and fulfilled to the uttermost of our powers, with divers other matters remaining of record in our treasury house among other things." "Those records," quod my lord, "would I gladly see; and those seen and digested, I shall then show you further of my mind."

And thus of this matter they ceased communication and passed forth in other matters. So that my lord assigned them a day to bring in their records, at which day they brought with them their register book of record, wherein was written their constitutions and ancient rules, whereunto all the fathers and ministers of the Church of York were most chiefly bound both to see it done and performed and also to perform and observe the same themselves. And when my lord had seen, read, and considered the effect of their records and debated with them substantially therein, he determined to be stalled there in the minster the next Monday after All Hallow Day. Against which day there was made necessary preparation for the furniture[1] thereof, but not in so sumptuous a wise as his predecessors did before him, ne yet in such a sort as the common fame[2] was blown abroad of him to his great slander, and to the reporters much more dishonesty, to forge such lies and

7. installed.   8. with one voice.   9. request.   1. furnishing.
2. rumor.

blasphemous reports, wherein there is nothing more untrue. The truth whereof I perfectly know, for I was made privy to the same and sent to York to foresee all thing to prepare according[3] for the same, which should have been much more mean and base[4] than all other of his predecessors heretofore hath done.

It came so to pass that upon All Hallow Day one of the head officers of the church, which should, by virtue of his office, have most doings in this stallation,[5] came to dine with my lord at Cawood; and sitting at dinner they fell in communication for the order of his stallation. Who said to my lord that he ought to go upon cloth from Saint James's Chapel (standing without the gates of the City of York) unto the minster, the which should be distributed among the poor. My lord, hearing this, made answer to the same in this wise. "Although," quod he, "that our predecessors went upon cloth right sumptuously, we do intend (God willing) to go afoot from thence without any such glory, in the vamps of my hosen.[6] For I take God to be my very judge that I presume not to go thither for any triumph or vainglory, but only to fulfill the observances and rules of the church, to the which, as ye say, I am bound. And therefore I shall desire you all to hold you contented with my simplicity; and also I command all my servants to go as humbly without any other sumptuous apparel than they be customably used,[7] and that is comely and decent to wear. For I do assure you I do intend to come to York upon Sunday at night and lodge there in the Dean's house, and upon Monday to be stalled; and there to make a dinner for you of the close and for other worshipful gentlemen that shall chance to come to me at that time; and the next day to dine with the Mayor, and so return home again to Cawood that night, and thus to finish the same, whereby I may at all times resort to York Minster without either scripulosity[8] or offence to any of you."

This day could not be unknown to all the country, but that

3. in accordance.   4. *mean and base:* humble and low.   5. installation.
6. *in . . . hosen:* in my stocking feet.
7. *than . . . used:* than they customarily wear.   8. scruple.

some must needs have knowledge thereof, whereby that notice was given unto the gentlemen of the country, and they being thereof as well advertized, as abbots, priors and other, of the day of this solemnization, sent in such provision of dainty victuals that it is almost incredible—whereof I omit to declare unto you the certainty[9] thereof, as of great and fat beefs, muttons, wildfowl, and venison both red and fallow, and divers other dainty meats such as the time of the year did serve, sufficient to furnish a great and sumptuous feast. All which things were unknown to my lord, for as much as he being prevented and disappointed of his reasonable purposed intent, because he was arrested, as ye shall hear hereafter. So that the most part of this provision was sent to York that same day that he was arrested and the next day following; for his arrest was kept as close and secret from the country as it could be, because they doubted [1] the people, which had him in great love and estimation for his accustomed charity and liberality used daily among them with familiar gesture and countenance—which be the very means to allure the love and hearts of the people in the north parties.

Or ever I wade any farther in this matter I do intend to declare unto you what chanced him before this his last trouble at Cawood, as a sign or token given by God what should follow of his end or of trouble which did shortly ensue, the sequel whereof was of no man then present either premeditate[2] or imagined. Therefore for as much as it is a notable thing to be considered I will (God willing) declare it as truly as it chanced, according to my simple remembrance, at the which I myself was present.

My lord's accustomed enemies in the court about the King had now my lord in more doubt than they had before his fall, considering the continual favor that the King bare him; [they] thought that at length the King might call him home again and, if he so did, they supposed that he would rather imagine[3] against them than to remit or forget their cruelty which they most unjustly imagined against him. Wherefore they compassed [4] in their heads that they would either by some means

9. exact quantity.   1. feared.   2. conceived.   3. plot.   4. planned.

dispatch him by some sinister accusation of treason, or to bring him into the King's high indignation by some other ways. This was their daily imagination and study, having as many spials[5] and as many eyes to attend upon his doings as the poets feign Argus to have; so that he could neither work or do anything but that his enemies had knowledge thereof shortly after. Now at the last they espied a time wherein they caught an occasion to bring their purpose to pass, thinking thereby to have of him a great advantage; for, the matter being once disclosed unto the King in such a vehemency as they purposed, they thought the King would be moved against him with great displeasure. And that by them executed and done, the King upon their information thought it good that he should come up to stand to his trial—which they liked nothing at all. Notwithstanding he was sent for after this sort: first they devised that he should come up upon arrest in ward,[6] the which they knew right well would so sore[7] grieve him that he might be the weaker to come into the King's presence to make answer. Wherefore they sent Sir Walter Walsh knight, one of the gentlemen of the King's privy chamber, down into the country unto the Earl of Northumberland (who was brought up in my lord's house) with a commission, and they twain being in commission jointly to arrest my lord of hault[8] treason. This conclusion fully resolved, they caused Master Walsh to prepare himself to this journey with this commission and certain instructions annexed to the same; who made him ready to ride and took his horse at the court gate about one of the clock at noon upon All Hallow Day towards the North. Now am I come to the place where I will declare the thing that I promised you before of a certain token of my lord's trouble—which was this.

My lord sitting at dinner upon All Hallow Day in Cawood Castle, having at his board's[9] end divers of his most worthiest chaplains sitting at dinner to keep him company for lack of strangers; ye shall understand that my lord's great cross of silver accustomably[1] stood in the corner at the table's end, lean-

5. spies.   6. *in ward:* under guard.   7. deeply.   8. high.   9. table's.
1. customarily.

ing against the tappet[2] or hanging of the chamber. And when
the table's end was taken up and a convenient time for them to
arise; and in arising from the table one Doctor Augustine,[3] the
physician, being a Venetian born, having a boystors[4] gown of
black velvet upon him, as he would have come out at the table's
end, his gown overthrew the cross that stood there in the
corner. And the cross, railing[5] down along the tappet, it
chanced to fall upon Doctor Bonner's[6] head, which stood
among other by the tappet, making of curtsy to my lord, and
with one of the points of the cross razed his head a little that
the blood ran down. The company standing there were greatly
astoned [7] with the chance. My lord sitting in his chair, looking
upon them, perceived the chance, demanded of me, being next
him, what the matter meant of their sudden abashment. I
showed him how the cross fell upon Doctor Bonner's head.
"Hath it," quod he, "drawn any blood?" "Yea, forsooth, my
lord," quod I, "as it seemeth me." With that he cast down his
head, looking very soberly upon me a good while without any
word, speaking at the last, quod he, shaking of his head,
"*Malum omen*"; and therewith said grace and rose from the
table and went into his bedchamber there, lamenting, making
his prayers.

Now mark the signification, how my lord expounded this
matter unto me afterward at Pomfret Abbey. First ye shall
understand that by the cross, which belonged to the dignity of
York, he understood to be himself. And by Augustine he
understood, that overthrew the cross, to be he that should accuse him, by means whereof he should be overthrown. The
falling upon Master Bonner's head (who was master of my
lord's faculties and spiritual jurisdictions) which was damnified [8] by the overthrowing of the cross by the physician, and
by the drawing of blood, betokened death—which shortly
after came to pass. About the same very time of the day of
this mischance Master Walsh took his horse at the court gate,

2. tapestry.   3. Agostino d'Agostini, in Wolsey's service since 1527. He
seems, after his arrest, to have turned King's evidence against the
Cardinal.   4. "boisterous," of rough texture.   5. falling.
6. Edmund Bonner (1500?–1569), later Bishop of London under Queen
Mary.   7. amazed.   8. *which was damnified:* who was physically
injured.

as nigh as it could be judged. And thus my lord took it for a very sign or token of that which after ensued, if the circumstance be equally considered and noted, although no man was there present at that time that had any knowledge of Master Walsh's coming down or what should follow. Wherefore, as it was supposed, that God showed him more secret knowledge of his latter days and end of his trouble than all men supposed; which appeared right well by divers talks that he had with me at divers times of his last end. And now that I have declared unto you the effect of this prodigy and sign, I would return again to my matter.

The time drawing nigh of his stallation, sitting at dinner, upon the Friday[9] next before Monday on the which he intended to be stalled at York, the Earl of Northumberland and Master Walsh, with a great company of gentlemen, as well of the Earl's servants as of the country, which he had gathered together to accompany him in the King's name (not knowing to what purpose or to what intent), came into the hall at Cawood, the officers sitting at dinner and my lord not fully dined, but being at his fruits, nothing knowing of the Earl's being in his hall. The first thing that the Earl did after he came into the castle, commanded the porter to deliver him the keys of the gates; who would in no wise deliver him the keys, although he were very roughly commanded in the King's name to deliver them to one of the Earl's servants. Saying unto the Earl, "Sir, ye do intend to deliver them to one of your servants to keep them and the gates and to plant another in my room. I know no cause why ye should so do, and this I assure you, that your lordship hath no one servant but that I am as able to keep them as he, to what purpose so ever it be. And also the keys were delivered me by my lord my master with a charge both by oath and by other precepts and commandments; therefore I beseech your lordship to pardon me, though I refuse your commandment. For what so ever ye shall command me to do that belongeth to my office, I shall do it with a right good will as justly as any other of your servants."

With that quod the gentlemen there present unto the Earl,

9. November 4, 1530.

hearing him speak so stoutly, like a man, and with so good reason, "Sir," quod they, "he is a good fellow and speaketh like a faithful servant unto his master and like an honest man. Therefore give him your charge and let him keep still the gates; who, we doubt not, will be obedient to your lordship's commandment." "Well then," quod the Earl, "hold him a book and command him to lay his hand upon the book." Whereat the porter made some doubt, but being persuaded by the gentlemen there present, was contented, and laid his hand upon the book. To whom, quod the Earl, "thou shall swear to keep well and truly these gates to the King's our sovereign lord's use, and to do all such things as we shall command thee in the King's name, being his highness's commissioners, and as it shall seem to us at all times good as long as we shall be here in the castle; and that ye shall not let in nor out at these gates but such as ye shall be commanded by us from time to time." And upon this oath he received the keys at the Earl's and Master Walsh's hands.

Of all these doings knew my lord nothing, for they stopped the stairs that went up into my lord's chamber where he sat, so that no man could pass up again that was come down. At the last, one of my lord's servants chanced to look down into the hall at a loop[1] that was upon the stairs, and returned to my lord, that showed him that my Lord of Northumberland was in the hall. Whereat my lord marvelled and would not believe him at the first; but commanded a gentleman, being his gentleman usher, to go down and bring him perfect word. Who going down the stairs, looking down at the loop, where he saw the Earl, who then returned to my lord and showed him that it was very[2] he. "Then," quod my lord, "I am sorry that we have dined, for I fear that our officers be not stored of any plenty of good fish to make him such honorable cheer as to his estate is convenient.[3] Notwithstanding he shall have such as we have with a right good will and loving heart. Let the table be standing still and we will go down and meet him and bring him up, and then he shall see how far forth we be at our dinner."

1. loophole.   2. really, truly.   3. suitable.

With that he put the table from him and rose up; going down, he encountered the Earl upon the midst of the stairs coming up, with all his men about him. And as soon as my lord espied the Earl, he put off his cap and said to him, "my lord, ye be most heartily welcome." And therewith they embraced each other. "Although my lord," quod he, "that I have often desired and wished in my heart to see you in my house, yet if ye had loved me as I do you, ye would have sent me word before of your coming to the intent that I might have received you according to your honor and mine. Notwithstanding ye shall have such cheer as I am able to make you with a right good will, trusting that ye will accept the same of me as of your very old and loving friend, hoping hereafter to see you oftener when I shall be more able and better provided to receive you with better fare." And then my lord took my Lord of Northumberland by the hand and led him up into the chamber; whom followed all the Earl's servants, where the table stood in the estate[4] that my lord left it when he rose, saying unto the Earl, "Sir, now ye may perceive how far forth we were at our dinner."

My lord led the Earl to the fire, saying, "my lord, ye shall go into my bedchamber, where is a good fire made for you, and there ye may shift[5] your apparel until your chamber be made ready. Therefore let your male[6] be brought up; and or ever I go, I pray you give me leave to take these gentlemen, your servants, by the hands." And when he had taken them all by the hands, he returned to the Earl and said, "Ah, my lord, I perceive well that ye have observed my old precepts and instructions which I gave you when ye were abiding with me in your youth, which was to cherish your father's old servants, whereof I see here present with you a great number. Surely, my lord, ye do therein very well, and nobly, and like a wise gentleman, for these be they that will not only serve and love you, but they will also live and die with you, and be true and faithful servants to you, and glad to see you prosper in honor, the which I beseech God send you with long life."

This said, he took the Earl by the hand and led him into

4. condition.   5. change.   6. bag.

his bedchamber. And they being there all alone (save only I that kept the door according to my duty, being gentleman usher), these two lords standing at a window by the chimney in my lord's bedchamber, the Earl trembling said with a very faint and soft voice unto my lord, laying his hand upon his arm, "my lord," quod he, "I arrest you of high treason." With which words my lord was marvellously astonied,[7] standing both still a long space without any further words. But at the last, quod my lord, "what moveth you or by what authority do you this?" "Forsooth, my lord, I have a commission to warrant me and my doings." "Where is your commission?" quod my lord, "let me see it." "Nay, sir, that you may not," quod the Earl. "Well then," quod my lord, "I will not obey your arrest; for there hath been between some of your predecessors and mine great contention and debate grown upon an ancient grudge, which may succeed in you with like inconvenience[8] as it hath done heretofore. Therefore unless I see your authority and commission I will not obey you."

Even as they were debating this matter between them in the chamber, so busily was Master Walsh arresting of Doctor Augustine, the physician, at the door within the portal; whom I heard say unto him, "go in, thou traitor, or I shall make thee!" And with that I opened the portal door, and the same being open, Master Walsh thrust Doctor Augustine in before him with violence. These matters on both the sides astonied me very sore,[9] musing what all this should mean. Until at the last Master Walsh, being entered the chamber, began to pluck off his hood, the which he had made him with a coat of the same cloth of cotton, to the intent that he would not be known.

And after he had pluck it off he kneeled down to my lord, to whom my lord spake first, saying thus, commanding him to stand up, "Sir, here my Lord of Northumberland hath arrested me of treason, but by what authority or commission he showeth me not, but sayeth he hath one. If ye be privy thereto[1] or be joined with him therein, I pray you show me." "Indeed,

7. *marvellously astonied*: struck dumb with amazement.
8. harm, injury.   9. grievously.
1. *privy thereto*: secretly cognizant of it.

my lord," quod Master Walsh, "if it please your grace, it is true that he hath one." "Well then," said my lord, "I pray you let me see it." "Sir, I beseech your grace hold us excused," quod Master Walsh, "there is annexed unto our commission a schedule with certain instructions which you may in no wise be privy unto."

"Why," quod my lord, "be your instructions such that I may not see them? Peradventure if I might be privy to them I could the better help you to perform them. It is not unknown unto you both, I am assured, but I have been privy and of counsel in as weighty matters as this is; for I doubt not for my part but I shall prove and clear myself to be a true man against the expectation of all my cruel enemies. I have an understanding whereupon all this matter groweth. Well, there is no more to do. I trow,[2] gentleman, ye be one of the King's privy chamber. Your name, I suppose, is Walsh. I am content to yield unto you, but not to my Lord of Northumberland without[3] I see his commission. And also you are a sufficient commission yourself in that behalf in as much as ye be one of the King's privy chamber; for the worst person there is a sufficient warrant to arrest the greatest peer of this realm by the King's only commandment[4] without any commission. Therefore I am ready to be ordered and disposed at your will. Put therefore the King's commission and your authority in execution, a[5] God's name, and spare not, and I will obey the King's will and pleasure. For I fear more the cruelty of my unmerciful enemies than I do my truth and allegiance; wherein I take God to witness I never offended the King's majesty in word or deed. And therein I dare stand face to face with any man alive having indifferency[6] without partiality."

Then came my Lord of Northumberland unto me, standing at the portal door, and commanded me to avoid [7] the chamber. And being loth to depart from my master, [I] stood still and would not remove; to whom he spake again and said, "there is no remedy, ye must needs depart." With that I looked upon

2. believe.   3. unless.   4. *only commandment:* commandment alone.
5. in.   6. *having indifferency:* who is unprejudiced.   7. leave.

my lord, as who sayeth,[8] "shall I go?" Upon whom my lord
looked very heavily[9] and shook at me his head. Perceiving by
his countenance it booted me not to abide, and so I departed
the chamber, and went into the next chamber, where abode
many gentlemen of my fellows and other to learn of me some
news of the matter within. To whom I made report what I
saw and heard, which was to them great heaviness to hear.

Then the Earl called divers gentlemen into the chamber,
which were for the most part of his own servants. And after
the Earl and Master Walsh had taken the keys of all my lord's
coffers from him, they gave the charge and custody of my
lord's person unto these gentlemen. They departed and went
about the house to set all things in order that night against[1]
the next morning, intending then to depart from thence with
my lord, being Saturday. The which they deferred until Sunday because all things could not be brought to pass as they
would have it. They went busily about to convey Doctor Augustine away to Londonward with as much speed as they
could, sending with him divers honest persons to conduct him,
who was tied under the horse belly. And this done, when it was
night, these commissioners assigned two grooms of my lord's to
attend upon him in his chamber that night, where they lay.
And the most part of the rest of the Earl's gentlemen servants
watched in the next chamber and about the house continually
until the morrow. And the porter kept the gates so that no man
could go in ne out until the next morning.

At which time my lord rose up, supposing that he should
have departed that day. Howbeit he was kept close secretly in
his chamber, expecting continually his departure from thence.
Then the Earl sent for me into his own chamber. And being
there, he commanded me to go into my lord and there to give
attendance upon him; and charged me upon an oath that I
should observe certain articles. And going away from him towards my lord, I met with Master Walsh in the court, who
called me unto him and led me into his chamber; and there
showed me that the King's highness bare towards me his

8. *as who sayeth:* like one who says.   9. sadly.   1. in preparation for.

princely favor for my diligent and true service that I daily ministered towards my lord and master. "Wherefore," quod he, "the King's pleasure is that ye shall be about your master as most chiefest person, in whom his highness putteth great confidence and assured trust; whose pleasure is therefore that ye shall be sworn unto his majesty to observe certain articles in writing, the which I would deliver you." "Sir," quod I, "my Lord of Northumberland hath already sworn me to divers articles." "Yea," quod he, "but my lord could not deliver you the articles in writing as I am commanded specially to do. Therefore I deliver you this bill with these articles, to the which ye shall be sworn to fulfill." "Sir, then," quod I, "I pray you to give me leave to peruse them or ever I be sworn, to see if I be able to perform them." "With a right good will," quod he. And when I had perused them and understood that they were but reasonable and tolerable, I answered that I was contented to obey the King's pleasure and to be sworn to the performance of them. And so he gave me a new oath. And then I resorted to my lord, where he was in his chamber, sitting in a chair, the table being covered ready for him to go to dinner.

But as soon as he perceived me coming in, he fell into such a woeful lamentation with such rueful terms and watery eyes that it would have caused the flintiest heart to have relented [2] and burst for sorrow. And as I and other could, comforted him —but it would not be. "For now," quod he, "that I see this gentleman (meaning by me),[3] how faithful, how diligent, and how painful, since the beginning of my trouble he hath served me, abandoning his own country, his wife and children, his house and family, his rest and quietness, only to serve me; and remembering with myself that I have nothing to reward him for his honest merits, grieveth me not a little. And also the sight of him putteth me in remembrance of the number of my faithful servants that I have here remaining with me in this house, whom I did intend to have preferred [4] and advanced to the best of my power from time to time as occasion should serve.

2. melted.   3. *meaning by me:* referring to me.   4. promoted.

But now, alas, I am prevented and have nothing left me to reward them; for all is deprived me and I am left here their desolate and miserable master, bare and wretched, without help or succor but of God alone. Howbeit," quod he to me (calling me by my name), "I am a true man and therefore ye shall never receive shame of me for your service."

I, perceiving his heaviness[5] and lamentable words, said thus unto him, "my lord, I mistrust nothing your truth. And for the same I dare and will be sworn before the King's person and his honorable council." Wherefore (kneeling upon my knee before him) [I] said, "my lord, comfort yourself and be of good cheer. The malice of your uncharitable enemies nor their untruth shall never prevail against your truth and faithfulness. For I doubt not but coming once to your answer, my hope is such that ye shall so acquit and clear yourself of all their surmised and feigned accusations that it shall be to the King's contentation and much to your advancement and restitution of your former dignity and estate." "Yea," quod he, "if I may come to mine answer I fear no man alive; for he liveth not upon the earth that shall look upon this face (pointing to his own face) shall be able to accuse me of any untruth. And that knoweth mine enemies full well, which will be an occasion that I shall not have indifferent[6] justice, but will rather seek some other sinister ways to destroy me." "Sir," quod I, "ye need not therein to doubt the King, being so much your good lord as he hath always showed himself to be in all your troubles."

With that came up my lord's meat, and so we left our communication. I gave him water and sat him down to dinner, with whom sat divers of the Earl's gentlemen. Notwithstanding my lord did eat very little meat, but would many times burst out suddenly in tears with the most sorrowfullest words that hath been heard of any woeful creature. And at the last he fetched a great sigh from the bottom of his heart, saying these words of scripture, "*O constantia martirum laudabilis, O charitas inextinguibilis, O patientia invincibilis, quae licet inter pressuras persequentium visa sit despicabilis, invenietur in laudem et*

5. sadness.   6. impartial.

gloriam et honorem in tempore tribulationis." [7] And thus passed he forth his dinner in great lamentation and heaviness, who was more fed and moisted [8] with sorrow and tears than with either pleasant meats or delicate drinks. I suppose there was not a dry eye among all the gentlemen sitting at the table with him. And when the table was taken up, it was showed my lord that he could not remove that night (who expected none other[9] all that day). Quod he, "even when it shall seem my Lord of Northumberland good." [1]

The next day my lord prepared himself (being Sunday) to ride when he should be commanded. And after dinner, by that time that the Earl had appointed all thing in good order within the castle, it drew fast to night. There was assigned to attend upon him five of us his own servants and no more, that was to say, I, one chaplain, his barber, and two grooms of his chamber. And when he should go down the stairs out of the great chamber my lord demanded [2] for the rest of his servants; the Earl answered that they were not far, the which he had enclosed within the chapel because they should not disquiet[3] his departure. "Sir, I pray you," quod my lord, "let me see them or ever I depart or else I will never go out of this house." "Alack, my lord," quod the Earl, "they should trouble you; therefore I beseech you to content yourself." "Well," quod my lord, "then will I not depart out of this house but I will see them and take my leave of them in this chamber." And his servants being enclosed in the chapel, having understanding of my lord's departing away and that they should not see him before his departure, began to grudge and to make such a rueful noise that the commissioners doubted [4] some tumult or inconvenience[5] to arise by reason thereof, thought it good to let

7. "scripture" for Cavendish meant any holy writing, not just the Bible. Wolsey quotes from a tenth-century liturgical hymn, the *O Constantia Martirum,* composed by King Robert of France. The lines may be translated as follows: "O praiseworthy perseverance of the martyrs! O inextinguishable charity! O unconquerable patience, which, though it may seem contemptible amid the rigors of persecution, will be found to merit praise and glory and honor in the time of tribulation."
8. moistened.   9. *expected none other:* had expected to leave etc.
1. *seem . . . good:* seem good to my Lord of Northumberland.
2. asked.   3. *because . . . disquiet:* so that they would not upset.
4. feared.   5. harm, injury.

them pass out to my lord. And that done, they came to him into the great chamber where he was and there they kneeled down before him, among whom was not one dry eye, but pitifully lamented their master's fall and trouble. To whom my lord gave comfortable words and worthy praises for their diligent faithfulness and honest truth towards him, assuring them that what chances so ever should happen unto him that he is a true man and a just to his sovereign lord. And thus with a lamentable manner shaking each of them by the hands, was fain to depart, the night drew so fast upon them.

My lord's mule and our horses were ready, brought into the inner court, where we mounted; and coming to the gate, which was shut, the porter opened the same to let us pass, where was ready attending a great number of gentlemen with their servants (such as the Earl assigned) to conduct and attend upon his person that night to Pomfret and so forth, as ye shall hear hereafter. But to tell you of the number of people of the country that were assembled at the gates which lamented his departing was wondrous, which was about the number of three thousand persons; who at the opening of the gates, after they had a sight of his person, cried all with a loud voice, "God save your grace, God save your grace, the foul evil take all them that hath thus taken you from us! We pray God that a very vengeance may light upon them!" Thus they ran crying after him through the town of Cawood, they loved him so well; for surely they had a great loss of him, both the poor and the rich; for the poor had of him great relief and the rich lacked his counsel in any business that they had to do, which caused him to have such love among them in the country.

Then rode he with his conductors towards Pomfret; and by the way as he rode, he asked me if I had any familiar acquaintance among these gentlemen that rode with him. "Yea, sir," said I, "what is your pleasure?" "Marry," quod he, "I have left a thing behind me which I would fain have." "Sir," said I, "if I knew what it were I would send for it out of hand." [6] "Then," said he, "let the messenger go to my Lord of Northumberland, and desire him to send me the red buckram bag lying in my al-

6. *out of hand:* immediately.

monry[7] in my chamber sealed with my seal." With that I departed from him and went straight unto Sir Roger Lascelles, knight, who was then steward to the Earl of Northumberland, being among the rout[8] of horsemen as one of the chiefest rulers, whom I desired to send some of his servants back unto the Earl his master for that purpose; the which granted most gently my request and sent incontinent[9] one of his servants unto my lord to Cawood for the said bag. Who did so honestly his message that he brought the same to my lord immediately after he was in his chamber within the Abbey of Pomfret, where he lay all night. In which bag was no other thing enclosed but three shirts of hair, which he delivered to the chaplain, his ghostly father,[1] very secretly.

Furthermore as we rode toward Pomfret my lord demanded of me whither they would lead him that night. "Forsooth, sir," quod I, "but to Pomfret." "Alas," quod he, "shall I go to the castle and lie there and die like a beast?" [2] "Sir, I can tell you no more what they do intend, but, sir, I will inquire here among these gentlemen of a special friend of mine who is chief of all their counsel." With that I repaired unto the said Sir Roger Lascelles, knight, desiring him most earnestly that he would vouchsafe to show me whither my lord should go to be lodged that night. Who answered me again that my lord should be lodged within the Abbey of Pomfret and in none other place. And so I reported to my lord, who was glad thereof; so that within night we came to Pomfret Abbey and there lodged. And the Earl remained still all that night in Cawood Castle to see the dispatch of the household and to establish all the stuff in some surety within the same.

The next day they removed with my lord towards Doncaster, desiring that he might come thither by night because the people followed him weeping and lamenting, and so they did nevertheless although he came in by torchlight, crying "God save your grace, God save your grace, my good Lord Cardinal," running before him with candles in their hands;

7. place where alms were dispensed.   8. retinue.   9. at once.
1. confessor.
2. Wolsey was thinking of the fact that Pontefract (or "Pomfret") Castle had been the scene of state executions in the past.

who caused me therefore to ride hard by his mule to shadow him from the people, and yet they perceived him, cursing his enemies. And thus they brought him to the Black Friars, within the which they lodged him that night.

And the next day we removed to Sheffield Park, where the Earl of Shrewsbury lay within the lodge, and all the way thitherward the people cried and lamented as they did in all places as we rode before. And when we came to the park of Sheffield nigh to the lodge, my Lord of Shrewsbury with my lady his wife, a train of gentlewomen, and all my lord's gentlemen and yeomen, standing without the gates of the lodge to attend my lord's coming to receive him with much honor; whom the Earl embraced, saying these words, "my lord," quod he, "your grace is most heartily welcome unto me, and glad to see you in my poor lodge, the which I have often desired; and much more gladder if you had come after another sort." "Ah, my gentle Lord of Shrewsbury," quod my lord, "I heartily thank you. And although I have no cause to rejoice, yet as a sorrowful heart may joy, I rejoice my chance, which is so good to come into the hands and custody of so noble a person, whose approved honor and wisdom hath been always right well known to all noble estates. And, sir, how so ever my ungentle accusers hath used their accusations against me, yet I assure you, and so before your lordship and all the world I do protest that my demeanor[3] and proceedings hath been just and loyal towards my sovereign and liege[4] lord, of whose behavior and doings your lordship hath had good experience; and even according to my truth and faithfulness so I beseech God help me in this my calamity."

"I doubt nothing of your truth," quod the Earl, "therefore, my lord, I beseech you be of good cheer and fear not; for I have received letters from the King of his own hand in your favor and entertaining,[5] the which you shall see. Sir, I am nothing sorry but that I have not wherewith worthily to receive you and to entertain you according to your honor and my

3. behavior.   4. faithful.
5. *and entertaining:* regarding the manner in which you are to be entertained.

good will; but such as I have, ye are most heartily welcome thereto, desiring you to accept my good will accordingly, for I will not receive you as a prisoner but as my good lord and the King's true, faithful subject. And here is my wife, come to salute you." Whom my lord kissed bareheaded and all her gentlewomen, and took my lord's servants by the hands as well gentlemen and yeomen as other. Then these two lords went arm in arm into the lodge, conducting my lord into a fair chamber at the end of a goodly gallery within a new tower, where my lord was lodged. There was also in the midst of the same gallery a traverse of sarcenet[6] drawn so that the one part was preserved for my lord and the other part for the Earl.

Then departed all the great number of gentlemen and other that conducted my lord to the Earl of Shrewsbury's. And my lord being there, continued there eighteen days[7] after; upon whom the Earl appointed divers gentlemen of his servants to serve my lord, for as much as he had a small number of servants there to serve; and also to see that he lacked nothing that he would desire, being served in his own chamber at dinner and supper as honorably and with as many dainty dishes as he had most commonly in his own house, being at liberty. And once every day the Earl would resort unto him and sit with him, communing upon a bench in a great window in the gallery. And though the Earl would right heartily comfort him, yet would he lament so piteously that it would make the Earl very sorry and heavy for his grief. "Sir," said he, "I have and daily do receive letters from the King commanding me to entertain you as one that he loveth and highly favoreth; whereby I perceive ye do lament without any great cause, much more than ye need to do. And though ye be accused, as I think in good faith unjustly, yet the King can do no less but put you to your trial, the which is more for the satisfying of some persons, than he hath for any mistrust[8] in your doings."

"Alas," quod my lord, to the Earl, "is it not a piteous case that any man should so wrongfully accuse me unto the King's

6. *traverse of sarcenet*: compartment curtained with fine silk.
7. In actuality from November 8 to November 24.
8. *than he . . . mistrust*: than for any mistrust which he hath.

person, and [I] not to come to mine answer before his majesty? For I am well assured, my lord, that there is no man alive or dead that looketh in this face of mine is able to accuse me of any disloyalty towards the King. Oh how much then doth it grieveth me that the King should have any suspicious opinion in me to think that I would be false or conspire any evil to his royal person; who may well consider that I have no assured friend in all the world in whom I put my trust but only in his grace; for if I should go about to betray my sovereign lord and prince, in whom is all my trust and confidence before all other persons, all men might justly think and report that I lacked not only grace, but also both wit and discretion. Nay, nay, my lord, I would rather adventure[9] to shed my heart blood in his defense, as I am bound to do by mine allegiance and also for the safeguard of myself, than to imagine[1] his destruction. For he is my staff that supporteth me, and the wall that defendeth me against my malignant enemies and all other, who knoweth best my truth before all men and hath had thereof best and longest experience. Therefore to conclude, it is not to be thought that ever I would go about or intend maliciously or traitorously to travail[2] or wish any prejudice or damage to his royal person or imperial dignity; but, as I said, defend it with the shedding of my heart blood, and procure all men so to do, and[3] it were but only for the defense of mine own person and simple estate, the which my enemies think I do so much esteem, having none other refuge to flee to for defense or succor in all adversity, but under the shadow of his majesty's wing.

"Alas, my lord, I was in a good estate now, and in case of a quiet living,[4] right well content therewith; but the enemy that never sleepeth, but studieth and continually imagineth, both sleeping and waking, my utter destruction, perceiveth the contentation of my mind, doubted[5] that their malicious and cruel dealing would at length grow to their shame and rebuke, goeth about therefore to prevent the same with shedding of my blood. But from God, that knoweth the secrets of their hearts

9. hazard, dare.　1. plot.　2. labor for.　3. even if.
4. *in case . . . living:* enjoying a quiet life.　5. feared.

and of all others, it cannot be hid, ne yet unrewarded when he shall see opportunity. For, my good lord, if ye will show yourself so much my good friend as to require[6] the King's majesty by your letters that my accusers may come before my face in his presence, and there that I may make answer, I doubt not but ye shall see me acquit myself of all their malicious accusations and utterly confound them; for they shall never be able to prove by any due probations[7] that ever I offended the King in will, thought, and deed. Therefore, sir, I desire you and most heartily require your good lordship to be a mean for me that I may answer unto my accusers before the King's majesty. The case is his. And if their accusations should be true, then should it touch no man but him most earnestly; wherefore it were most convenient that he should hear it himself in proper[8] person.

"But I fear me that they do intend rather to dispatch me than I should come before him in his presence; for they be well assured and very certain that my truth should vanquish their untruth and surmised accusations, which is the special cause that moveth me so earnestly to desire to make my answer before the King's majesty. The loss of goods, the slander of my name, ne yet all my trouble grieveth me nothing so much as the loss of the King's favor, and that he should have in me such an opinion, without desert, of untruth, that hath with such travail and pain served his highness so justly, so painfully, and with so faithful an heart to his profit and honor at all times. And also, again, the truth of my doings against their unjust accusations proved most just and loyal, should be much to my honesty, and do me more good than to attain great treasure; as I doubt not but it will if they might be indifferently heard. Now, my good lord, weigh ye my reasonable request and let charity and truth move your noble heart with pity to help me in all this my truth, wherein ye shall take no manner[9] of slander or rebuke (by the grace of God)."

"Well then," quod my Lord of Shrewsbury, "I will write to the King's majesty in your behalf, declaring to him by my let-

6. request.   7. proofs.   8. his own.
9. *take no manner:* receive no taint.

ters how grievously ye lament his displeasure and indignation; and what request ye make for the trial of your truth towards his highness." Thus after these communications and divers others (as between them daily was accustomed),[1] they departed asunder.

Where my lord continued the space after of a fortnight, having goodly and honorable entertainment; whom the Earl would often require him[2] to kill a doe or two there in the park, who always refused all manner of earthly pleasures and disports either in hunting or in other games, but applied [3] his prayers continually, very devoutly. So that it came to pass at certain season,[4] sitting at dinner in his own chamber, having at his board's end that same day, as he divers times had to accompany him, a mess[5] of the Earl's gentlemen and chaplains, and eating of roasted wardens[6] at the end of his dinner, before whom I stood at the table, dressing of those wardens for him, beholding of him, perceived his color often to change and alter divers times—whereby I judged him not to be in health. Which caused me to lean over the table, saying unto him softly, "sir, me seems your grace is not well at ease?" He answered again and said, "forsooth, no more I am, for I am," quod he, "suddenly taken about my stomach with a thing that lieth overthwart[7] my breast as cold as a whetstone—the which is but wind. Therefore I pray you take up the cloth and make ye a short dinner and resort shortly again unto me."

And after that the table was taken up I went and sat the waiters to dinner without[8] in the gallery, and resorted again to my lord, where I found him still sitting where I left him, very evil [9] at ease. Notwithstanding he was in communications with the gentlemen sitting at the board's end. And as soon as I was entered the chamber he desired me to go down to the pothecary,[1] and to inquire of him whether he had anything that would break wind upward. And according to his commandment I went my way towards the pothecary; and by the way I remembered one article of mine oath before made unto Master

1. the custom.   2. *require him*: request.   3. kept to.
4. *certain season*: a certain time.   5. group.   6. baking pears.
7. across.   8. outside.   9. ill.   1. druggist.

Walsh, which caused me first to go to the Earl, and showed him both what estate he was in and also what he desired at the pothecary's hand for his relief. With that the Earl caused the pothecary to be called incontinent before him, of whom he demanded whether he had anything to break wind that troubleth one in his breast. And he answered that he had such gear.[2] "Then," quod the Earl, "fetch me some hither." The which the pothecary brought in a white paper—a certain white confection[3]—unto the Earl; who commanded me to give the essay[4] thereof to the pothecary, and so I did before him. And then I departed therewith, bringing it to my lord, before whom I took also the assay thereof, and delivered the same to my lord, who received the same wholly, altogether at once. And immediately after he had received the same, surely he avoided [5] exceeding much wind upward. "Lo," quod he, "now ye may see that it was but wind, but by the means of this receipt[6] I am, I thank God, well eased." And so he rose from the table and went to his prayers, as he accustomedly[7] did after dinner. And being at his prayers, there came upon him such a laske,[8] that it caused him to go to his stool.

And being there, the Earl sent for me, and at my coming he said, "for as much as I have always perceived in you to be a man in whom my lord your master hath great affiance;[9] and for my experience, knowing you to be an honest man," (with many more words of commendations than needs here to be rehearsed)—said, "it is so that my lord your lamentable master hath often desired me to write to the King's majesty that he might come unto his presence to make answer to his accusations. And even so have I done; for this day have I received letters from his grace by Sir William Kingston,[1] knight, whereby I do perceive that the King hath in him a very good opinion. And upon my often[2] request he hath sent for him by the said Sir William Kingston to come up to answer, according to his own desire—who is in his chamber. Wherefore now is

2. stuff.   3. medicinal preparation.   4. trial.   5. belched.
6. prescription.   7. customarily.   8. attack of diarrhoea.   9. trust.
1. Kingston (d. 1540) had been Constable of the Tower since 1524.
2. frequent.

the time come that my lord hath often desired to try himself
and his truth, as I trust, much to his honor. And I put no
doubts in so doing that it shall be for him the best journey
that ever he made in all his life. Therefore now I would have
you to play the part of a wise man, to break first this matter
unto him so wittily[3] and in such a sort that he might take it
quietly in good part; for he is ever so full of sorrow and
dolor in my company that I fear me he will take it in evil part.
And then he doth not well; for, I assure you (and so show
him) that the King is his good lord and hath given me the most
worthy thanks for his entertainment, desiring and commanding
me so to continue, not doubting but that he will right nobly
acquit himself towards his highness. Therefore go your ways to
him, and so persuade with him that I may find him in good
quiet at my coming, for I will not tarry long after you."

"Sir," quod I, "I shall if it please your lordship endeavor me
to accomplish your commandment to the best of my power.
But, sir, I doubt one thing, that when I shall name 'Sir William
Kingston' he will mistrust[4] that all is not well; because he is
Constable of the Tower, and Captain of the Guard, having
twenty-four of the guard to attend upon him." "Marry, it is
truth," quod the Earl, "what thereof, though he be Constable
of the Tower, yet he is the most meetest[5] man for his wisdom
and discretion to be sent about any such message. And for the
guard, it is for none other purpose but only to defend him
against all them that would intend him any evil either in word
or deed. And also they be all or for the most part such of his
old servants as the King took of late into his service to the
intent that they should attend upon him most justly, and doth
know best how to serve him." "Well, sir, I will do what I can."
And so departed toward my lord.

And at my repair I found him sitting at the upper end of the
gallery upon a trussing chest[6] of his own with his beads and
staff in his hands. And espying me coming from the Earl, he
demanded of me, "what news now?" quod he. "Forsooth, sir,"
quod I, "the best news that ever came to you, if your grace

3. *so wittily:* in such an intelligent way.
4. suspect.   5. suitable.   6. *trussing chest:* chest used for packing.

can take it well." "I pray God it be—what is it?" quod he. "Forsooth," quod I, "my Lord of Shrewsbury, perceiving by your often communication[7] that ye were always desirous to come before the King's majesty, and now as your most assured friend, hath travailed so with his letters unto the King that the King hath sent for you by Master Kingston and twenty-four of the guard, to conduct you to his highness." "Master Kingston," quod he, rehearsing[8] his name once or twice; and with that clapped his hand upon his thigh and gave a great sigh.

"Sir," quod I, "if your grace could or would take all things in good part, it should be much better for you. Content yourself therefore, for God's sake, and think that God and your friends hath wrought for you according to your own desire. Did ye not always wish that ye might clear yourself before the King's person? Now that God and your friends hath brought your desire to pass, ye will not take it thankfully. If ye consider your truth and loyalty unto our sovereign lord, against the which your enemies cannot prevail (the King being your good lord, as he is), you know well that the King can do no less than he doth, you being to his highness accused of some heinous crime, but cause you to be brought to your trial, and there to receive according to your demerits;[9] the which his highness trusteth, and saith no less but that you shall prove yourself a just man to his majesty, wherein ye have more cause to rejoice than thus to lament or mistrust his favorable justice. For, I assure you, your enemies be more in doubt and fear of you than you of them; that they wish that thing that, I trust, they shall never be able to bring to pass with all their wits, the King (as I said before) being your indifferent[1] and singular good lord and friend. And to prove that he so is, see ye not how he hath sent gentle Master Kingston for you with such men as were your old true servants and yet be, as far as it becometh them to be, only to attend upon you for the want[2] of your own servants; willing also Master Kingston to reverence you with as much honor as was due to you in your high

7. *often communication:* frequent conversations.   8. repeating.
9. deserving.   1. impartial.   2. *for the want:* because of the lack.

estate, and to convey you by such easy journeys as ye shall
command him to do, and that ye shall have all your desires and
commandments by the way in every place, to your grace's
contentation and honor. Wherefore, sir, I humbly beseech
your grace to imprint all these just persuasions with many
other eminent occasions in your discretion; and be of good
cheer, I most humbly with my faithful heart require your
grace, wherewith ye shall principally comfort yourself, and
next give all your friends and to me and other of your servants
good hope of your good speed." "Well, well, then," quod he,
"I perceive more than ye can imagine or do know. Experience
of old hath taught me."

And therewith he rose up and went into his chamber to his
close stool,[3] the flux troubled him so sore.[4] And when he had
done, he came out again, and immediately my Lord of Shrewsbury came into the gallery unto him, with whom my lord met.
And then they both sitting down upon a bench in a great window, the Earl asked him how he did. And he most lamentably,
as he was accustomed, answered, thanking him for his gentle
entertainment. "Sir," quod the Earl, "if ye remember, ye have
often wished in my company to make answer before the
King. And I, as desirous to help your request as you to wish,
bearing toward you my good will, hath written especially to
the King in your behalf, making him also privy of your
lamentable sorrow that ye inwardly receive for his high displeasure; who accepteth all things and your doings therein as
friends be accustomed to do in such cases. Wherefore I would
advise you to pluck up your heart and be not aghast of your
enemies, who I assure you have you in more doubt[5] than ye
would think, perceiving that the King is fully minded to have
the hearing of your case before his own person. Now, sir, if ye
can be of good cheer, I doubt not but this journey which ye
shall take towards his highness shall be much to your advancement, and an overthrow of your enemies. The King hath sent
for you by that worshipful knight, Master Kingston, and with
him twenty-four of your old servants, which be now of the

3. *close stool:* chamber pot enclosed in a box.   4. seriously.
5. *have you . . . doubt:* are more afraid of you.

guard, to defend you against your unknown enemies, to the intent that ye may safely come unto his majesty."

"Sir," quod my lord, "as I suppose, Master Kingston is Constable of the Tower?" "Yea, what of that?" quod the Earl. "I assure you he is only appointed by the king for[6] one of your friends and for a discreet gentleman, as most worthy to take upon him the safe-conduct of your person; for without fail the King favoreth you much more, and beareth towards you a special secret favor far otherwise than ye do take it." "Well, sir," quod my lord, "as God will, so be it. I am subject to Fortune, and to Fortune I commit myself, being a true man, ready to accept such ordinance[7] as God hath provided for me. And there an end. Sir, I pray you, where is Master Kingston?" "Marry," quod the Earl, "if ye will, I will send for him, who would most gladly see you." "I pray you then," quod he, "send for him."

At whose message he came incontinent, and as soon as my lord espied him coming into the gallery, he made haste to encounter him. Master Kingston came towards him with much reverence. At his approach he kneeled down and saluted him on the King's behalf; whom my lord, bareheaded, offered to take up, but he still kneeled. Then quod my lord, "Master Kingston, I pray you stand up and leave your kneeling unto a very wretch, replete with misery, not worthy to be esteemed but for a vile abject, utterly cast away without desert. And therefore, good Master Kingston, stand up, or I will myself kneel down by you." With that Master Kingston stood up, saying with humble reverence, "sir, the King's majesty hath him commended unto you." "I thank his highness," quod my lord, "I trust he be in health and merry, the which I beseech God long continue."

"Yea, without doubt," quod Master Kingston, "and, sir, he hath commanded me first to say unto you that you should assure yourself that he beareth you as much good will and favor as ever he did, and willeth you to be of good cheer. And where report hath been made unto him that ye should commit against

6. because he is.   7. a fate.

his royal majesty certain heinous crimes, which he thinketh to
be untrue, yet for the ministration of justice in such cases requisite, and to avoid all suspect partiality, can do no less at
the least than to send for you to your trial, mistrusting nothing
your truth and wisdom, but that ye shall be able to acquit yourself against all complaints and accusations exhibited against
you; and to take your journey towards him at your own
pleasure, commanding me to be attendant upon you with
ministration of due reverence, and to see your person preserved
from all damage[8] and inconveniences[9] that might ensue; and
to elect all such your old servants (now his) to serve you by
the way, who hath most experience of your diet. Therefore,
sir, I beseech your grace to be of good cheer; and when it
shall be your good pleasure to take your journey, I shall give
mine attendance."

"Master Kingston," quod my lord, "I thank you for your
good news. And, sir, hereof assure yourself, that if I were
as able and as lusty as I have been but of late, I would not fail
to ride with you in post;[1] but, sir, I am diseased with a flux that
maketh me very weak. But, Master Kingston, all these comfortable words which ye have spoken be but for a purpose to bring
me in a fool's paradise. I know what is provided for me. Notwithstanding I thank you for your good will and pains taken
about me, and I shall with all speed make me ready to ride
with you tomorrow." And thus they fell into other communication, both the Earl and Master Kingston, with my lord; who
commanded me to foresee and provide that all things might
be made ready to depart the morrow after. I caused all things
to be thrust up[2] and made in a readiness as fast as they could
conveniently.

When night came that we should go to bed, my lord waxed
very sick through his new disease, the which caused him continually from time to time to go to the stool all that night; in
so much from the time that his disease took him unto the
next day he had above fifty stools, so that he was that day very
weak. The matter that he avoided[3] was wondrous black, the

8. harm.   9. injury.   1. post haste.
2. *thrust up:* trussed up, packed.   3. excreted.

which physicians call choler adustum.⁴ And when he perceived it he said unto me, "if I have not," quod he, "some help shortly, it will cost me my life." With that I caused one Doctor Nicholas, a physician being with the Earl, to look upon the gross⁵ matter that he avoided. Upon sight whereof he determined how he should not live past four or five days. Yet notwithstanding he would have ridden with Master Kingston that same day if the Earl of Shrewsbury had not been.⁶ Therefore in consideration of his infirmity they caused him to tarry all that day.

And the next day he took his journey with Master Kingston and the guard. And as soon as they espied their old master in such a lamentable estate, lamented him with weeping eyes; whom my lord took by the hands, and divers times by the way as he rode, he would talk with them, sometime with one and sometime with another. At night he was lodged at an house of the Earl of Shrewsbury's called Hardwick Hall, very evil at ease. The next day he rode to Nottingham, and there lodged that night, more sicker. And the next day we rode to Leicester Abbey; and by the way he waxed so sick that he was divers time likely to have fallen from his mule. And being night or we came to the Abbey aforesaid, where at his coming in at the gates, the Abbot of the place with all his convent⁷ met him with the light of many torches, whom they right honorably received with great reverence. To whom my lord said, "Father Abbot, I am come hither to leave my bones among you." Whom they brought on his mule to the stairs' foot of his chamber, and there lighted,⁸ and Master Kingston then took him by the arm and led him up the stairs—who told me afterward that he never carried so heavy a burden in all his life. And as soon as he was in his chamber, he went incontinent to his bed, very sick. This was upon Saturday at night; and there he continued, sicker and sicker.

Upon Monday in the morning as I stood by his bedside, about eight of the clock, the windows being close shut, hav-

4. *choler adustum:* name given in sixteenth-century medicine to bile excreted in dysentery.   5. thick.
6. *if the . . . been:* i.e. if the Earl had not prevented him.   7. monks.
8. alighted.

ing wax lights burning upon the cupboard, I beheld him as me seemed drawing fast to his end. He perceived my shadow upon the wall by his bedside, asked who was there. "Sir, I am here," quod I; "how do you?" quod he to me. "Very well, sir, if I might see your grace well." "What is it of the clock?" quod he to me. "Forsooth, sir," quod I, "it is past eight of the clock in the morning." "Eight of the clock," quod he, "that cannot be," rehearsing[9] divers time, "eight of the clock, eight of the clock. Nay, nay," quod he at the last, "it cannot be eight of the clock, for by eight of the clock ye shall lose your master; for my time draweth near that I must depart out of this world." With that Master Doctor Palmes, a worshipful gentleman, being his chaplain and ghostly father,[1] standing by, bade me secretly demand [2] of him if he would be shriven,[3] and to be in a readiness towards God what so ever should chance. At whose desire I asked him that question. "What have you to do," quod he, "to ask me any such question?" And began to be very angry with me for my presumption, until at the last Master Doctor took my part and talked with him in Latin and so pacified him.

And after dinner Master Kingston sent for me into his chamber. And at my being there, said to me, "so it is that the King hath sent me letters by this gentleman, Master Vincent,[4] one of your old companions, who hath been late in trouble in the Tower of London for money that my lord should have at his last departing from him, which now cannot be found. Wherefore the King, at this gentleman's request for the declaration of his truth, hath sent him hither with his grace's letters directed unto me, commanding me by virtue thereof to examine my lord in that behalf, and to have your counsel herein, how it may be done that he may take it well and in good part. This is the chief cause of my sending for you; wherefore I pray you what is your best counsel to use in this matter for the true acquittal of this gentleman?" "Sir," quod I, "as touching that matter my simple advice shall be this: that ye your own person

9. repeating.   1. confessor.   2. ask.   3. confessed.
4. David Vincent, formerly a groom in Wolsey's privy chamber. He had left Wolsey in September and had been arrested on suspicion of having stolen the money mentioned below.

shall resort unto him and visit him, and in communication break the matter unto him. And if he will not tell the truth, there be that can satisfy the King's pleasure therein. And in any wise speak nothing of my fellow Vincent. And I would not advise you to tract[5] the time with him, for he is very sick; I fear me he will not live past tomorrow in the morning."

Then went Master Kingston unto him and asked first how he did, and so forth proceeded in communication; wherein Master Kingston demanded [6] of him the said money, saying that my Lord of Northumberland hath found a book at Cawood that reporteth "how ye had but late fifteen hundred pounds in ready money, and one penny thereof will not be found, who hath made the King privy by his letters thereof. Wherefore the King hath written unto me to demand it of you, if ye do know where it is become; for it were pity that it should be embezzled from you both. Therefore I shall require you in the King's name to tell me the truth herein, to the intent that I may make just report unto his majesty what answer ye make therein."

With that my lord paused a while and said, "ah, good Lord! how much doth it grieve me that the King should think in me such deceit, wherein I should deceive him of any one penny that I have. Rather than I would, Master Kingston, embezzle or deceive him of a mite, I would it were molt[7] and put in my mouth!"—which words he spake twice or thrice very vehemently—"I have nothing ne never had, God being my judge, that I esteemed or had in it any such delight or pleasure but that I took it for the King's goods, having but the bare use of the same during my life; and after my death to leave it to the King, wherein he hath but prevented[8] mine intent and purpose. And for this money that ye demand of me, I assure you it is none of mine, for I borrowed it of divers of my friends to bury me and to bestow among my servants, which hath taken great pains about me like true and faithful men. Notwithstanding, if it be his pleasure to take this money from me, I must hold me therewith content. Yet I would most humbly beseech

5. delay.   6. asked.   7. melted.   8. anticipated.

his majesty to see them satisfied of whom I borrowed the same
for the discharge of my conscience."

"Who be they?" quod Master Kingston. "That shall I show
you: I borrowed two hundred pounds thereof of Sir John
Alyn of London;[9] and two hundred pounds of Sir Richard
Gresham;[1] and two hundred pounds of the Master of Savoy;[2]
and two hundred pounds of Doctor Hickden,[3] Dean of my
college in Oxford; and two hundred pounds of the Treasurer
of the Church of York;[4] and two hundred pounds of the
Dean of York;[5] and two hundred pounds of Parson Ellis,[6]
my chaplain; and an hundred pounds of my steward,[7] whose
name I have forgotten, trusting that the King will restore
them again their money, for it is none of mine." "Sir," quod
Master Kingston, "there is no doubt in the King (ye need
not to mistrust that), but when the King shall be advertized
thereof, to whom I shall make report of your request, that
his grace will do as shall become him. But sir, I pray you,
where is this money?" "Master Kingston," quod he, "I will
not conceal it from the King; I will declare it to you or I die,
by the grace of God. Take a little patience with me, I pray
you." "Well, sir, then I will trouble you no more at this time,
trusting that ye will show me tomorrow." "Yea, that I will,
Master Kingston, for the money is safe enough, and in an
honest man's keeping, who will not keep one penny from the
King." And then Master Kingston went to his supper.

Howbeit my lord waxed very sick, most likeliest to die that
night, and often swooned;[8] and as me thought drew toward
fast his end, until it was four of the clock in the morning, at
which time I asked him how he did. "Well," quod he, "if
I had any meat. I pray you give me some." "Sir, there is none
ready." "Iwis,[9] ye be the more to blame, for you should have

9. a prominent London alderman, Mayor in 1526.
1. Gresham (1485?–1549) was a London mercer who had extensive
dealings with Wolsey.
2. William Holgill, Wolsey's surveyor. The Savoy was a London
hospital.   3. John Higden, Dean of Cardinal College until 1531.
4. Launcelot Collynson (d. 1538).
5. Brian Higden (d. 1539), probably the brother of John.
6. Probably Nicholas Ellis, a priest in Wolsey's household in 1529.
7. Thomas Donington, of whom little else is known.   8. fainted.
9. indeed.

always some meat for me in a readiness to eat when my stomach serveth me. Therefore I pray you get me some; for I intend this day, God willing, to make me strong to the intent I may occupy myself in confession and make me ready to God." "Then, sir," quod I, "I will call up the cooks to provide some meat for you; and will also, if it be your pleasure, call for Master Palmes, that ye may commune with him until your meat be ready." "With a good will," quod he. And therewith I went first and called up the cook, commanding him to prepare some meat for my lord. And then I went to Master Palmes and told him what case my lord was in, willing him to rise and to resort to him with speed.

And then I went to Master Kingston and gave him warning that, as I thought, he would not live; advertizing[1] him that if he had anything to say to him that he should make haste, for he was in great danger. "In good faith," quod Master Kingston, "ye be to blame, for ye make him believe that he is sicker and in more danger than he is." "Well, sir," quod I, "ye shall not say another day but that I gave you warning as I am bound to do in discharge of my duty. Therefore I pray you what so ever shall chance, let no negligence be ascribed to me herein; for I assure you his life is very short. Do therefore now as ye think best." Yet nevertheless he arose and made him ready and came to him. After he had eaten of a cullis[2] made of a chicken a spoonful or two, at the last quod he, "whereof was this cullis made?" "Forsooth, sir," quod I, "of a chicken." "Why," quod he, "it is fasting day and Saint Andrew's Eve." [3] "What though, sir," quod Doctor Palmes, "ye be excused by reason of your sickness." "Yea," quod he, "what though? I will eat no more."

Then was he in confession the space of an hour. And when he had ended his confession, Master Kingston bade him good morrow (for it was about seven of the clock in the morning), and asked him how he did. "Sir," quod he, "I tarry but the will and pleasure of God, to render unto Him my simple soul into His divine hands." "Not yet so, sir," quod Master Kingston, "with the grace of God ye shall live and do very well,

1. informing.   2. a strong broth.   3. Tuesday, November 29, 1530.

if ye will be of good cheer." "Master Kingston, my disease is such that I cannot live. I have had some experience in my disease, and thus it is: I have a flux with a continual fever, the nature whereof is this; that if there be no alteration with me of the same within eight days, then must either ensue excoriation of the entrails, or frenzy, or else present[4] death. And the best thereof is death. And, as I suppose, this is the eighth day, and if ye see in me no alteration, then is there no remedy (although I may live a day or twain) but death, which is the best remedy of the three." "Nay, sir, in good faith," quod Master Kingston, "ye be in such dolor and pensiveness, doubting[5] that thing that indeed ye need not to fear, which maketh you much worse than ye should be."

"Well, well, Master Kingston," quod he, "I see the matter against me how it is framed. But if I had served God as diligently as I have done the King, he would not have given me over in my grey hairs. Howbeit this is the just reward that I must receive for my worldly diligence and pains that I have had to do him service, only to satisfy his vain pleasures, not regarding my godly duty. Wherefore I pray you with all my heart to have me most humbly commended unto his royal majesty, beseeching him in my behalf to call to his most gracious remembrance all matters proceeding between him and me from the beginning of the world unto this day, and the progress of the same. And most chiefly in the weighty matter yet depending (meaning the matter newly begun between him and good Queen Catherine)—then shall his conscience declare whether I have offended him or no. He is sure a prince of a royal corage,[6] and hath a princely heart; and rather than he will either miss or want any part of his will or appetite, he will put the loss of one half of his realm in danger. For I assure you I have often kneeled before him in his privy chamber on my knees the space of an hour or two to persuade him from his will and appetite; but I could never bring to pass to dissuade him therefro. Therefore, Master Kingston, if it chance hereafter you to be one of his privy council (as for your wisdom and other qualities ye be meet[7]

4. immediate.   5. fearing.   6. temper.   7. fit.

so to be) I warn you to be well advised and assured what matter ye put in his head; for ye shall never pull it out again.

"And say furthermore that I require his grace, in God's name, that he have a vigilant eye to depress[8] this new perverse sect of the Lutherans, that it do not increase within his dominions through his negligence, in such a sort as that he shall be fain at length to put harness[9] upon his back to subdue them; as the King of Bohemia[1] did, who had good game to see his rude commons (then infected with Wycliffe's[2] heresies) to spoil[3] and murder the spiritual men and religious persons[4] of his realm; the which fled to the King and his nobles for succors[5] against their frantic rage; of whom they could get no help of defense or refuge, but laughed them to scorn, having good game at their spoil and consumption, not regarding their duties nor their own defense. And when these erroneous heretics had subdued all the clergy and spiritual persons, taking the spoil of their riches, both of churches, monasteries, and all other spiritual things, having no more to spoil, caught such a courage of their former liberty,[6] that then they disdained their prince and sovereign lord with all other noble personages and the head governors of the country, and began to fall in hand[7] with the temporal lords to slay and spoil them without pity or mercy most cruelly. In so much that the King and other his nobles[8] were constrained to put harness upon their backs to resist the ungodly powers of these traitorous heretics, and to defend their lives and liberties. Who pitched a field royal[9] against them, in which field these traitors so stoutly encountered that the part of them were so cruel and vehement that, in fine,[1] they were victors and slew the King, the lords, and all the gentlemen of the realm, leaving not one person that bare the name or port[2] of a gentleman alive, or

8. suppress.   9. armor.
1. Wolsey refers to the early fifteenth-century Hussite revolt in Bohemia.   2. John Wycliffe (1320?–1384).   3. plunder.
4. *spiritual . . . persons:* members of the clergy.   5. succor, aid.
6. *caught . . . liberty:* became so encouraged by the liberty they had gained.   7. *fall in hand:* join forces.
8. *other his nobles:* his other nobles.
9. *pitched . . . royal:* began a battle royal.   1. *in fine:* in conclusion.
2. dignity.

of any person that had any rule or authority in the common-weal. By means of which slaughter they have lived ever since in great misery and poverty without an head or governor, but lived all in common like wild beasts, abhorred of all Christian nations.

"Let this be to him an evident example to avoid the like danger, I pray you, good Master Kingston. There is no trust in routs[3] or unlawful assemblies of the common people; for when the riotous multitude be assembled there is among them no mercy or consideration of their bounden duty; as in the history of King Richard the Second, one of his noble progen-itors, which in that same time of Wycliffe's seditious opinions did not the commons, I pray you, rise against the King[4] and nobles of the realm of England? Whereof some they appre-hended, whom they without mercy or justice put to death. And did they not fall to spoiling[5] and robbery to the intent they might bring all thing in common? And at the last, without discretion or reverence, spared not in their rage to take the King's most royal person out of the Tower of London and carried him about the City most presumptuously, causing him, for the preservation of his life, to be agreeable to their lewd[6] proclamations. Did not also that traitorous heretic, Sir John Oldcastle,[7] pitch a field[8] against King Harry the Fifth, against whom the King was constrained to encounter in his royal person, to whom God gave the victory?

"Alas! Master Kingston, if these be not plain precedents and sufficient persuasions to admonish a prince to be circum-spect against the semblable mischief;[9] and if he be negligent then will God strike and take from him his power and diminish his regally,[1] taking from him his prudent counsellors and valiant captains, and leave us in our own hands without his help and aid. And then will ensue mischief upon mischief, incon-

3. mobs.
4. Wat Tyler's rebellion of June 1381, in the course of which Richard II was held for a time by the rebels.   5. plundering.   6. villainous.
7. Sir John Oldcastle (1378?–1417) became a Lollard about 1410. He was executed on December 14, 1417.
8. *pitch a field:* commence a battle.   9. *semblable mischief:* similar evils.
1. royal authority.

venience[2] upon inconvenience, barrenness and scarcity of all things for lack of good order in the commonwealth, to the utter destruction and desolation[3] of this noble realm—from which mischiefs God for His tender mercy defend us.

"Master Kingston, farewell. I can no more but wish all thing to have good success. My time draweth on fast. I may not tarry with you. And forget not, I pray you, what I have said and charged you withal; for when I am dead ye shall peradventure[4] remember my words much better." And even with these words he began to draw his speech at length and his tongue to fail, his eyes being set in his head, whose sight failed him. Then we began to put him in remembrance of Christ's passion and sent for the Abbot of the place to anneal[5] him, who came with all speed and ministered unto him all the service to the same belonging. And caused also the guard to stand by, both to hear him talk before his death and also to be witness of the same. And incontinent the clock strake[6] eight, at which time he gave up the ghost and thus departed he this present life. And calling to our remembrance his words the day before, how he said that at eight of the clock we should lose our master, one of us looking upon another, supposing that he prophesied of his departure.

Here is the end and fall of pride and arrogancy[7] of such men, exalted by Fortune to honor and high dignities; for I assure you in his time of authority and glory he was the haultest[8] man in all his proceedings that then lived, having more respect to the worldly honor of his person than he had to his spiritual profession, wherein should be all meekness, humility, and charity; the process[9] whereof I leave to them that be learned and seen[1] in the divine laws.

After that he was departed, Master Kingston sent an empost[2] to the King to advertize him of the death of the late Cardinal of York, by one of the guard that both saw and heard him talk and die. And then Master Kingston, calling me unto him, and to the Abbot went to consultation for the order of his burial.

2. injury.   3. ruin.   4. perchance.
5. administer the sacrament of Extreme Unction to.   6. struck.
7. arrogance.   8. proudest.   9. relation.   1. knowledgeable.
2. express messenger.

After divers communications it was thought good that he should be buried the next day following, for Master Kingston would not tarry the return of the empost. And it was further thought good that the Mayor of Leicester and his brethren should be sent for to see him personally[3] dead, in avoiding of false rumors that might hap to say that he was not dead but still living. Then was the Mayor and his brethren sent for; and in the meantime the body was taken out of the bed where he lay dead. Who had upon him next his body a shirt of hair besides his other shirt, which was of very fine linen holland cloth. This shirt of hair was unknown to all his servants being continually attending upon him in his bedchamber, except to his chaplain, which was his ghostly father; wherein he was buried and laid in a coffin of boards, having upon his dead corpse all such vestures[4] and ornaments as he was professed in when he was consecrated bishop and archbishop, as miter, crozier,[5] ring, and pall,[6] with all other things appurtenant[7] to his profession. And lying thus all day in his coffin open and barefaced that all men might see him lie there dead without feigning—then when the Mayor, his brethren, and all other had seen him lying thus until four or five of the clock at night, he was carried so down into the church with great solemnity by the Abbot and covent[8] with many torches light, singing such service as is due for such funerals.

And being in the church the corpse was set in Our Lady Chapel, with many divers tapers of wax burning about the hearse, and diverse poor men sitting about the same, holding of torches light in their hands, who watched about the dead body all night whilst the canons sang *dirige*[9] and other devout orisons.[1] And about four of the clock in the morning they sang Mass. And that done and the body interred, Master Kingston with us, being his servants, were present at his said funerals and offered at his Mass. And by that time that all things was finished and all ceremonies that to such a person was decent and convenient,[2] it was about six of the clock in the morning.

3. in person.   4. robes.   5. bishop's staff.   6. pallium.   7. belonging.
8. group of monks.   9. the dirge.   1. prayers.
2. *decent and convenient:* fitting and suitable.

Then prepared we to horseback, being Saint Andrew's Day the apostle, and so took our journey towards the court, being at Hampton Court where the King then lay. And after we came thither, which was upon Saint Nicholas' Eve,[3] we gave attendance upon the council for our dispatch.

Upon the morrow I was sent for by the King to come to his grace; and being in Master Kingston's chamber in the court, had knowledge thereof. And repairing to the King, I found him shooting at the rounds in the park on the backside of the garden. And perceiving him occupied in shooting, thought it not my duty to trouble him, but leaned to a tree, intending to stand there and to attend his gracious pleasure, being in a great study. At the last, the King came suddenly behind me where I stood and clapped his hand upon my shoulder. And when I perceived him, I fell upon my knee. To whom he said, calling me by my name, "I will," quod he, "make an end of my game, and then will I talk with you." And so departed to his mark, whereat the game was ended. Then the King delivered his bow to the yeoman of his bows and went his way inward to the place, whom I followed. Howbeit he called for Sir John Gage, with whom he talked until he came at the garden postern gate, and there entered, the gate being shut after him, which caused me to go my ways.

And being gone but a little distance, the gate was opened again, and there Sir Harry Norris called me again, commanding me to come into the King, who stood behind the door in a nightgown of russet velvet furred with sables. Before whom I kneeled down, being with him there all alone the space of an hour and more, during which time he examined me of divers weighty matters concerning my lord, wishing that lever[4] than twenty thousand pounds he had lived. Then he asked me for the fifteen hundred pounds (which Master Kingston moved to my lord[5] before his death). "Sir," said I, "I think that I can tell your grace partly where it is." "Yea, can,"[6] quod the King, "then I pray you tell me and you

3. December 5.   4. rather.
5. *moved to my lord:* questioned my lord about.   6. *Yea, can:* can ye?

shall do us much pleasure, nor it shall not be unrewarded."
"Sir," said I, "if it please your highness, after the departure
of David Vincent from my lord at Scroby, who had then
the custody thereof, leaving the same with my lord in divers
bags sealed with my lord's seal, delivered the same money in
the same bags sealed unto a certain priest (whom I named to
the King) safely to keep to his use." "Is this true?" quod
the King. "Yea, sir," quod I, "without all doubt; the priest
shall not be able to deny it in my presence, for I was at the
delivery thereof."

"Well then," quod the King, "let me alone. Keep this gear[7]
secret between yourself and me and let no man be privy[8]
thereof. For if I hear any more of it, then I know by whom
it is come to knowledge. Three may," quod he, "keep counsel,
if two be away. And if I thought that my cap knew my
counsel, I would cast it into the fire and burn it. And for your
truth and honesty, ye shall be one of our servants and in that
same room[9] with us that ye were with your old master.
Therefore go to Sir John Gage, our vice-chamberlain, to
whom I have spoken already, to give you your oath and to
admit you our servant in the same room. And then go to my
Lord of Norfolk, and he shall pay you all your whole year's
wages, which is ten pounds—is it not so?" quod the King.
"Yes, forsooth, sir," quod I, "and I am behind thereof for
three quarters of a year." "That is true," quod the King, "for
so we be informed. Therefore ye shall have your whole
year's wages with our reward delivered you by the Duke of
Norfolk." The King also promised me furthermore to be my
singular good and gracious lord whensoever occasion should
serve. And thus I departed from him.

And as I went I met with Master Kingston coming from
the council, who commanded me in their names to go straight
unto them, for whom they have sent for by him. "And in any
wise," quod he, "for God's sake, take good heed what ye
say; for ye shall be examined of such certain words as my
lord your late master had at his departure. And if you tell
them the truth," quod he, "what he said, you should undo

7. business.   8. aware.   9. office.

yourself, for in any wise they would not hear of it. Therefore be circumspect what answer ye make to their demand." "Why, sir," quod I, "how have ye done therein yourself?" "Marry," quod he, "I have utterly denied that ever I heard any such words. And he that opened the matter first is fled for fear, which was the yeoman of the guard that rode empost[1] to the King from Leicester. Therefore go your ways, God send you good speed; and when ye have done come to me into the chamber of presence, where I shall tarry[2] your coming to see how you speed and to know how ye have done with the King."

Thus I departed and went directly to the council chamber door; and as soon as I was come I was called in among them. And being there, my Lord of Norfolk spake to me first and bade me welcome to the court, and said, "my lords, this gentleman hath both justly and painfully served the Cardinal his master like an honest and diligent servant. Therefore I doubt not but of such questions as ye shall demand of him, he will make just report. I dare undertake the same for him. How say ye? It is reported that your master spake certain words even[3] before his departure out of this life, the truth whereof I doubt not ye know. And as ye know I pray you report and fear not for no man. Ye shall not need to swear him. Therefore, go to, how say you? Is it true that is reported?"

"Forsooth, sir, I was so diligent attending more to the preservation of his life than I was to note and mark every word that he spake; and sir, indeed he spake many idle words as men in such extremes, the which I cannot now remember. If it please your lordships to call before you Master Kingston he will not fail to show you the truth." "Marry, so have we done already," quod they, "who hath been here presently[4] before us, and hath denied utterly that ever he heard any such words spoken by your master at the time of his death or at any time before." "Forsooth, my lords," quod I, "then I can say no more, for if he heard them not, I could not hear them. For he heard as much as I, and I as much as he. Therefore, my lords, it were much folly for me to declare anything

1. in post haste.   2. await.   3. just.   4. just now.

of untruth, which I am not able to justify." "Lo!" quod my
Lord of Norfolk, "I told you as much before. Therefore go
your ways," quod he to me, "you are dismissed. And come
again to my chamber anon[5] for I must needs talk with you."

I most humbly thanked them and so departed; and went
into the chamber of presence to meet with Master Kingston,
whom I found standing in communication with an ancient[6]
gentleman usher of the King's privy chamber called Master
Ratcliff. And at my coming Master Kingston demanded of
me if I had been with the council and what answer I made
them. I said again that I had satisfied them sufficiently with
my answer, and told him the manner of it. And then he asked
me how I sped with the King. I told him partly of our communication and of his grace's benevolence and princely liberality, and how he commanded me to go to my Lord of
Norfolk. As we were speaking of him, he came from the
council into the chamber of presence. As soon as he espied
me he came into the window where I stood with Master
Kingston and Master Ratcliff, to whom I declared the King's
pleasure. These two gentlemen desired him to be my good
lord. "Nay," quod he, "I will be better unto him than ye
ween,[7] for if I could have spoken with him before he came
to the King I would have had him to my service. The King
excepted, he should have done no man service in all England
but only me. And look, what I may do for you, I will do it
with a right good will."

"Sir, then," quod I, "will it please your grace to move the
King's majesty in my behalf to give me one of the carts and
horses that brought up my stuff with my lord's, which is now in
the Tower, to carry it into my country?" "Yea, marry, will I,"
quod he, and returned again to the King; for whom I tarried
still with Master Kingston and Master Ratcliff, who said that
he would go in and help my lord in my suit with the King.
And incontinent[8] my lord came forth and showed me how the
King was my good and gracious lord; and hath given me six
of the best horse that I can choose amongst all my lord's cart
horse, with a cart to carry my stuff and five marks for my

5. in a little while.   6. aged.   7. think.   8. at once.

costs homewards. "And [he] hath commanded me," quod he, "to deliver you ten pounds for your wages, being behind unpaid, and twenty pounds for a reward." Who commanded to call for Master Secretary to make a warrant for all these things.

Then was it told him that Master Secretary was gone to Hanworth for that night. Then commanded he one of the messengers of the chamber to ride unto him in all haste for these warrants, and willed me to meet with him the next day at London, and there to receive both my money, my stuff, and horse that the King gave me. And so I did. Of whom I received all things according;[9] and then I returned into my country. And thus ended the life of my late lord and master, the rich and triumphant legate and Cardinal of England, on whose soul Jesu have mercy, Amen.

Finis Quod G. C.

Who list[1] to read and consider with an indifferent[2] eye this history may behold the wondrous mutability of vain honors, the brittle assurance of abundance, the uncertainty of dignities, the flattering of feigned friends, and the tickle[3] trust to worldly princes. Whereof this Lord Cardinal hath felt both of the sweet and the sour in each degrees—as fleeting[4] from honors, losing of riches, deposed from dignities, forsaken of friends, and the inconstantness of princes' favor. Of all which things he hath had in this world the full felicity as long as that Fortune smiled upon him; but when she began to frown, how soon was he deprived of all these dreaming joys and vain pleasures! The which in twenty years with great travail, study, and pains obtained, were in one year and less, with heaviness,[5] care, and sorrow, lost and consumed. O madness, O foolish desire, O fond hope, O greedy desire of vain honors, dignities, and riches, O what inconstant trust and assurance is in rolling Fortune! Wherefore the prophet said

9. accordingly.   1. *who list:* whoever cares.   2. impartial.
3. insecure, uncertain.   4. gliding away from.   5. grief.

full well, *"Thesaurizat, et ignorat cui congregabit ea."* [6] Who is certain to whom he shall leave his treasure and riches that he hath gathered together in this world? It may chance him to leave it unto such as he hath purposed. But the wise man saith, "that another person who peradventure[7] he hated in his life shall spend it out and consume it." [8]

6. Psalms 38: 7.   7. perchance. The allusion must be to Henry VIII.
8. *that another . . . consume it:* cf. Ecclesiastes 6: 2.

The Life of
Sir Thomas More

by William Roper

FORASMUCH AS SIR THOMAS MORE, KNIGHT, sometime Lord Chancellor of England, a man of singular virtue and of a clear, unspotted conscience, as witnesseth Erasmus, more pure and white than the whitest snow, and of such an angelical wit as England (he saith) never had the like before, nor never shall again, universally, as well in the laws of our own realm, a study in effect able to occupy the whole life of a man, as in all other sciences[1] right well studied, was in his days accompted[2] a man worthy perpetual famous memory:

I, William Roper, though most unworthy, his son-in-law by marriage of his eldest daughter,[3] knowing—at this day—no one man living that of him and of his doings understood so much as myself, for that I was continually resident in his house by the space of sixteen years and more,[4] thought it therefore my part to set forth such matters touching his life as I could at this present call to remembrance.

Among which things, very many notable things (not meet[5] to have been forgotten) through negligence and long continuance of time are slipped out of my mind. Yet to the intent the same should not all utterly perish, I have at the desire of divers worshipful friends of mine, though very far from the grace and worthiness of them, nevertheless as far forth as my mean wit, memory, and knowledge would serve me, declared so much thereof as in my poor judgment seemed worthy to be remembered.

This Sir Thomas More, after he had been brought up in the Latin tongue at Saint Anthony's[6] in London, was by his father's[7] procurement received into the house of the right

1. branches of knowledge.   2. accounted.
3. Margaret, More's favorite daughter, married Roper on July 2, 1521.
4. Since More was executed in July 1535, Roper must therefore have entered his service in the year 1518. He was then about twenty years old.
5. fit, proper.
6. A free school associated with the Hospital of St. Anthony.
7. Judge John More (1451?–1530).

reverend, wise, and learned prelate, Cardinal Morton.[8] Where, though he was young of years, yet would he at Christmas-tide suddenly sometimes step in among the players, and never studying for the matter, make a part of his own there presently among them, which made the lookers-on more sport than all the players beside. In whose wit and towardness the Cardinal much delighting would often say of him unto the nobles that divers times dined with him, "This child here waiting at the table, whosoever shall live to see it, will prove a marvellous man."

Whereupon for his better furtherance in learning, he placed him at Oxford, where when he was both in the Greek and Latin tongue sufficiently instructed, he was then for the study of the law of the realm put to an Inn of Chancery called New Inn, where for his time he very well prospered, and from thence was admitted to Lincoln's Inn, with very small allowance, continuing there his study until he was made and accompted a worthy utter[9] barrister. After this, to his great commendation, he read for a good space a public lecture of Saint Augustine, *De Civitate Dei,* in the Church of Saint Lawrence in the old Jewry, whereunto there resorted Doctor Grocyn,[1] an excellent cunning man, and all the chief learned of the City of London. Then was he made Reader of Furnival's Inn,[2] so remaining by the space of three years and more.

After which time he gave himself to devotion and prayer in the Charterhouse of London,[3] religiously living there without vow[4] about four years, until he resorted to the house of one Master Colt, a gentleman of Essex, that had oft invited him thither, having three daughters, whose honest conversation[5] and virtuous education provoked him there specially to set his affection. And albeit his mind most served him to the second daughter, for that he thought her the fairest and best favored, yet when he considered that it would be both great

8. Lord Chancellor of England (1487–1500). More entered the Cardinal's household in 1490.   9. fully qualified.
1. Vicar of St. Lawrence, and one of the most learned men of his time.
2. An Inn of Chancery attached to Lincoln's Inn. *Reader:* i.e. a lecturer on law.   3. A Carthusian monastery.
4. *Religiously . . . vow:* i.e. he never took orders but did participate regularly in the religious life of the community.   5. behavior.

grief and some shame also to the eldest to see her younger sister in marriage preferred before her, he then of a certain pity framed his fancy towards her, and soon after married her[6] —neverthemore discontinuing his study of the law at Lincoln's Inn, but applying still the same, until he was called to the bench, and had read[7] there twice, which is as often as ordinarily any judge of the law doth read.

Before which time he had placed himself and his wife at Bucklersbury in London, where he had by her three daughters and one son, in virtue and learning brought up from their youth, whom he would often exhort to take virtue and learning for their meat, and play for their sauce.

Who, ere ever he had been reader in Court,[8] was in the latter time of King Henry the Seventh made a burgess of the Parliament, wherein there were by the King demanded (as I have heard reported) about three-fifteenths[9] for the marriage of his eldest daughter, that then should be the Scottish queen; at the last debating whereof he made such arguments and reasons there against, that the King's demands thereby were clean overthrown. So that one of the King's privy chamber, named Master Tyler, being present thereat, brought word to the King out of the Parliament House that a beardless boy had disappointed all his purpose. Whereupon the King, conceiving great indignation towards him, could not be satisfied until he had some way revenged it. And forasmuch as he, nothing having, nothing could lose, his grace devised a causeless quarrel against his father, keeping him in the Tower until he had made him pay to him an hundred pounds fine.

Shortly hereupon it fortuned[1] that this Sir Thomas More, coming in a suit to Doctor Foxe, Bishop of Winchester, one of the King's privy council, the Bishop called him aside and pretending great favor towards him, promised him that if he would be ruled by him he would not fail into the King's favor again to restore him, meaning, as it was after conjectured, to

6. More's marriage to Jane Colt took place in, or shortly before, January 1505. She died in 1511. More remarried almost immediately, this time a widow, Alice Middleton, the "Dame Alice" of the biography. 7. given a series of lectures.   8. Inn of Court.
9. A personal property tax amounting to three-fifteenths of the value of the property.   1. chanced.

cause him thereby to confess his offense against the King, whereby his highness might with the better color[2] have occasion to revenge his displeasure against him.

But when he came from the Bishop, he fell in communication with one Master Whitford, his familiar friend, then chaplain to that Bishop, and after a Father of Sion,[3] and showed him what the Bishop had said unto him, desiring to have his advice therein, who for the Passion of God prayed him in no wise to follow his counsel. "For my lord, my master," quoth he, "to serve the King's turn, will not stick to agree to his own father's death." So Sir Thomas More returned to the Bishop no more. And had not the King soon after died,[4] he was determined to have gone over the sea, thinking that, being in the King's indignation, he could not live in England without great danger.

After this he was made one of the undersheriffs[5] of London, by which office and his learning together (as I have heard him say), he gained without grief not so little as four hundred pounds by the year, sith there was at that time in none of the prince's courts of the laws of this realm any matter of importance in controversy wherein he was not with the one part of counsel. Of whom, for his learning, wisdom, knowledge, and experience, men had such estimation that, before he came to the service of King Henry the Eighth, at the suit and instance of the English merchants, he was by the King's consent made twice ambassador in certain great causes between them and the merchants of the Steel-yard.[6] Whose wise and discreet dealing therein, to his high commendation, coming to the King's understanding, provoked his highness to cause Cardinal Wolsey, then Lord Chancellor, to procure him to his service.

And albeit the Cardinal, according to the King's request, earnestly travailed[7] with him therefore—among many other his persuasions alleging unto him how dear his service must

2. appearance of right.   3. Bridgettine monastery of Sion in Middlesex.
4. Henry VII died in April 1509.
5. Important executive officials responsible to the High Sheriff. Their duties included the supervision of prisoners, the execution of writs, and the imposition of death-sentences.
6. Hanseatic League colony in London.   7. labored.

needs be unto his majesty, which could not, with his honor, with less than he should yearly lose thereby seem to recompense him—yet he, loath to change his estate, made such means to the King by the Cardinal to the contrary[8] that his grace for that time was well satisfied.

Now happened there after this a great ship of his that then was Pope to arrive at Southampton, which the King claiming for a forfeiture, the Pope's ambassador, by suit unto his grace, obtained that he might for his master the Pope have counsel learned in the laws of this realm, and the matter in his own presence (being himself a singular civilian)[9] in some public place to be openly heard and discussed.

At which time there could none of our law be found so meet to be of counsel with this ambassador as Sir Thomas More, who could report to the ambassador in Latin all the reasons and arguments by the learned counsel on both sides alleged. Upon this, the counsellors of either part,[1] in presence of the Lord Chancellor and other the judges, in the Star Chamber[2] had audience accordingly. Where Sir Thomas More not only declared to the ambassador the whole effect of all their opinions, but also in defense of the Pope's side argued so learnedly himself that both was the foresaid forfeiture to the Pope restored, and himself among all the hearers, for his upright and commendable demeanor therein so greatly renowned, that for no entreaty would the King from thenceforth be induced any longer to forbear[3] his service. At whose first entry thereunto, he made him Master of the Requests,[4] having then no better room[5] void, and within a month after, knight and one of his privy council.

And so from time to time was he by the prince advanced, continuing in his singular favor and trusty service twenty

8. *by the . . . contrary:* i.e. the Cardinal conveyed to the King More's reluctance to enter the royal service.
9. one especially well-versed in civil law, in this case the Pope's ambassador.   1. both parties.
2. A famous court with jurisdiction chiefly, though not exclusively, over criminal cases. It was presided over by the King's Council. Abolished in 1641.   3. dispense with.
4. i.e. Judge in the Court of Requests, sometimes called the "Poor Man's Court." The appointment was made in late 1517.   5. office.

years and above—a good part whereof used the King upon holidays, when he had done his own devotions, to send for him into his traverse,[6] and there sometime in matters of astronomy, geometry, divinity, and such other faculties, and sometimes of his worldly affairs, to sit and confer with him. And other whiles would he in the night have him up into his leads,[7] there for to consider with him the diversities, courses, motions, and operations of the stars and planets.

And because he was of a pleasant disposition, it pleased the King and Queen after the council had supped, at the time of their supper, for their pleasure commonly to call for him to be merry with them. Whom when he perceived so much in his talk to delight that he could not once in a month get leave to go home to his wife and children, whose company he most desired, and to be absent from the court two days together but that he should be thither sent for again—he, much misliking this restraint of his liberty, began thereupon somewhat to dissemble his nature, and so by little and little from his former accustomed mirth to disuse[8] himself, that he was of them from thenceforth at such seasons no more so ordinarily sent for.

Then died one Master Weston, Treasurer of the Exchequer, whose office after his death the King, of his own offer, without any asking, freely gave unto Sir Thomas More.[9]

In the fourteenth year of his grace's reign was there a Parliament holden,[1] whereof Sir Thomas More was chosen Speaker. Who, being very loath to take that room upon him, made an oration (not now extant) to the King's highness for his discharge[2] thereof. Whereunto when the King would not consent, he spake unto his grace in the form following:

> Sith I perceive, most redoubted Sovereign, that it standeth not with your high pleasure to reform[3] this election and cause it to be changed, but have by the mouth of the

6. a screened-off apartment.   7. lead roof.   8. disengage.
9. A mistake on Roper's part. In May 1521 More was made Under-Treasurer, not Treasurer, of the Exchequer. Furthermore, his predecessor was not Weston but Sir John Cutte.   1. In April 1523.
2. relief from that obligation (to be Speaker).   3. revoke.

most reverend father in God, the legate, your highness's Chancellor, thereunto given your most royal assent, and have of your benignity determined—far above that I may bear—to enable me, and for this office to repute me meet,[4] rather than you should seem to impute unto your Commons that they had unmeetly chosen, I am therefore, and always shall be, ready obediently to conform myself to the accomplishment of your high commandment—in my most humble wise beseeching your most noble majesty that I may with your grace's favor, before I farther enter thereunto, make mine humble intercession unto your highness for two lowly petitions: the one privately concerning myself, the other the whole assembly of your Common House.

For myself, gracious Sovereign, that if it mishap me[5] in anything hereafter that is on the behalf of your Commons in your high presence to be declared, to mistake my message, and in the lack of good utterance, by my misrehearsal[6] to pervert or impair their prudent instructions, it may then like your most noble majesty, of your abundant grace, with the eye of your accustomed pity, to pardon my simpleness—giving me leave to repair again to the Common House and there to confer with them, and to take their substantial advice what thing and in what wise I shall on their behalf utter and speak before your noble grace, to the intent their prudent devices and affairs be not by my simpleness and folly hindered or impaired. Which thing, if it should so mishap, as it were well likely to mishap in me, if your gracious benignity relieved not my oversight, it could not fail to be during my life a perpetual grudge[7] and heaviness to my heart. The help and remedy whereof, in manner aforesaid remembered, is, most gracious Sovereign, my first lowly suit and humble petition unto your most noble grace.

Mine other humble request, most excellent prince, is this: forasmuch as there be of your Commons, here by

4. *repute me meet:* declare me qualified.
5. *if . . . me:* if it is my bad luck. 6. misrepresentation. 7. uneasiness.

your high commandment assembled for your Parliament, a great number which are after the accustomed manner appointed in the Common House to treat and advise of the common affairs among themselves apart; and albeit, most dear liege-lord, that according to your prudent advice, by your honorable writs everywhere declared, there hath been as due diligence used in sending up to your highness's Court of Parliament the most discreet persons out of every quarter that men could esteem meet thereunto—whereby it is not to be doubted but that there is a very substantial assembly of right wise and politick persons; yet, most victorious prince, sith among so many wise men neither is every man wise alike, nor among so many men, like well-witted, every man like well-spoken. And it often happeneth that, likewise, as much folly is uttered with painted, polished speech; so many boisterous and rude in language see deep indeed, and give right substantial counsel.

And sith also in matters of great importance, the mind is often so occupied in the matter that a man rather studieth what to say than how, by reason whereof the wisest man and the best spoken in a whole country for-tuneth among,[8] while his mind is fervent in the matter, somewhat to speak in such wise as he would afterward wish to have been uttered otherwise, and yet no worse will had when he spake it than he hath when he would so gladly change it; therefore, most gracious Sovereign, considering that in your high Court of Parliament is nothing entreated[9] but matter of weight and importance concerning your realm and your own royal estate, it could not fail to let[1] and put to silence from the giving of their advice and counsel many of your discreet Commons, to the great hindrance of the common affairs, except that every of your Commons were utterly discharged[2] of all doubt and fear how anything that it should happen them to speak should happen of your highness to be

8. now and then.   9. treated.   1. hinder.   2. relieved.

taken.[3] And in this point, though your well known and proved benignity putteth every man in right good hope, yet such is the weight of the matter, such is the reverend[4] dread[5] that the timorous hearts of your natural subjects conceive toward your high majesty, our most redoubted King and undoubted Sovereign, that they cannot in this point find themselves satisfied, except your gracious bounty therein declared put away the scruple of their timorous minds, and animate and encourage them, and put them out of doubt.

It may therefore like your most abundant grace, our most benign and godly King, to give all your Commons here assembled your most gracious license and pardon, freely, without doubt of your dreadful displeasure, every man to discharge his conscience, and boldly in every thing incident among us to declare his advice. And whatsoever happen any man to say that it may like your noble majesty, of your inestimable goodness, to take all in good part, interpreting every man's words, how uncunningly[6] soever they be couched, to proceed yet of good zeal towards the profit of your realm and honor of your royal person, the prosperous estate and preservation whereof, most excellent Sovereign, is the thing which we all, your most humble loving subjects, according to the most bounden duty of our natural allegiance, most highly desire and pray for.

At this Parliament Cardinal Wolsey found himself much grieved with the burgesses thereof, for that nothing was so soon done or spoken therein but that it was immediately blown abroad in every alehouse. It fortuned at that Parliament a very great subsidy[7] to be demanded, which the Cardinal fearing would not pass the Common House, determined for the furtherance thereof to be personally present there. Before whose coming, after long debating there, whether it were better but

3. interpreted.   4. reverenced.   5. fear.   6. unskilfully.
7. money granted by Parliament to the Crown to meet specific needs.

with a few of his lords (as the most opinion of the house was) or with his whole train royally to receive him there amongst them—"Masters," quoth Sir Thomas More, "forasmuch as my Lord Cardinal lately, ye wot well, laid to our charge the lightness[8] of our tongues for things uttered out of this house, it shall not in my mind be amiss with all his pomp to receive him, with his maces, his pillars, his pole-axes, his crosses, his hat, and Great Seal, too—to the intent, if he find the like fault with us hereafter, we may be the bolder from ourselves to lay the blame on those that his grace bringeth hither with him." Whereunto the house wholly agreeing, he was received accordingly.

Where, after that he had in a solemn oration by many reasons proved how necessary it was the demand there moved to be granted, and further showed that less would not serve to maintain the prince's purpose, he—seeing the company sitting still silent, and thereunto nothing answering and contrary to his expectation showing in themselves towards his requests no towardness of inclination,[9] said unto them:

"Masters, you have many wise and learned men among you, and since I am from the King's own person sent hither unto you for the preservation of yourselves and all the realm, I think it meet you give me some reasonable answer."

Whereat every man holding his peace, then began he to speak to one Master Marney, after Lord Marney: "How say you," quoth he, "Master Marney?" Who making him no answer neither, he severally asked the same question of divers others accompted the wisest of the company.

To whom, when none of them all would give so much as one word, being before agreed, as the custom was, by their speaker to make answer—"Masters," quoth the Cardinal, "unless it be the manner of your house, as of likelihood it is, by the mouth of your speaker, whom you have chosen for trusty and wise, as indeed he is, in such cases to utter your minds, here is without doubt a marvellous obstinate silence."

And thereupon he required answer of Master Speaker. Who

8. looseness.
9. *towardness of inclination*: readiness to accede (to Wolsey's requests).

first reverently upon his knees excusing the silence of the
house, abashed at the presence of so noble a personage, able
to amaze[1] the wisest and best learned in a realm, and after by
many probable arguments proving that for them to make
answer was it neither expedient nor agreeable with the ancient
liberty of the house, in conclusion for himself showed that
though they had all with their voices trusted him, yet except
every one of them could put into his one head all their several
wits,[2] he alone in so weighty a matter was unmeet[3] to make
his grace answer.

Whereupon the Cardinal, displeased with Sir Thomas More,
that had not in this Parliament in all things satisfied his desire,
suddenly arose and departed.

And after the Parliament ended, in his gallery at Whitehall
in Westminster, uttered unto him his griefs, saying: "Would
to God you had been at Rome, Master More, when I made
you Speaker!"

"Your grace not offended, so would I too, my lord," quoth
he. And to wind such quarrels out of the Cardinal's head, he
began to talk of that gallery and said: "I like this gallery of
yours, my lord, much better than your gallery at Hampton
Court." Wherewith so wisely brake he off the Cardinal's
displeasant talk that the Cardinal at that present (as it seemed)
wist[4] not what more to say to him. But for revengement of
his displeasure counselled the King to send him ambassador
into Spain, commending to his highness his wisdom, learning,
and meetness for that voyage; and, the difficulty of the cause
considered, none was there, he said, so well able to serve his
grace therein.

Which, when the King had broken to Sir Thomas More,
and that he had declared unto his grace how unfit a journey
it was for him, the nature of the country and disposition of
his complexion[5] so disagreeing together, that he should never
be likely to do his grace acceptable service there, knowing
right well that if his grace sent him thither, he should send him

1. confound.   2. minds.   3. unqualified.   4. knew.
5. More apparently felt that the Spanish climate might fatally affect
his constitution ("complexion").

to his grave. But showing himself nevertheless ready, according to his duty (all were it with the loss of his life), to fulfill his grace's pleasure in that behalf.

The King, allowing well[6] his answer, said unto him: "It is not our meaning, Master More, to do you hurt, but to do you good would we be glad. We will therefore for this purpose devise upon some other, and employ your service otherwise." And such entire favor did the King bear him that he made him Chancellor of the Duchy of Lancaster upon the death of Sir Richard Wingfield,[7] who had that office before.

And for the pleasure he took in his company would his grace suddenly sometimes come home to his house at Chelsea to be merry with him. Whither on a time, unlooked for, he came to dinner to him; and after dinner, in a fair garden of his, walked with him by the space of an hour, holding his arm about his neck.

As soon as his grace was gone, I, rejoicing thereat, told Sir Thomas More how happy he was, whom the King had so familiarly entertained, as I never had seen him to do to any other except Cardinal Wolsey, whom I saw his grace once walk with, arm in arm. "I thank our Lord, son," quoth he, "I find his grace my very good lord indeed; and I believe he doth as singularly favor me as any subject within this realm. Howbeit, son Roper, I may tell thee I have no cause to be proud thereof, for if my head could win him a castle in France (for then was there war between us) it should not fail to go."

This Sir Thomas More, among all other his virtues, was of such meekness that, if it had fortuned him with any learned men resorting to him from Oxford, Cambridge, or elsewhere, as there did divers,[8] some for desire of his acquaintance, some for the famous report of his wisdom and learning, and some for suits of[9] the universities, to have entered into argument (wherein few were comparable unto him) and so far to have discoursed with them therein that he might perceive they

6. *allowing well:* accepting as satisfactory.
7. Interestingly enough, shortly after he arrived in Spain, Sir Richard (who replaced More on the mission) was taken ill in Toledo and died there in July 1525. More succeeded him as Chancellor of the Duchy in the same year.   8. on sundry occasions.   9. *suits of:* petitions from.

could not, without some inconvenience, hold out much further disputation with him, then lest he should discomfort them—as he that sought not his own glory but rather would seem conquered than to discourage students in their studies, ever showing himself more desirous to learn than to teach—would he by some witty device courteously break off into some other matter and give over.

Of whom for his wisdom and learning had the King such an opinion that at such time as he attended upon his highness, taking his progress[1] either to Oxford or Cambridge, where he was received with very eloquent orations, his grace would always assign him, as one that was prompt and ready therein, *ex tempore* to make answer thereunto. Whose manner was, whensoever he had occasion either here or beyond the sea to be in any university, not only to be present at the readings and disputations there commonly used, but also learnedly to dispute among them himself. Who being Chancellor of the Duchy was made ambassador twice, joined in commission with Cardinal Wolsey—once to the Emperor Charles into Flanders, the other time to the French King into France.

Not long after this, the Water-bailly of London,[2] sometime his servant, hearing (where he had been at dinner) certain merchants liberally[3] to rail against his old master, waxed so discontented therewith that he hastily came to him and told him what he had heard. "And were I, sir," quoth he, "in such favor and authority with my prince as you are, such men surely should not be suffered so villainously and falsely to misreport and slander me. Wherefore I would wish you to call them before you, and to their shame for their lewd[4] malice to punish them."

Who, smiling upon him, said: "Why, Master Water-bailly, would you have me punish those by whom I receive more benefit than by you all that be my friends? Let them, a God's name, speak as lewdly as they list of me and shoot never so many arrows at me. As long as they do not hit me, what am I

1. formal state journey.
2. An important official, one of four attendants upon the Lord Mayor of London.   3. unrestrainedly.   4. villainous.

the worse? But if they should once hit me, then would it indeed not a little trouble me. Howbeit I trust, by God's help, there shall none of them all once be able to touch me. I have more cause, I assure thee, Master Water-bailly, to pity them than to be angry with them." Such fruitful communication had he oft-times with his familiar friends.

So on a time, walking with me along the Thames-side at Chelsea,[5] in talking of other things he said unto me: "Now would to our Lord, son Roper, upon condition that three things were well established in Christendom, I were put in a sack and here presently cast into the Thames."

"What great things be those, sir," quoth I, "that should move you so to wish?"

"Wouldst thou know what they be, son Roper?" quoth he.

"Yea, marry, with good will, sir, if it please you," quoth I.

"In faith, son, they be these," said he. "The first is that where the most part of Christian princes be at mortal war, they were all at an universal peace. The second, that where the Church of Christ is at this present sore afflicted with many errors and heresies, it were settled in a perfect uniformity of religion. The third, that where the King's matter of his marriage is now come in question, it were to the glory of God and quietness of all parts brought to a good conclusion." Whereby, as I could gather, he judged that otherwise it would be a disturbance to a great part of Christendom.

Thus did it by his doings throughout the whole course of his life appear that all his travail and pains, without respect of earthly commodities[6] either to himself or any of his, were only upon the service of God, the prince, and the realm, wholly bestowed and employed. Whom I heard in his later time to say that he never asked the King for himself the value of one penny.

As Sir Thomas More's custom was daily, if he were at home, besides his private prayers, with his children to say the Seven

5. The site of More's beloved country estate. In his day Chelsea was about ten miles up the Thames River from the City of London. All contemporary authors who allude in any detail to the estate rhapsodize over its idyllic setting and character.   6. benefits or profits.

Psalms, Litany and Suffrages following, so was his guise[7] nightly before he went to bed, with his wife, children, and household, to go to his chapel and there upon his knees ordinarily to say certain psalms and collects[8] with them. And because he was desirous for godly purposes sometime to be solitary, and sequester himself from worldly company, a good distance from his mansion house builded he a place called the New Building, wherein there was a chapel, a library, and a gallery. In which, as his use was upon other days to occupy himself in prayer and study together, so on the Friday there usually continued he from morning to evening, spending his time only in devout prayers and spiritual exercises.

And to provoke[9] his wife and children to the desire of heavenly things, he would sometimes use these words unto them:

"It is now no mastery[1] for you children to go to heaven, for everybody giveth you good counsel, everybody giveth you good example—you see virtue rewarded and vice punished. So that you are carried up to heaven even by the chins. But if you live the time that no man will give you good counsel, nor no man will give you good example, when you shall see virtue punished and vice rewarded, if you will then stand fast and firmly stick to God, upon pain of my life, though you be but half good, God will allow you for whole good."

If his wife or any of his children had been diseased or troubled, he would say unto them: "We may not look at our pleasure to go to heaven in featherbeds. It is not the way, for our Lord himself went thither with great pain and by many tribulations, which was the path wherein he walked thither. For the servant may not look to be in better case than his master."

And as he would in this sort persuade them to take their troubles patiently, so would he in like sort teach them to withstand the devil and his temptations valiantly, saying:

"Whosoever will mark the devil and his temptations shall find him therein much like to an ape. For, like as an ape,

7. custom.   8. short prayers.   9. stimulate.   1. achievement.

not well looked unto, will be busy and bold to do shrewd turns[2] and contrariwise, being spied, will suddenly leap backward and adventure no farther, so the devil finding a man idle, slothful, and without resistance ready to receive his temptations, waxeth so hardy that he will not fail still to continue with him until to his purpose he have thoroughly brought him. But, on the other side, if he see a man with diligence[3] persevere to prevent and withstand his temptations, he waxeth so weary that in conclusion he utterly forsaketh him. For as the devil of disposition is a spirit of so high a pride that he cannot abide to be mocked, so is he of nature so envious that he feareth any more to assault him, lest he should thereby not only catch a foul[4] fall himself but also minister to the man more matter of merit."

Thus delighted he evermore not only in virtuous exercises to be occupied himself, but also to exhort his wife, children, and household to embrace and follow the same.

To whom for his notable virtue and godliness, God showed, as it seemed, a manifest miraculous token of his special favor towards him, at such time as my wife, as many other that year were, was sick of the sweating sickness.[5] Who, lying in so great extremity of that disease as by no invention or devices that physicians in such cases commonly use (of whom she had divers both expert,[6] wise, and well-learned, then continually about her) she could be kept from sleep. So that both physicians and all other there despaired of her recovery and gave her over.

Her father, as he that most entirely tendered[7] her, being in no small heaviness for her, by prayer at God's hand sought to get her remedy. Whereupon going up, after his usual manner, into his foresaid New Building, there in his chapel, upon his knees, with tears most devoutly besought almighty God that it would like His goodness, unto whom nothing was impos-

2. *shrewd turns:* harmful tricks.
3. *a man with diligence:* i.e. the diligent, wary man.   4. ignominious.
5. A terrible epidemic disease, which swept England periodically during the fifteenth and sixteenth centuries and later; characterized by heavy sweating and a general debility. The incidence of death was extremely high.   6. experienced.   7. loved.

sible, if it were His blessed will, at his mediation to vouchsafe graciously to hear his humble petition. Where incontinent[8] came into his mind that a clyster[9] should be the only way to help her. Which, when he told the physicians, they by and by[1] confessed that, if there were any hope of health, that was the very best help indeed, much marvelling of themselves that they had not before remembered it.

Then was it immediately ministered unto her sleeping, which she could by no means have been brought unto waking. And albeit after that she was thereby thoroughly awaked, God's marks,[2] an evident undoubted token of death plainly appeared upon her, yet she, contrary to all their expectations, was as it was thought by her father's fervent prayer miraculously recovered, and at length again to perfect health restored. Whom, if it had pleased God at that time to have taken to His mercy, her father said he would never have meddled with worldly matters after.

Now while Sir Thomas More was Chancellor of the Duchy, the See of Rome chanced to be void, which was cause of much trouble. For Cardinal Wolsey, a man very ambitious and desirous (as good hope and likelihood he had) to aspire unto that dignity, perceiving himself of his expectation disappointed, by means of the Emperor Charles[3] so highly commending one Cardinal Adrian,[4] sometime his schoolmaster, to the cardinals of Rome, in the time of their election, for his virtue and worthiness, that thereupon was he chosen Pope. Who from Spain where he was then resident, coming on foot to Rome, before his entry into the city, did put off his hosen and shoes, barefoot and barelegged passing through the streets towards his palace with such humbleness that all the people had him in great reverence—Cardinal Wolsey, I say, waxed so wood[5] therewith that he studied to invent all ways of revengement of his grief against the Emperor; which, as it

8. all of a sudden.   9. enema.   1. *by and by:* immediately.
2. visible marks of the plague.
3. Charles V, 1500–1558. He became Emperor of the Holy Roman Empire in June 1519.
4. Adrian VI, 1459–1523. He was elected Pope in January 1522.
5. *waxed so wood:* became so angry.

was the beginning of a lamentable tragedy, so some part of it as not impertinent to my present purpose I reckoned requisite here to put in remembrance.

This Cardinal, therefore, not ignorant of the King's inconstant and mutable disposition, soon inclined to withdraw his devotion from his own most noble, virtuous, and lawful wife, Queen Catherine—aunt to the Emperor—upon every light[6] occasion. And upon other,[7] to her in nobility, wisdom, virtue, favor, and beauty far incomparable, to fix his affection, meaning to make this his so light[8] disposition an instrument to bring about his ungodly intent, devised to allure the King, then already (contrary to his mind, nothing less looking for) falling in love with the Lady Anne Boleyn, to cast fantasy[9] to one of the French King's sisters. Which thing, because of the enmity and war that was at that time between the French King and the Emperor—whom for the cause afore remembered he mortally maligned—he was very desirous to procure. And for the better achieving thereof, requested Longland,[1] Bishop of Lincoln, and ghostly father to the King, to put a scruple into his grace's head, that it was not lawful for him to marry his brother's wife.

Which the King, not sorry to hear of, opened it first to Sir Thomas More, whose counsel he required therein, showing him certain places of scripture that somewhat seemed to serve his appetite.[2] Which when he had perused and thereupon, as one that had never professed the study of divinity, himself excused to be unmeet many ways to meddle with such matters, the King, not satisfied with this answer, so sore still pressed upon him therefore, that in conclusion he condescended[3] to his grace's motion.[4] And further, forasmuch as the case was of such importance as needed great advisement and deliberation, he besought his grace of sufficient respite advisedly to consider of it. Wherewith the King, well-contented, said unto him that

6. trivial.   7. another.   8. wanton.   9. *cast fantasy:* take a fancy.
1. John Longland, Bishop of Lincoln from 1520 to 1547, confessor to the King, and a close friend of Cardinal Wolsey.   2. wilful purpose.
3. assented.   4. proposal.

Tunstal and Clerk,[5] Bishops of Durham and Bath, with other learned of his privy council, should also be dealers therein.

So Sir Thomas More departing conferred[6] those places of scripture with expositions of divers of the old holy doctors. And at his coming to the court, in talking with his grace of the aforesaid matter, he said: "To be plain with your grace, neither my Lord of Durham nor my Lord of Bath, though I know them both to be wise, virtuous, learned, and honorable prelates, nor myself, with the rest of your council, being all your grace's own servants, for your manifold benefits daily bestowed on us so most bounden to you, be in my judgment meet counsellors for your grace herein. But if your grace mind to understand the truth, such counsellors may you have devised, as neither for respect of their own worldly commodity[7] nor for fear of your princely authority, will be inclined to deceive you." To whom he named then Saint Jerome, Saint Augustine, and divers other old holy doctors, both Greeks and Latins, and, moreover, showed him what authorities he had gathered out of them. Which, although the King (as disagreeable with his desire) did not very well like of, yet were they by Sir Thomas More who, in all his communication with the King in that matter, had always most discreetly behaved himself, so wisely tempered, that he both presently took them in good part and oft-times had thereof conference with him again.

After this were there certain questions among his council proponed,[8] whether the King needed in this case to have any scruple at all; and if he had what way were best to be taken to deliver him of it. The most part of whom were of opinion that there was good cause of scruple and that, for discharging of it, suit were meet to be made to the See of Rome, where the King hoped by liberality[9] to obtain his purpose. Wherein, as it after appeared, he was far deceived.

5. Cuthbert Tunstal was Bishop of London from 1522 to 1530. In the summer of 1529 he and More were appointed joint ambassadors to go to Cambrai. See below, p. 217. John Clerk was Bishop of Bath from 1523 to 1541.   6. compared.   7. convenience, profit.   8. proposed.
9. either "by a generous interpretation," or "through gift-giving on his own (the King's) part."

Then was there for the trial and examination of this matrimony procured from Rome a commission, in which Cardinal Campeggio[1] and Cardinal Wolsey were joined commissioners. Who, for the determination thereof, sat at the Blackfriars in London, where a libel[2] was put in for the annulling of the said matrimony, alleging the marriage between the King and Queen to be unlawful. And for proof of the marriage to be lawful was there brought in a dispensation, in which after divers disputations thereon holden, there appeared an imperfection which, by an instrument[3] or brief, upon search found in the Treasury of Spain and sent to the commissioners into England, was supplied. And so should judgment have been given by the Pope accordingly—had not the King, upon intelligence thereof, before the same judgment, appealed to the next general council. After whose appellation,[4] the Cardinal upon that matter sat no longer.

It fortuned before the matter of the said matrimony brought in question when, I, in talk with Sir Thomas More, of a certain joy commended unto him the happy estate of this realm that had so catholic a prince that no heretic durst show his face, so virtuous and learned a clergy, so grave and sound a nobility, and so loving, obedient subjects all in one faith agreeing together, "Truth, it is indeed, son Roper," quoth he, and in commending all degrees and estates of the same went far beyond me. "And yet, son Roper, I pray God," said he, "that some of us, as high as we seem to sit upon the mountains treading heretics under our feet like ants, live not in the day that we gladly would wish to be at a league and composition with them to let them have their churches quietly to themselves, so that they would be content to let us have ours quietly to ourselves."

After that I had told him many considerations why he had no cause so to say—"Well," said he, "I pray God, son Roper, some of us live not till that day," showing me no reason why

1. Lorenzo Campeggio (1464–1539), distinguished Italian Cardinal. Arriving in London on October 9, 1528, he represented the Pope in the divorce proceedings. The Pope at this time was Clement VII, who had succeeded Adrian VI after his death in 1523.   2. plea.
3. An instrument was a formal legal document; a brief, a short, compendious papal letter.   4. action of appeal.

he should put any doubt therein. To whom I said, "by my troth, sir, it is very desperately[5] spoken." That vile term, I cry God mercy, did I give him. Who by these words perceiving me in a fume[6] said merrily unto me: "Well, well, son Roper, it shall not be so, it shall not be so." Whom, in sixteen years and more, being in house conversant[7] with him, I could never perceive as much as once in a fume.

But now to return again where I left. After the supplying of the imperfections of the dispensation sent, as is before rehearsed, to the commissioners into England, the King taking the matter for ended and then meaning no farther to proceed in that matter, assigned the Bishop of Durham and Sir Thomas More to go ambassadors to Cambrai,[8] a place neither imperial nor French, to treat[9] a peace between the Emperor, the French King, and him. In the concluding whereof, Sir Thomas More so worthily handled himself, procuring in our league far more benefits unto this realm than at that time by the King or his Council was thought possible to be compassed,[1] that for his good service in that voyage, the King, when he after made him Lord Chancellor, caused the Duke of Norfolk openly to declare unto the people (as you shall hear hereafter more at large) how much all England was bound unto him.

Now upon the coming home of the Bishop of Durham and Sir Thomas More from Cambrai, the King was as earnest in persuading Sir Thomas More to agree unto the matter of his marriage as before, by many and divers ways provoking[2] him thereunto. For the which cause, as it was thought, he the rather[3] soon after made him Lord Chancellor.

And further declaring unto him that, though at his going over sea to Cambrai, he was in utter despair thereof, yet he had conceived since some good hope to compass it.[4] For albeit his marriage being against the positive laws of the Church and the written laws of God was holpen[5] by the dispensation, yet was there another thing found out of late, he said, whereby

5. despairingly.   6. fit of irritation.   7. intimately dwelling.
8. a town in the north of France. The Treaty of Cambrai was signed in 1529.   9. negotiate.   1. achieved.
2. urging.   3. *the rather:* all the more quickly.
4. i.e. to secure More's agreement to the divorce proceedings.
5. helped, promoted.

his marriage appeared to be so directly against the law of nature, that it could in no wise by the Church be dispensable —as Doctor Stokesley,[6] whom he had then preferred to be Bishop of London and in that case chiefly credited, was able to instruct him—with whom he prayed him in that point to confer. But, for all his conference with him, he saw nothing of such force as could induce him to change his opinion therein. Which notwithstanding, the Bishop showed himself in his report of him to the King's highness so good and favorable that he said he found him in his grace's cause very toward [7] and desirous to find some good matter wherewith he might truly serve his grace to his contentation.

This Bishop Stokesley, being by the Cardinal not long before in the Star Chamber openly put to rebuke and awarded to the Fleet,[8] not brooking this contumelious usage, and thinking that forasmuch as the Cardinal, for lack of such forwardness in setting forth the King's divorce as his grace looked for, was out of his highness's favor, he had now a good occasion offered him to revenge his quarrel against him, further to incense the King's displeasure towards him, busily travailed to invent some colorable[9] device for the King's furtherance in that behalf. Which, as before is mentioned, he to his grace revealed, hoping thereby to bring the King to the better liking of himself, and the more misliking of the Cardinal; whom his highness therefore soon after of his[1] office displaced, and to Sir Thomas More, the rather to move him to incline to his side, the same in his stead committed.[2]

Who, between the Dukes of Norfolk and Suffolk being brought through Westminster Hall to his place in the Chancery, the Duke of Norfolk in audience of all the people there assembled showed that he was from the King himself straitly charged, by special commission, there openly in presence of them all to make declaration how much all England was beholding to Sir Thomas More for his good service, and how worthy he was to have the highest room in the realm, and how dearly

6. John Stokesley was made Bishop of London in 1530.
7. favorably inclined.   8. *awarded . . . Fleet:* sentenced to Fleet Prison.
9. specious.   1. i.e. Wolsey's.
2. More was made Chancellor in October 1529.

his grace loved and trusted him, for which—said the Duke—
he had great cause to rejoice. Whereunto Sir Thomas More,
among many other his humble and wise sayings not now in
my memory, answered: that although he had good cause to
take comfort of the highness's singular favor towards him—
that he had far above his deserts so highly commended him,
to whom therefore he acknowledged himself most deeply
bounden—yet, nevertheless, he must for his own part needs
confess that in all things by his grace alleged he had done no
more than was his duty. And further disabled himself as
unmeet for that room, wherein, considering how wise and
honorable a prelate had lately before taken so great a fall, he
had, he said, thereof no cause to rejoice.

And as they had before, on the King's behalf, charged him
uprightly to minister indifferent[3] justice to the people, without
corruption or affection,[4] so did he likewise charge them again
that, if they saw him at any time in any thing digress from
any part of his duty in that honorable office, even as they
would discharge their own duty and fidelity to God and the
King, so should they not fail to disclose it to his grace, who
otherwise might have just occasion to lay his fault wholly
to their charge.

While he was Lord Chancellor, being at leisure (as seldom
he was) one of his sons-in-law[5] on a time said merrily unto
him: "When Cardinal Wolsey was Lord Chancellor, not only
divers of his privy chamber, but such also as were his door-
keepers got great gain." And since he had married one of his
daughters, and gave still[6] attendance upon him, he thought
he might of reason look for some; where he indeed, because
he was so ready himself to hear every man, poor and rich,
and kept no doors shut from them, could find none, which
was to him a great discourage.[7] And whereas else, some for
friendship, some for kindred, and some for profit, would gladly
have had his furtherance in bringing them to his presence, if
he should now take anything of them, he knew, he said, he
should do them great wrong. For that they might do as much

3. impartial.   4. bias.
5. William Daunce, who married More's daughter Elizabeth in 1525.
6. constant.   7. discouragement.

for themselves as he could do for them. Which condition, although he thought in Sir Thomas More very commendable, yet to him, said he, being his son, he found it nothing profitable.

When he had told him this tale: "You say well, son," quoth he. "I do not mislike that you are of conscience so scrupulous, but many other ways be there, son, that I may both do yourself good and pleasure your friend also. For sometime may I by my word stand your friend in stead, and sometime may I by my letter help him; or if he have a cause depending[8] before me, at your request I may hear him before another. Or if his cause be not all the best, yet may I move the parties to fall to some reasonable end by arbitrement.[9] Howbeit this one thing, son, I assure thee on my faith, that if the parties will at my hands call for justice, then all were it my father stood on the one side and the devil on the other, his cause being good, the devil should have right." So offered he his son, as he thought, he said, as much favor as with reason he could require.

And that he would for no respect digress from justice well appeared by a plain example of another of his sons-in-law called Master Heron.[1] For when he, having a matter before him in the Chancery and presuming too much of his favor, would by him in no wise be persuaded to agree to any indifferent[2] order, then made he in conclusion a flat decree against him.

This Lord Chancellor used commonly every afternoon to sit in his open hall to the intent that, if any persons had any suit unto him, they might the more boldly come to his presence and there open their complaints before him. Whose manner was also to read every bill himself ere he would award any *sub poena*, which, bearing matter sufficient worthy a *sub poena*, would he set his hand unto, or else cancel it.

8. pending.   9. arbitration.
1. Giles Heron, son of Sir John Heron, Treasurer of the Chamber to Henry VIII, married More's youngest daughter, Cecily, in September 1525. He was executed at Tyburn in August 1540, for high treason, although the specific charges are nowhere documented, and there is good reason to believe that he was the victim of trumped-up accusations.
2. impartial.

Whensoever he passed through Westminster Hall to his place in the Chancery by the court of the King's Bench, if his father, one of the judges thereof, had been sate[3] ere he came, he would go into the same court, and there reverently kneeling down in the sight of them all, duly ask his father's blessing. And if it fortuned that his father and he at readings in Lincoln's Inn met together, as they sometime did, notwithstanding his high office, he would offer in argument the pre-eminence to his father, though he for his office's sake would refuse to take it. And for the better declaration of his natural affection towards his father, he not only while he lay on his death bed, according to his duty, oft-times with comfortable words most kindly came to visit him, but also at his departure out of the world, with tears taking him about the neck, most lovingly kissed and embraced him, commending him into the merciful hands of almighty God, and so departed from him.

And as few injunctions[4] as he granted while he was Lord Chancellor, yet were they by some of the judges of the law misliked which I, understanding, declared the same to Sir Thomas More, who answered me that they should have little cause to find fault with him therefore. And thereupon caused he one Master Crooke, chief of the six clerks, to make a docket containing the whole number and causes of all such injunctions as either in his time had already passed or at that present depended in any of the King's courts at Westminster before him.

Which done, he invited all the judges to dine with him in the council chamber at Westminster, where after dinner, when he had broken with them what complaints he had heard of his injunctions, and moreover showed them both the number and causes of everyone of them in order, so plainly that, upon full debating of those matters, they were all enforced to confess that they in like case could have done no otherwise themselves. Then offered he this unto them. That if the justices of every court—unto whom the reformation of the rigor of

3. *had been sate:* had sat down.
4. orders to stop legal proceedings until the Court had established their equity.

the law, by reason of their office, most especially appertained —would upon reasonable considerations by their own discretion, as they were as he thought in conscience bound, mitigate and reform the rigor of the law themselves, there should from thenceforth by him no more injunctions be granted. Whereunto when they refused to condescend,[5] then said he unto them: "Forasmuch as yourselves, my lords, drive me to that necessity for awarding out injunctions to relieve the people's injury, you cannot hereafter any more justly blame me."

After that he said secretly unto me: "I perceive, son, why they like not so to do, for they see that they may by the verdict of the jury cast off all quarrels from themselves upon them, which they accompt[6] their chief defense. And therefore am I compelled to abide the adventure[7] of all such reports."

And as little leisure as he had to be occupied in the study of Holy Scripture and controversies upon religion and such other virtuous exercises, being in manner continually busied about the affairs of the King and the realm, yet such watch[8] and pain, in setting forth of divers profitable works in defense of the true Christian religion against heresies secretly sown abroad in the realm, assuredly sustained he,[9] that the Bishops— to whose pastoral care[1] the reformation thereof principally appertained—thinking themselves by his travail, wherein by their own confession they were not able with him to make comparison, of their duties in that behalf discharged; and considering that for all his prince's favor he was no rich man nor in yearly revenues advanced as his worthiness deserved— therefore, at a convocation among themselves and other of the clergy, they agreed together and concluded upon a sum of four or five thousand pounds at the least, to my remembrance, for his pains to recompense him. To the payment whereof every bishop, abbot, and the rest of the clergy were —after the rate of their abilities—liberal contributories, hoping this portion should be to his contentation.

Whereupon Tunstal, Bishop of Durham, Clerk, Bishop of

5. assent.   6. reckon.   7. risk.   8. vigilance.
9. *assuredly . . . he:* he maintained with such assurance.
1. spiritual jurisdiction.

Bath, and as far as I can call to mind, Vaysey, Bishop of Exeter,[2] repaired unto him, declaring how thankfully for his travails, to their discharge in God's cause bestowed, they reckoned themselves bounden to consider him. And that albeit they could not, according to his deserts so worthily as they gladly would, requite him therefore, but must reserve that only to the goodness of God, yet for a small part of recompense (in respect of his estate so unequal to his worthiness) in the name of their whole convocation they presented unto him that sum, which they desired him to take in good part.[3]

Who, forsaking[4] it, said, that like as it was no small comfort unto him that so wise and learned men so well accepted his simple doings, for which he never intended to receive reward but at the hands of God only, to whom alone was the thank thereof chiefly to be ascribed, so gave he most humble thanks to their honors all, for their so bountiful and friendly consideration.

When they for all their importune pressing upon him, that few would have went[5] he could have refused it, could by no means make him to take it, then besought they him to be content yet that they might bestow it upon his wife and children. "Not so, my lords," quoth he, "I had rather see it all cast into the Thames than I or any of mine should have thereof the worth of one penny. For though your offer, my lords, be indeed very friendly and honorable, yet set I so much by my pleasure and so little by my profit that I would not, in good faith, for so much, and much more too, have lost the rest of so many nights' sleep as was spent upon the same. And yet wish would I, for all that, upon condition that all heresies were suppressed, that all my books were burned and my labor utterly lost." Thus departing were they fain to restore unto every man his own again.

This Lord Chancellor, albeit he was to God and the world well-known of notable virtue, though not so of every man considered, yet for the avoiding of singularity would he

2. For Tunstal and Clerk, see above, p. 215, n. 5. John Vaysey or Veysey was Bishop of Exeter from 1519 to 1551, and from 1553 to 1554. 3. *in good part:* without offense.   4. declining.   5. supposed.

appear none otherwise than other men in his apparel and other behavior. And albeit outwardly he appeared honorable like one of his calling, yet inwardly he, no such vanities esteeming, secretly next his body wore a shirt of hair. Which my sister More,[6] a young gentlewoman, in the summer as he sat at supper singly[7] in his doublet and hose, wearing thereupon a plain shirt without ruff or collar, chancing to spy began to laugh at it. My wife, not ignorant of his manner, perceiving the same, privily told him of it. And he, being sorry that she saw it, presently amended it.

He used also sometimes to punish his body with whips, the cords knotted, which was known only to my wife, his eldest daughter, whom for her secrecy above all other he specially trusted, causing her as need required to wash the same shirt of hair.

Now shortly upon his entry into the high office of the chancellorship, the King yet eftsoons[8] again moved him to weigh and consider his great matter. Who, falling down upon his knees, humbly besought his highness to stand his gracious sovereign, as he ever since his entry into his grace's service had found him, saying there was nothing in the world had been so grievous unto his heart as to remember that he was not able, as he willingly would, with the loss of one of his limbs—for that matter anything to find whereby he could, with his conscience safely, serve his grace's contentation, as he that always bore in mind the most goodly words that his highness spake unto him at his first coming into his noble service, the most virtuous lesson that ever prince taught his servant, willing him first to look unto God, and after God to him. As in good faith he said he did, or else might his grace well accompt[9] him his most unworthy servant. To this the King answered that if he could not therein with his conscience serve him, he was content to accept his service otherwise. And using the advice of other of his learned council, whose consciences could well enough agree therewith, would nevertheless continue his gracious favor

6. Anne Cresacre, wife of More's son, John.   7. simply.
8. *yet eftsoons:* soon afterwards.   9. reckon.

towards him and never with that matter molest his conscience after.

But Sir Thomas More in process of time, seeing the King fully determined to proceed forth in the marriage of Queen Anne and when he with the bishops and nobles of the higher house of Parliament were, for the furtherance of that marriage, commanded by the King to go down to the Common House to show unto them both what the universities, as well of other parts beyond the seas as of Oxford and Cambridge, had done in that behalf, and their seals also testifying the same— all which matters, at the King's request, not showing of what mind himself was therein, he opened to the lower house of the Parliament. Nevertheless, doubting[1] lest further attempts after should follow which, contrary to his conscience, by reason of his office he was likely to be put unto, he made suit unto the Duke of Norfolk, his singular[2] dear friend, to be a mean[3] to the King that he might, with his grace's favor, be discharged of that chargeable room[4] of the chancellorship wherein, for certain infirmities of his body, he pretended himself unable any longer to serve.

This Duke, coming on a time to Chelsea to dine with him, fortuned to find him at the church, singing in the choir, with a surplice on his back. To whom after service as they went homeward together, arm-in-arm, the Duke said: "God body, God body, my Lord Chancellor, a parish clerk! You dishonor the King and his office."

"Nay," quoth Sir Thomas More, smiling upon the Duke: "Your grace may not think that the King, your master and mine, will with me for serving of God, his master, be offended or thereby count his office dishonored!"

When the Duke, being thereunto often solicited, by importunate suit had at length of the King obtained for Sir Thomas More a clear discharge of his office, then at a time convenient, by his highness's appointment, repaired he to his grace to yield up unto him the Great Seal.[5] Which as his grace, with thanks

1. fearing.   2. intimate.   3. *be a mean:* act as an intercessor.
4. *chargeable room:* burdensome office.
5. emblematic of the authority of the High Chancellor.

and praise for his worthy service in that office, courteously at his hands received, so pleased it his highness further to say unto him that, for the service that he before had done him, in any suit which he should after have unto him that either should concern his honor (for that word it liked [6] his highness to use unto him) or that should appertain unto his profit, he should find his highness good and gracious lord unto him.

After he had thus given over the chancellorship[7] and placed all his gentlemen and yeomen with bishops and noblemen, and his eight watermen with the Lord Audeley, that in the same office succeeded him, to whom also he gave his great barge; then, calling us all that were his children unto him and asking our advice how we might now in this decay of his ability[8]—by the surrender of his office so impaired that he could not, as he was wont and gladly would, bear out the whole charge[9] of them all himself—from thenceforth be able to live and continue together, as he wished we should. When he saw us silent and in that case not ready to show our opinions to him—"Then will I," said he, "show my poor mind unto you. I have been brought up," quoth he, "at Oxford, at an Inn of Chancery, at Lincoln's Inn, and also in the King's court—and so forth from the lowest degree to the highest; and yet have I in yearly revenues at this present left me little above an hundred pounds by the year. So that now must we hereafter, if we like[1] to live together, be contented to become contributaries together. But, by my counsel, it shall not be best for us to fall to the lowest fare first. We will not, therefore, descend to Oxford fare, nor to the fare of New Inn. But we will begin with Lincoln's Inn diet, where many right worshipful and of good years do live full well. Which, if we find not ourselves the first year able to maintain, then will we the next year go one step down to New Inn fare, wherewith many an honest man is well contented. If that exceed our ability too, then will we the next year after descend to Oxford fare, where many grave, learned, and ancient fathers be continually conversant.[2] Which, if our

6. pleased.   7. More resigned from the Chancellorship in May 1532. Sir Thomas Audeley succeeded him and served until 1544.
8. wealth, estate.   9. expenses.   1. wish.   2. dwelling.

power stretch not to maintain neither, then may we yet, with bags and wallets, go a-begging together, and hoping that for pity some good folk will give us their charity, at every man's door to sing *Salve Regina*,[3] and so still keep company and be merry together."

And whereas you have heard before, he was by the King from a very worshipful living taken into his grace's service, with whom in all the great and weighty causes that concerned his highness or the realm, he consumed and spent with painful cares, travails, and troubles as well beyond the seas as within the realm, in effect the whole substance of his life, yet with all the gain he got thereby, being never wasteful spender thereof, was he not able after the resignation of his office of the Lord Chancellor, for the maintenance of himself and such as necessarily belonged unto him, sufficiently to find meat, drink, fuel, apparel, and such other necessary charges. All the land that ever he purchased, which also he purchased before he was Lord Chancellor, was not, I am well assured, above the value of twenty marks by the year. And after his debts paid he had not, I know, his chain[4] excepted, in gold and silver left him the worth of one hundred pounds.

And whereas upon the holidays during his high chancellorship one of his gentlemen, when service at the church was done, ordinarily used to come to my Lady his wife's pew and say unto her, "Madam, my lord is gone,"—the next holiday after the surrender of his office and departure of his gentlemen, *he*[5] came unto my Lady his wife's pew himself, and making a low curtsy, said unto her: "Madam, my lord is gone!"

In the time somewhat before his trouble, he would talk with his wife and children of the joys of heaven and the pains of hell, the lives of holy martyrs, of their grievous martyrdoms, of their marvellous patience, and of their passions and deaths that they suffered rather than they would offend God. And what an happy and blessed thing it was, for the love of God, to suffer loss of goods, imprisonment, loss of lands, and life also. He

3. "Hail Holy Queen," a very popular medieval hymn to the Virgin.
4. The chain of gold worn about the neck was the symbol of high civic office.   5. italics mine.

would further say unto them that, upon his faith, if he might perceive his wife and children would encourage him to die in a good cause, it should so comfort him that, for very joy thereof, it would make him merrily run to death. He showed unto them afore what trouble might after fall unto him. Wherewith and the like virtuous talk he had so long before his trouble encouraged them that when he after fell into the trouble indeed, his trouble to them was a great deal the less, *Quia spicula previsa minus laedunt.*[6]

Now upon this resignment of his office came Master Thomas Cromwell,[7] then in the King's high favor, to Chelsea to him with a message from the King. Wherein when they had thoroughly commoned[8] together, "Master Cromwell," quoth he, "you are now entered into the service of a most noble, wise, and liberal prince. If you will follow my poor advice, you shall, in your counsel-giving unto his grace, ever tell him what he ought to do but never what he is able to do. So shall you show yourself a true faithful servant and a right worthy counsellor. For if a lion knew his own strength, hard were it for any man to rule him."

Shortly thereupon was there a commission directed to Cranmer,[9] then Archbishop of Canterbury, to determine the matter of the matrimony between the King and Queen Catherine at Saint Albans, where according to the King's mind it was thoroughly determined. Who, pretending he had no justice at the Pope's hands, from thenceforth sequestered himself from the See of Rome, and so married the Lady Anne Boleyn.[1] Which Sir Thomas More understanding, said unto me: "God give

6. "Because anticipated spears hurt less."
7. Thomas Cromwell, 1485?–1540. From a middle class status, Cromwell rose rapidly and with ruthless efficiency until he was appointed Secretary in 1534. He is most notorious for the part he played in the Dissolution of the Monasteries and the subsequent distribution of Church lands and valuables. Attainted for treason in 1540, he was beheaded on July 28 of the same year.   8. held familiar discourse.
9. Thomas Cranmer, Archbishop of Canterbury from 1533 to 1556. In both a theological and literary sense, one of the prime architects of the Reformation in England. He was burned at the stake during the reign of Queen Mary.
1. Anne and Henry VIII were secretly married about January 25, 1533. On June 1, she was crowned Queen of England.

grace, son, that these matters within a while be not confirmed with oaths." I, at that time seeing no likelihood thereof, yet fearing lest for his forespeaking it would the sooner come to pass, waxed therefore for his so saying much offended with him.

It fortuned not long before the coming of Queen Anne through the streets of London from the Tower to Westminster to her coronation that he received a letter from the Bishops of Durham, Bath, and Winchester, requesting him both to keep them company from the Tower to the coronation and also to take twenty pounds that by the bearer thereof they had sent him to buy him a gown with. Which he thankfully receiving, and at home still tarrying, at their next meeting said merrily unto them:

"My lords, in the letters which you lately sent me, you required two things of me; the one whereof, sith I was so well content to grant you, the other therefore I might be the bolder to deny you. And like as the one—because I took you for no beggars and myself I knew to be no rich man—I thought I might the rather fulfill, so the other did put me in remembrance of an emperor[2] that had ordained a law that whosoever committed a certain offense (which I now remember not) except it were a virgin, should suffer the pains of death. Such a reverence had he to virginity. Now so it happened that the first committer of that offense was indeed a virgin, whereof the emperor hearing was in no small perplexity, as he that by some example fain would have had that law to have been put in execution. Whereupon when his council had sat long, solemnly debating this case, suddenly arose there up one of his council—a good plain man among them—and said: 'Why make you so much ado, my lords, about so small a matter? Let her first be deflowered and then after may she be devoured!'

"And so, though your lordships have in the matter of the matrimony hitherto kept yourselves pure virgins, yet take good

2. Tiberius Caesar. See the story of Sejanus' daughter as related by Tacitus (*Annals*, VI). More's version is, of course, considerably adapted.

heed, my lords, that you keep your virginity still. For some there be that by procuring[3] your lordships first at the coronation to be present, and next to preach for the setting forth of it, and finally to write books to all the world in defense thereof, are desirous to deflower you; and when they have deflowered you, then will they not fail soon after to devour you. Now, my lords," quoth he, "it lieth not in my power but that they may devour me. But God, being my good Lord, I will provide that they shall never deflower me!"

In continuance: when the King saw that he could by no manner of benefits win him to his side, then, lo, went he about by terrors and threats to drive him thereunto. The beginning of which trouble grew by occasion of a certain nun dwelling in Canterbury,[4] for her virtue and holiness among the people not a little esteemed. Unto whom, for that cause, many religious persons, doctors of divinity and divers others of good worship[5] of the laity used to resort. Who, affirming that she had revelations from God to give the King warning of his wicked life and of the abuse of the sword and authority committed unto him by God; and understanding my Lord of Rochester, Bishop Fisher,[6] to be a man of notable virtuous living and learning, repaired to Rochester and there disclosed to him all her revelations, desiring his advice and counsel therein.

Which the Bishop perceiving might well stand with the laws of God and his Holy Church, advised her (as she before had warning and intended) to go to the King herself and to let him understand the whole circumstance thereof. Whereupon she went to the King and told him all her revelations, and so returned home again. And in short space after, she, making a

---

3. prevailing upon.
4. Elizabeth Barton, known as "the Holy Maid of Kent," 1506?–1534. She predicted that, if Henry VIII divorced Catherine, he would "die a villain's death." She was executed for treason at Tyburn in April 1534.
5. of good worship: respected members.
6. John Fisher, Bishop of Rochester from 1504 to 1536. One of the most remarkable men of his time, in terms of both achievement and integrity, he incurred the wrath of Henry VIII by refusing to subscribe to the Oath of Supremacy. He was beheaded on Tower Hill on June 22, 1535, just two weeks before More was led out to the scaffold.

voyage to the nuns of Sion, by means of one Master Reynolds,[7] a father of the same house, there fortuned concerning such secrets as had been revealed unto her—some part whereof seemed to touch the matter of the King's supremacy and marriage, which shortly thereupon followed—to enter into talk with Sir Thomas More. Who, notwithstanding he might well at that time without danger of any law—though after, as himself had prognosticated before, those matters were established by statutes and confirmed by oaths—freely and safely have talked with her therein; nevertheless, in all the communication between them, as in process[8] it appeared, had always so discreetly demeaned [9] himself that he deserved not to be blamed, but contrariwise to be commended and praised.

And had he not been one that in all his great offices and doings for the King and the realm so many years together had from all corruption of wrong-doing or bribes-taking kept himself so clear that no man was able therewith once to blemish him, or make any just quarrel against him, it would without doubt in this troublous time of the King's indignation towards him, have been deeply laid to his charge and of the King's highness most favorably accepted, as in the case of one Parnell it most manifestly appeared. Against whom, because Sir Thomas More while he was Lord Chancellor, at the suit of one Vaughan, his[1] adversary, had made a decree. This Parnell to his highness most grievously complained that Sir Thomas More, for making the same decree, had of the same Vaughan, unable for the gout to travel abroad himself, by the hands of his wife taken a fair great gilt cup for a bribe.

Who thereupon, by the King's appointment, being called before the whole council, where that matter was heinously laid to his charge, forthwith confessed that, forasmuch as that cup was long after the foresaid decree brought him for a New Year's gift, he, upon her importunate pressing upon him, therefore of courtesy refused not to receive it.

Then the Lord of Wiltshire[2]—for hatred of his religion

7. Dr. Richard Reynolds. Executed on May 4, 1535. From a window in his Tower cell, More watches as he is conducted to his death. See below, p. 242.   8. in due time.   9. conducted.   1. i.e. Parnell's adversary.   2. Sir Thomas Boleyn, the father of Anne.

preferrer[3] of this suit—with much rejoicing said unto the lords: "Lo, did I not tell you, my lords, that you should find this matter true?" Whereupon Sir Thomas More desired their lordships that as they had courteously heard him tell the one part of his tale, so they would vouchsafe of their honors indifferently[4] to hear the other. After which obtained, he further declared unto them that, albeit he had indeed with much work received that cup, yet immediately thereupon he caused his butler to fill it with wine, and of that cup drank to her; and that when he had so done and she pledged him, then as freely as her husband had given it to him, even so freely gave he the same unto her again to give unto her husband for his New Year's gift. Which at his instant[5] request, though much against her will, at length yet she was fain to receive, as herself and certain other there presently before them deposed. Thus was the great mountain turned scant to[6] a little molehill.

So I remember that at another time, upon a New Year's Day, there came to him one Mistress Crocker, a rich widow, for whom with no small pain he had made a decree in the Chancery against the Lord of Arundel, to present him with a pair of gloves and forty pounds in angels[7] in them for a New Year's gift. Of whom he thankfully receiving the gloves but refusing the money said unto her: "Mistress, since it were against good manners to forsake a gentlewoman's New Year's gift, I am content to take your gloves but, as for your money, I utterly refuse." So, much against her mind, enforced he her to take her gold again.

And one Master Gresham, likewise, having at the same time a cause depending[8] in the Chancery before him, sent him for a New Year's gift a fair gilted cup, the fashion whereof he very well liking, caused one of his own (though not in his fantasy of so good a fashion, yet better in value) to be brought him out of his chamber, which he willed the messenger in recompense to deliver to his master. And under other condition would he in no wise receive it.

3. promoter.   4. impartially.   5. urgent.   6. *scant to:* to barely.
7. a gold coin, whose value varied from 6s. 8d. to 10s.   8. pending.

Many things more of like effect, for the declaration of his innocency and clearness from all corruption or evil affection,[9] could I here rehearse besides; which for tediousness omitting, I refer to the readers by these few before remembered examples, with their own judgments wisely to weigh and consider the same.

At the Parliament following was there put into the Lords' House a bill to attaint[1] the nun and divers other religious persons of high treason, and the Bishop of Rochester, Sir Thomas More, and certain others of misprision of treason.[2] The King presupposing of likelihood that this bill would be to Sir Thomas More so troublous and terrible that it would force him to relent and condescend[3] to his request—wherein his grace was much deceived. To which bill Sir Thomas More was a suitor personally to be received in his own defense to make answer. But the King, not liking that, assigned the Bishop of Canterbury, the Lord Chancellor, the Duke of Norfolk, and Master Cromwell, at a day and place appointed, to call Sir Thomas More before them. At which time I, thinking that I had a good opportunity, earnestly advised him to labor unto those lords for the help of his discharge[4] out of that Parliament bill. Who answered me he would.

And at his coming before them, according to their appointment, they entertained him very friendly, willing him to sit down with them, which in no wise he would. Then began the Lord Chancellor to declare unto him how many ways the King had showed his love and favor towards him, how fain he would have had him continue in his office, how glad he would have been to have heaped more benefits upon him, and finally how he could ask no worldly honor nor profit at his highness's hands that were likely to be denied him; hoping by the declaration of the King's kindness and affection towards him to provoke[5] him to recompense his grace with the like again. And unto those things that the Parliament, the bishops, and universities had already passed to add his consent.

9. bias.   1. accuse.
2. *misprision of treason:* the concealment of treasonable information.
3. assent.   4. the dismissal of the charges against More.   5. induce.

To this Sir Thomas More mildly made answer, saying: "No man living is there, my lords, that would with better will do the thing that should be acceptable to the King's highness than I, which must needs confess his manifold goodness and bountiful benefits most benignly bestowed on me. Howbeit, I verily hoped that I should never have heard of this matter more, considering that I have from time to time, always from the beginning, so plainly and truly declared my mind unto his grace, which his highness to me ever seemed like a most gracious prince very well to accept, never minding (as he said) to molest me more therewith. Since which time any further thing that was able to move me to any change could I never find. And if I could, there is none in all the world that would have been gladder of it than I."

Many things more were there of like sort uttered on both sides. But in the end, when they saw they could by no manner of persuasions remove him from his former determination, then began they more terribly to touch him, telling him that the King's highness had given them in commandment, if they could by no gentleness win him, in his name with his great ingratitude to charge him—that never was there servant to his sovereign so villainous, nor subject to his prince so traitorous as he. For he by his subtle, sinister sleights most unnaturally procuring and provoking[6] him to set forth a book of *The Assertion of the Seven Sacraments*[7]—and maintenance of the Pope's authority—had caused him to his dishonor throughout all Christendom to put a sword into the Pope's hands to fight against himself.

When they had thus laid forth all the terrors they could imagine against him: "My lords," quoth he, "these terrors be arguments for children and not for me. But to answer that wherewith you do chiefly burden me, I believe the King's highness of his honor will never lay that to my charge. For none is there that can in that point say in my excuse more than his highness himself, who right well knoweth that I never was procurer nor counsellor of his majesty thereunto; but after it

6. *procuring and provoking:* prevailing upon and urging.
7. published in 1521.

was finished, by his grace's appointment and consent of the makers of the same, only a sorter-out and placer of the principal matters therein contained. Wherein when I found the Pope's authority highly advanced and with strong arguments mightily defended, I said unto his grace: 'I must put your highness in remembrance of one thing and that is this: the Pope, as your grace knoweth, is a prince as you are, and in league with all other Christian princes. It may hereafter so fall out that your grace and he may vary upon some points of the league, whereupon may grow breach of amity and war between you both. I think it best, therefore, that that place be amended and his authority more slenderly touched.'

" 'Nay,' quoth his grace, 'that shall it not. We are so much bounden unto the See of Rome that we cannot do too much honor unto it.'

"Then did I further put him in remembrance of the Statute of Praemunire,[8] whereby a good part of the Pope's pastoral cure[9] here was pared away.

"To that answered his highness: 'Whatsoever impediment be to the contrary, we will set forth that authority to the uttermost. For we received from that See our crown imperial' —which till his grace with his own mouth told it me, I never heard of before. So that I trust when his grace shall be once truly informed of this and call to his gracious remembrance my doing in that behalf, his highness will never speak of it more but clear me thoroughly therein himself." And thus displeasantly departed they.

Then took Sir Thomas More his boat towards his house at Chelsea, wherein by the way he was very merry, and for that I was nothing sorry, hoping that he had got himself discharged out of the Parliament bill. When he was landed and come home, then walked we twain alone into his garden together; where I, desirous to know how he had sped, said: "I trust, sir, that all is well because you are so merry."

"It is so indeed, son Roper, I thank God," quoth he.

8. The Statute of Praemunire made it a treasonable offense to resort to the authority or jurisdiction of any foreign court, including that of the Vatican. Cf. above, p. 116.   9. spiritual jurisdiction.

"Are you then put out of the Parliament bill?" said I.

"By my troth, son Roper," quoth he, "I never remembered it."

"Never remembered it, sir!" said I, "a case that toucheth yourself so near, and us all for your sake. I am sorry to hear it. For I verily trusted, when I saw you so merry, that all had been well."

Then said he: "Wilt thou know, son Roper, why I was so merry?"

"That would I gladly, sir," quoth I.

"In good faith, I rejoiced, son," quoth he, "that I had given the devil a foul fall; and that with those lords I had gone so far as, without great shame, I could never go back again."

At which words waxed I very sad; for though himself liked it well, yet liked it me but a little.

Now upon the report made by the Lord Chancellor and the other lords to the King of all their whole discourse had with Sir Thomas More, the King was so highly offended with him that he plainly told them he was fully[1] determined that the aforesaid Parliament bill should undoubtedly proceed forth against him. To whom the Lord Chancellor and the rest of the lords said that they perceived the lords of the Upper House so precisely bent to hear him, in his own defense make answer himself, that if he were not put out of the bill, it would without fail be utterly an overthrow of all. But, for all this, needs would the King have his own will therein; or else he said that at the passing thereof, he would be personally present himself.

Then the Lord Audeley and the rest seeing him so vehemently set thereupon, on their knees most humbly besought his grace to forbear the same, considering that if he should, in his own presence, receive an overthrow, it would not only encourage his subjects ever after to contemn[2] him, but also throughout all Christendom redound to his dishonor forever; adding thereunto that they mistrusted not in time against him to find some meeter matter to serve his turn better. For in this case of the nun, he was accompted,[3] they said, so innocent and clear that for his dealing therein men reckoned him far

1. definitely.   2. disdain.   3. reckoned.

worthier of praise than reproof. Whereupon at length, through their earnest persuasion, he was content to condescend [4] to their petition.

And on the morrow after, Master Cromwell, meeting me in the Parliament House, willed me to tell my father that he was put out of the Parliament bill. But because I had appointed to dine that day in London, I sent the message by my servant to my wife to Chelsea. Whereof when she informed her father, "In faith, Meg," quoth he, "*quod differtur non aufertur.*" [5]

After this, as the Duke of Norfolk and Sir Thomas More chanced to fall in familiar talk together, the Duke said unto him: "By the Mass, Master More, it is perilous striving with princes. And therefore I would wish you somewhat to incline to the King's pleasure. For, by God body, Master More, *Indignatio principis mors est.*" [6]

"Is that all, my lord?" quoth he. "Then in good faith is there no more difference between your grace and me, but that I shall die today and you tomorrow."

So fell it out, within a month or thereabouts after the making of the statute for the Oath of the Supremacy and matrimony, that all the priests of London and Westminster—and no temporal [7] men but he—were sent for to appear at Lambeth before the Bishop of Canterbury, the Lord Chancellor, and Secretary Cromwell, commissioners appointed there to tender the oath unto them.

Then Sir Thomas More, as his accustomed manner was always, ere he entered into any matter of importance, as when he was first chosen of the King's privy council, when he was sent ambassador, appointed Speaker of the Parliament, made Lord Chancellor, or when he took any like weighty matter upon him, to go to church and be confessed, to hear Mass, and be houseled,[8] so did he likewise in the morning early the selfsame day that he was summoned to appear before the Lords at Lambeth.

And whereas he evermore used before at his departure from

4. agree.   5. "what is put aside is not put off."
6. "The indignation of the prince is death." Cf. above, p. 141.
7. secular.   8. receive the Eucharist.

his wife and children, whom he tenderly loved, to have them bring him to his boat, and there to kiss them all and bid them farewell; then would he suffer none of them forth of the gate to follow him, but pulled the wicket after him and shut them all from him. And with an heavy heart, as by his countenance it appeared, with me and our four servants there took he his boat towards Lambeth. Wherein sitting still sadly a while, at the last he suddenly rounded [9] me in the ear and said: "Son Roper, I thank our Lord the field is won." What he meant thereby I then wist[1] not, yet loath to seem ignorant, I answered: "Sir, I am thereof very glad." But as I conjectured afterwards, it was for that the love he had to God wrought in him so effectually that it conquered all his carnal affections[2] utterly.

Now at his coming to Lambeth, how wisely he behaved himself before the commissioners, at the ministration of the oath unto him, may be found in certain letters of his sent to my wife remaining in a great book of his works.[3] Where by the space of four days he was betaken to the custody of the Abbot of Westminster, during which time the King consulted with his council what order were meet to be taken with him. And albeit in the beginning they were resolved that with an oath not to be acknowen[4] whether he had to the Supremacy been sworn (or what he thought thereof) he should be discharged, yet did Queen Anne by her importunate clamor so sore exasperate the King against him that, contrary to his former resolution, he caused the said Oath of the Supremacy to be ministered unto him. Who, albeit he made a discreet qualified answer, nevertheless was forthwith committed to the Tower.

Whom, as he was going thitherward, wearing as he commonly did a chain of gold about his neck, Sir Richard Cromwell [5] that had the charge of his conveyance thither, advised

9. whispered.   1. knew.
2. *all . . . affections*: all his worldly feelings and emotions.
3. More's *English Works* were printed in 1557. Roper may have had an advance copy or he may have been referring to a manuscript collection of More's writing. The latter hypothesis seems to be the more likely one.
4. confessed.
5. The son of Sir Thomas Cromwell's sister. On entering his uncle's service, he assumed the surname of Cromwell.

him to send home his chain to his wife or to some of his children. "Nay, sir," quoth he, "that I will not. For if I were taken in the field by my enemies, I would they should somewhat fare the better by me."

At whose landing, Master Lieutenant at the Tower-gate was ready to receive him, where the porter demanded of him his upper garment. "Master Porter," quoth he, "here it is." And took off his cap and delivered it him, saying: "I am very sorry it is no better for you." "No, sir," quoth the porter, "I must have your gown."

And so was he by Master Lieutenant conveyed to his lodging where he called unto him one John a Wood, his own servant, there appointed to attend upon him (who could neither write nor read); and sware him before the Lieutenant that if he should hear or see him at any time speak or write any manner of thing against the King, the council, or the state of the realm, he should open it to the Lieutenant, that the Lieutenant might incontinent[6] reveal it to the council.

Now when he had remained in the Tower a little more than a month, my wife, longing to see her father, by her earnest suit at length got leave to go to him. At whose coming, after the Seven Psalms and Litany said—which, whensoever she came to him, ere he fell in talk of any worldly matters, he used accustomably[7] to say with her—among other communication he said unto her: "I believe, Meg, that they that have put me here ween[8] they have done me a high displeasure. But I assure thee, on my faith, my own good daughter, if it had not been for my wife and you that be my children, whom I accompt the chief part of my charge, I would not have failed long ere this to have closed myself in as strait a room—and straiter, too. But since I am come hither without mine own desert, I trust that God of His goodness will discharge me of my care, and with His gracious help supply my lack among you. I find no cause, I thank God, Meg, to reckon myself in worse case here than in my own house. For me thinketh God maketh me a wanton,[9] and setteth me on His lap and dandleth me."

Thus by his gracious demeanor[1] in tribulation appeared it

6. immediately.   7. customarily.   8. suppose.   9. pampered pet.
1. bearing.

that all the troubles that ever chanced unto him, by his patient sufferance thereof, were to him no painful punishments but, of[2] his patience, profitable exercises.

And at another time, when he had first questioned with my wife a while of the order of his wife, children, and state of his own house in his absence, he asked her how Queen Anne did. "In faith, father," quoth she, "never better." "Never better, Meg!" quoth he. "Alas, Meg, alas! It pitieth me to remember into what misery, poor soul, she shall shortly come."

After this, Master Lieutenant, coming into his chamber to visit him, rehearsed the benefits and friendship that he had many ways received at his hands, and how much bounden he was therefore friendly to entertain him and make him good cheer. Which, since the case standing as it did, he could not do without the King's indignation, he trusted, he said, he would accept his good will and such poor cheer as he had. "Master Lieutenant," quoth he again, "I verily believe, as you may, so you are my good friend indeed and would, as you say, with your best cheer entertain me, for the which I most heartily thank you. And assure yourself, Master Lieutenant, I do not mislike my cheer. But whensoever I so do, then thrust me out of your doors."

Whereas the oath confirming the Supremacy and matrimony was by the first statute in few words comprised, the Lord Chancellor and Master Secretary did of their own heads add more words unto it, to make it appear unto the King's ears more pleasant and plausible. And that oath, so amplified, caused they to be ministered to Sir Thomas More and to all other throughout the realm. Which Sir Thomas More perceiving, said unto my wife: "I may tell thee, Meg, they that have committed me hither for refusing of this oath not agreeable with the statute, are not by their own law able to justify my imprisonment. And, surely, daughter, it is great pity that any Christian prince should by a flexible council ready to follow his affections, and by a weak clergy lacking grace constantly to stand to their learning, with flattery be so shamefully abused." But at length the Lord Chancellor and Master Secre-

2. as a consequence of.

tary, espying their own oversight in that behalf, were fain afterwards to find the means that another statute should be made, for the confirmation of the oath so amplified with their additions.

After Sir Thomas More had given over his office and all other worldly doings therewith, to the intent he might from thenceforth the more quietly settle himself to the service of God, then made he a conveyance[3] for the disposition of all his lands, reserving to himself an estate thereof only for term of his own life. And after his decease assuring some part of the same to his wife, some to his son's wife, for a jointure,[4] in consideration that she was an inheritress in possession of more than an hundred pounds land by the year, and some to me and my wife in recompense of our marriage money—with divers remainders over. All which conveyance and assurance was perfectly finished long before that matter whereupon he was attained[5] was made an offense, and yet after by statute clearly avoided.[6] And so were all his lands that he had to his wife and children by the said conveyance in such sort assured, contrary to the order of law, taken away from them and brought into the King's hands—saving that portion which he had appointed to my wife and me.

Which, although he had in the foresaid conveyance reserved, as he did the rest, for term of life to himself, nevertheless, upon further consideration two days after by another conveyance, he gave the same immediately to my wife and me in possession. And so because the statute had undone only the first conveyance, giving no more to the King but so much as passed by that, the second conveyance—whereby it was given to my wife and me—being dated two days after, was without the compass of the statute, and so was our portion to us by that means clearly reserved.[7]

3. the transference of property, generally real estate, from one person to another.
4. the holding of property to the joint use of husband and wife for life.
5. accused.   6. made void.
7. After the attainder, the King seized upon those lands which by means of More's "conveyance" were to be distributed following his death. By a second "conveyance," however, More bestowed upon the Ropers their portion of his estate *before* his death, thus making their inheritance relatively safe from the threat of royal confiscation.

As Sir Thomas More in the Tower chanced on a time, looking out of his window, to behold one Master Reynolds, a religious, learned, and virtuous father of Sion and three monks of
the Charterhouse, for the matters of the matrimony and Supremacy, going out of the Tower to execution—he, as one
longing in that journey to have accompanied them, said unto
my wife, then standing there besides him: "Lo, dost thou not
see, Meg, that these blessed fathers be now as cheerfully going
to their deaths as bridegrooms to their marriage? Wherefore
thereby mayst thou see, mine own good daughter, what a great
difference there is between such as have in effect spent all their
days in a strait, hard, penitential, and painful life religiously,
and such as have in the world, like worldly wretches, as thy
poor father hath done, consumed all their time in pleasure and
ease licentiously. For God, considering their long-continued
life in most sore and grievous penance, will no longer suffer
them to remain here in this vale of misery and iniquity, but
speedily hence taketh them to the fruition of his everlasting
deity. Whereas thy silly[8] father, Meg, that like a most wicked
caitiff,[9] hath passed forth the whole course of his miserable
life most sinfully, God thinking him not worthy so soon to
come to that eternal felicity, leaveth him here yet still in the
world, further to be plunged and turmoiled with misery."

Within a while after, Master Secretary, coming to him into
the Tower from the King, pretended much friendship towards
him, and for his comfort told him that the King's highness was
his good and gracious lord, and minded not with any matter
wherein he should have any cause of scruple from henceforth
to trouble his conscience. As soon as Master Secretary was gone,
to express what comfort he conceived of his words, he wrote
with a coal—for ink then had he none—these verses following:

Aye, flattering Fortune, look thou never so fair,
Nor never so pleasantly begin to smile,
As though thou wouldst my ruin all repair,
During my life thou shalt not me beguile!
Trust I shall God to enter in a while

8. foolish.   9. wretch.

His haven of Heaven, sure and uniform:
Ever after thy calm, look I for a storm.

When Sir Thomas More had continued a good while in the Tower, my lady his wife obtained license to see him; who at her first coming, like a simple, ignorant woman and somewhat worldly too, with this manner of salutation bluntly saluted him:

"What the good-year,[1] Master More," quoth she, "I marvel that you that have been always hitherto taken for so wise a man will now so play the fool to lie here in this close, filthy prison and be content thus to be shut up among mice and rats when you might be abroad at your liberty and with the favor and good will both of the King and his council, if you would but do as all the bishops and best learned of this realm have done. And seeing you have at Chelsea a right fair house, your library, your books, your gallery, your garden, your orchard, and all other necessaries so handsome about you, where you might in the company of me your wife, your children, and household, be merry, I muse what, a God's name, you mean here still thus fondly[2] to tarry."

After he had a while quietly heard her, with a cheerful countenance he said unto her:

"I pray thee, good Mistress Alice, tell me one thing."

"What is that?" quoth she.

"Is not this house," quoth he, "as nigh heaven as my own?"

To whom she, after her accustomed homely fashion, not liking such talk, answered: "Tilly-valle, tilly-valle!"[3]

"How say you, Mistress Alice," quoth he, "is it not so?"

"*Bone deus, bone deus,* man, will this gear[4] never be left?" quoth she.

"Well, then, Mistress Alice, if it be so," quoth he, "it is very well. For I see no great cause why I should much joy either of my gay house or of anything belonging there unto, when, if I should but seven years lie buried under the ground and then arise and come thither again, I should not fail to find some therein that would bid me get me out of doors and tell me it

1. an exclamation connoting impatience.
2. foolishly.   3. a colloquialism suggesting impatience.
4. rubbish.

were none of mine. What cause have I then to like such an house as would so soon forget his master?"

So her persuasions moved him but a little.

Not long after came there to him the Lord Chancellor, the Dukes of Norfolk and Suffolk, with Master Secretary, and certain other of the privy council—at two several times—by all policies possible procuring[5] him either precisely[6] to confess the Supremacy or precisely to deny it. Whereunto as appeareth by his examinations in the said great book,[7] they could never bring him.

Shortly hereupon, Master Rich (afterwards Lord Rich), then newly-made the King's Solicitor, Sir Richard Southwell, and one Master Palmer, servant to the Secretary, were sent to Sir Thomas More into the Tower to fetch away his books from him. And while Sir Richard Southwell and Master Palmer were busy in the trussing-up of his books, Master Rich, pretending friendly talk with him, among other things, of a set course as it seemed, said thus unto him:

"Forasmuch as it is well known, Master More, that you are a man both wise and well-learned, as well in the laws of the realm as otherwise, I pray you therefore, sir, let me be so bold as of good will to put unto you this case. Admit there were, sir," quoth he, "an act of Parliament that all the realm should take me for King. Would not you, Master More, take me for King?"

"Yes, sir," quoth Sir Thomas More, "that would I."

"I put case further," quoth Master Rich, "that there were an act of Parliament that all the realm should take me for Pope. Would not you, then, Master More, take me for Pope?"

"For answer, sir," quoth Sir Thomas More, "to your first case. The Parliament may well, Master Rich, meddle with the state of temporal princes. But to make answer to your other case, I will put you this case: Suppose the Parliament would make a law that God should not be God. Would you, then, Master Rich, say that God were not God?"

"No, sir," quoth he, "that would I not, since no Parliament may make any such law."

5. inducing.   6. specifically.   7. See above, p. 238, n. 3.

"No more," said Sir Thomas More, as Master Rich reported of him, "could the Parliament make the King supreme head of the Church."

Upon whose only[8] report was Sir Thomas More indicted of treason upon the statute whereby it was made treason to deny the King to be supreme head of the Church. Into which indictment were put these heinous words—"Maliciously, traitorously, and diabolically."

When Sir Thomas More was brought from the Tower to Westminster Hall to answer the indictment, and at the King's Bench bar before the judges thereupon arraigned, he openly told them that he would upon that indictment have abidden in law,[9] but that he thereby should have been driven to confess of himself the matter indeed, that was the denial of the King's Supremacy, which he protested was untrue. Wherefore he thereto pleaded not guilty; and so reserved unto himself advantage to be taken of the body of the matter, after verdict, to avoid that indictment. And, moreover, added that if those only[1] odious terms—"Maliciously, traitorously, and diabolically"—were put out of the indictment, he saw therein nothing justly to charge him.

And for proof to the jury that Sir Thomas More was guilty of this treason, Master Rich was called forth to give evidence unto them upon his oath, as he did. Against whom thus sworn, Sir Thomas More began in this wise to say:

"If I were a man, my lords, that did not regard an oath, I needed not, as it is well known, in this place at this time nor in this case, to stand here as an accused person. And if this oath of yours, Master Rich, be true, then pray I that I never see God in the face, which I would not say, were it otherwise, to win the whole world." Then recited he to the court the discourse of all their communication in the Tower according to the truth and said: "In good faith, Master Rich, I am sorrier for your perjury than for my own peril. And you shall understand that neither I, nor no man else to my knowledge, ever took you to be a man of such credit as in any matter of importance

8. single.   9. *abidden in law:* abided by the law.
1. *those only:* only those.

I or any other would at any time vouchsafe to communicate with you. And I, as you know, of no small while have been acquainted with you and your conversation,[2] who have known you from your youth hitherto. For we long dwelled both in one parish together where, as yourself can tell (I am sorry you compel me to say) you were esteemed very light of your tongue, a great dicer and of no commendable fame.[3] And so in your house at the Temple,[4] where hath been your chief bringing-up, were you likewise accompted.

"Can it therefore seem likely unto your honorable lordships that I would, in so weighty a cause, so unadvisedly overshoot myself as to trust Master Rich, a man of me always reputed for one of so little truth as your lordships have heard, so far above my sovereign lord the King or any of his noble counsellors, that I would unto him utter the secrets of my conscience touching the King's Supremacy—the special point and only mark at my hands so long sought for? A thing which I never did, nor never would, after the statute thereof made, reveal either to the King's highness himself or to any of his honorable counsellors, as it is not unknown to your honors, at sundry several times sent from his grace's own person unto the Tower unto me for none other purpose. Can this, in your judgments, my lords, seem likely to be true?

"And yet if I had so done indeed, my lords, as Master Rich hath sworn, seeing it was spoken but in familiar secret talk, nothing affirming, and only in putting of cases without other displeasant circumstances, it cannot justly be taken to be spoken 'maliciously.' And where there is no malice, there can be no offense. And over[5] this I can never think, my lords, that so many worthy bishops, so many honorable personages, and so many other worshipful, virtuous, wise, and well-learned men as at the making of that law were in the Parliament assembled, ever meant to have any man punished by death in whom there could be found no malice—taking 'malitia' for 'malevolentia'; for if 'malitia' be generally taken for 'sin,' no

2. behavior.   3. reputation.
4. i.e. the Middle Temple, one of the Inns of Court.   5. besides.

man is there then that can thereof excuse himself: *Quia si dixerimus quod peccatum non habemus, nosmet ipsos seducimus, et veritas in nobis non est.*[6] And only this word '*maliciously*' is in the statute material [7]—as this term '*forcible*' is in the statute of forcible entries. By which statute, if a man enter peaceably, and put not his adversary out forcibly, it is no offense. But if he put him out forcibly, then by that statute it is an offense, and so shall he be punished by this term '*forcibly*.'

"Besides this the manifold goodness of the King's highness himself, that hath been so many ways my singular good lord and gracious sovereign, that hath so dearly loved and trusted me, even at my very first coming into his noble service with the dignity of his honorable privy council vouchsafing to admit me, and to offices of great credit and worship most liberally advanced me, and finally with that weighty room[8] of his grace's High Chancellor (the like whereof he never did to temporal [9] man before) next to his own royal person the highest officer in this noble realm, so far above my merits or qualities able and meet therefore, of his incomparable benignity honored and exalted me, by the space of twenty years and more showing his continual favor towards me. And, until at my own poor suit, it pleased his highness, giving me license with his majesty's favor, to bestow the residue of my life for the provision of my soul in the service of God—of his especial goodness thereof to discharge and unburthen me—most benignly heaped honors continually more and more upon me. All this his highness's goodness, I say, so long thus bountifully extended towards me, were in my mind, my lords, matter sufficient to convince[1] this slanderous surmise by this man so wrongfully imagined against me."

Master Rich, seeing himself so disproved and his credit so foully defaced, caused Sir Richard Southwell and Master Palmer, that at the time of their communication were in the chamber,[2] to be sworn what words had passed between them. Whereupon Master Palmer, upon his deposition, said that he

6. I John 1:8.   7. relevant.   8. office.   9. secular.   1. refute.
2. i.e. More's quarters in the Tower.

was so busy about the trussing-up of Sir Thomas More's books in a sack that he took no heed to their talk. Sir Richard Southwell likewise, upon his deposition, said that because he was appointed only to look unto the conveyance of his books, he gave no ear unto them.

After this were there many other reasons, not now in my remembrance, by Sir Thomas More in his own defense alleged, to the discredit of Master Rich's aforesaid evidence and proof of the clearness of his own conscience. All which notwithstanding, the jury found him guilty.

And incontinent upon³ their verdict, the Lord Chancellor, for that matter chief commissioner, beginning to proceed in judgment against him, Sir Thomas More said to him: "My Lord, when I was toward ⁴ the law, the manner in such case was to ask the prisoner before judgment, why judgment should not be given against him." Whereupon the Lord Chancellor, staying his judgment, wherein he had partly proceeded, demanded of him what he was able to say to the contrary. Who then in this sort most humbly made answer:

"Forasmuch as, my lord," quoth he, "this indictment is grounded upon an act of Parliament directly repugnant to the laws of God and His Holy Church, the supreme government of which, or of any part whereof, may no temporal prince presume by any law to take upon him, as rightfully belonging to the See of Rome, a spiritual pre-eminence by the mouth of Our Savior himself, personally present upon the earth, only to Saint Peter and his successors, Bishops of the same See, by special prerogative granted; it is therefore in law, amongst Christian men, insufficient to charge any Christian man."

And for proof thereof like as (among divers other reasons and authorities) he declared that this realm, being but one member and small part of the Church, might not make a particular law disagreeable with the general law of Christ's universal Catholic Church, no more than the City of London, being but one poor member in respect of the whole realm, might make a law against an act of Parliament to bind the whole realm. So

3. *incontinent upon:* immediately after.   4. engaged in the practice of.

farther showed he that it was contrary both to the laws and statutes of our own land yet unrepealed, as they might evidently perceive in Magna Charta: *Quod ecclesia Anglicana libera sit, et habeat omnia iura sua integra et libertates suas illaesas;*[5] and also contrary to that sacred oath which the King's highness and every Christian prince always with great solemnity received at their coronations. Alleging, moreover, that no more might this realm of England refuse obedience to the See of Rome than might the child refuse obedience to his own natural father.

For, as Saint Paul said of the Corinthians, "I have regenerated you my children in Christ," [6] so might Saint Gregory, Pope of Rome, of whom by Saint Augustine, his messenger, we first received the Christian faith, of us Englishmen truly say: "You are my children because I have given to you everlasting salvation, a far higher and better inheritance than any carnal father can leave to his child, and by regeneration made you my spiritual children in Christ."

Then was it by the Lord Chancellor thereunto answered that, seeing all the bishops, universities, and best learned of this realm had to this act agreed, it was much marvelled that he alone against them all would so stiffly stick[7] thereat, and so vehemently argue there against. To that Sir Thomas More replied, saying:

"If the number of bishops and universities be so material as your lordship seemeth to take it, then see I little cause, my lord, why that thing in my conscience should make any change. For I nothing doubt but that, though not in this realm, yet in Christendom about, of these well-learned bishops and virtuous men that are yet alive, they be not the fewer part that be of my mind therein. But if I should speak of those which already be dead, of whom many be now holy saints in heaven, I am very sure it is the far greater part of them that, all the while they lived, thought in this case that way that I think now. And therefore am I not bound, my lord, to conform my conscience

5. "That the English church may be free, and that it may exist with all its laws uncorrupted and its liberties unviolated."
6. I Corinthians 3:1.   7. *stiffly stick:* obstinately refuse.

to the council of one realm against the general council of Christendom."

Now when Sir Thomas More, for the avoiding of the indictment, had taken as many exceptions as he thought meet, and many more reasons than I can now remember alleged, the Lord Chancellor, loath to have the burthen of that judgment wholly to depend upon himself, there openly asked the advice of the Lord Fitz-James,[8] then Lord Chief Justice of the King's Bench, and joined in commission with him, whether this indictment were sufficient or not. Who, like a wise man, answered: "My lords all, by Saint Julian" (that was ever his oath), "I must needs confess that if the act of Parliament be not unlawful, then is not the indictment in my conscience insufficient."

Whereupon the Lord Chancellor said to the rest of the Lords: "Lo, my lords, lo, you hear what my Lord Chief Justice saith," and so immediately gave he judgment against him.

After which ended, the commissioners yet further courteously offered him, if he had anything else to allege for his defense, to grant him favorable audience. Who answered: "More have I not to say, my lords, but like as the blessed apostle Saint Paul, as we read in the Acts of the Apostles, was present and consented to the death of Saint Stephen, and kept their clothes that stoned him to death, and yet be they now both twain holy saints in heaven, and shall continue there friends forever, so I verily trust, and shall therefore right heartily pray, that though your lordships have now here in earth been judges to my condemnation, we may yet hereafter in heaven merrily all meet together, to our everlasting salvation."

Thus much touching Sir Thomas More's arraignment, being not thereat present myself, have I by the credible report partly of the right worshipful Sir Anthony Saint Leger, knight, and partly of Richard Heywood and John Webbe, gentlemen, with others of good credit, at the hearing thereof present themselves, as far as my poor wit and memory would serve me, here truly rehearsed unto you.

Now after this arraignment departed he from the bar to

8. Sir John Fitz-James (1470?–1542?) became Chief Justice in 1526.

the Tower again, led by Sir William Kingston,[9] a tall, strong, and comely knight, Constable of the Tower, and his very dear friend. Who, when he had brought him from Westminster to the Old Swan towards the Tower, there with an heavy heart, the tears running down by his cheeks, bade him farewell. Sir Thomas More, seeing him so sorrowful, comforted him with as good words as he could, saying: "Good Master Kingston, trouble not yourself but be of good cheer; for I will pray for you, and my good Lady, your wife, that we may meet in heaven together, where we shall be merry for ever and ever."

Soon after, Sir William Kingston, talking with me of Sir Thomas More, said: "In good faith, Master Roper, I was ashamed of myself that, at my departing from your father, I found my heart so feeble, and his so strong, that he was fain to comfort me which should rather have comforted him."

When Sir Thomas More came from Westminster to the Tower-ward again, his daughter—my wife—desirous to see her father, whom she thought she should never see in this world after, and also to have his final blessing, gave attendance about the Tower Wharf where she knew he should pass by before he could enter into the Tower—there tarrying for his coming home.

As soon as she saw him—after his blessing on her knees reverently received—she hasting towards him and, without consideration or care of herself, pressing in among the midst of the throng and company of the guard, that with halberds and bills[1] went round about him, hastily ran to him and there openly, in the sight of them all, embraced him, took him about the neck, and kissed him. Who, well liking her most natural and dear daughterly affection towards him, gave her his fatherly blessing and many goodly words of comfort besides.

From whom after she was departed she, not satisfied with the former sight of him and like one that had forgotten herself, being all-ravished with the entire love of her dear father, having respect neither to herself nor to the press of the people

9. After a distinguished military career, Sir William was made Constable of the Tower in 1524. He died in 1540. Cf. above, p. 173f.
1. *halberds and bills:* battle-axes and swords.

and multitude that were there about him, suddenly turned back again, ran to him as before, took him about the neck, and divers times together most lovingly kissed him—and at last, with a full heavy heart, was fain to depart from him. The beholding whereof was to many of them that were present thereat so lamentable that it made them for very sorrow thereof to mourn and weep.

So remained Sir Thomas More in the Tower more than a seven-night after his judgment. From whence, the day before he suffered,[2] he sent his shirt of hair—not willing to have it seen—to my wife, his dearly beloved daughter, and a letter written with a coal, contained in the foresaid book of his works, plainly expressing the fervent desire he had to suffer on the morrow, in these words following:

"I cumber[3] you, good Margaret, much; but I would be sorry if it should be any longer than tomorrow. For tomorrow is Saint Thomas's Even and the Utas of Saint Peter;[4] and therefore tomorrow long I to go to God. It were a day very meet and convenient for me, etc. I never liked your manner towards me better than when you kissed me last. For I like when daughterly love and dear charity hath no leisure to look to worldly courtesy."

And so upon the next morrow, being Tuesday, Saint Thomas's Even and the Utas of Saint Peter, in the year of our Lord one thousand five hundred thirty and five, according as he in his letter the day before had wished, early in the morning came to him Sir Thomas Pope, his singular friend, on message from the King and his council, that he should before nine of the clock the same morning suffer death. And that therefore forthwith he should prepare himself thereunto.

"Master Pope," quoth he, "for your good tidings I most heartily thank you. I have been always much bounden to the King's highness for the benefits and honors that he hath still from time to time most bountifully heaped upon me. And yet

2. i.e. with the implication of martyrdom.   3. trouble.
4. Saint Thomas's Even and the Utas (i.e. octave) of Saint Peter, a festivity of eight days, do indeed fall on July 6, the day of More's execution. But More was sentenced on July 1. Roper must therefore be in error when he states that More was in the Tower "more than a seven-night after his judgment."

more bound am I to his grace for putting me into this place, where I have had convenient time and space to have remembrance of my end. And so help me God, most of all, Master Pope, am I bound to his highness that it pleaseth him so shortly to rid me out of the miseries of this wretched world. And therefore will I not fail earnestly to pray for his grace, both here and also in another world."

"The King's pleasure is further," quoth Master Pope, "that at your execution you shall not use many words."

"Master Pope," quoth he, "you do well to give me warning of his grace's pleasure, for otherwise I had purposed at that time somewhat to have spoken, but of no matter wherewith his grace, or any other, should have had cause to be offended. Nevertheless, whatsoever I intended, I am ready obediently to conform myself to his grace's commandments. And I beseech you, good Master Pope, to be a mean unto his highness that my daughter Margaret may be at my burial."

"The King is content already," quoth Master Pope, "that your wife, children, and other your friends shall have liberty to be present thereat."

"O, how much beholden then," said Sir Thomas More, "am I to his grace that unto my poor burial vouchsafeth to have so gracious consideration."

Wherewithal Master Pope, taking his leave of him, could not refrain from weeping. Which Sir Thomas More perceiving, comforted him in this wise: "Quiet yourself, good Master Pope, and be not discomforted. For I trust that we shall, once in heaven, see each other full merrily, where we shall be sure to live and love together in joyful bliss eternally."

Upon whose departure, Sir Thomas More, as one that had been invited to some solemn feast, changed himself into his best apparel. Which Master Lieutenant espying, advised him to put it off, saying that he that should have it was but a javel.[5]

"What, Master Lieutenant," quoth he, "shall I accompt him a javel that shall do me this day so singular a benefit? Nay, I assure you, were it cloth-of-gold, I would accompt it well bestowed on him, as Saint Cyprian did, who gave his executioner thirty pieces of gold." And albeit at length, through

/5. rogue.

Master Lieutenant's importunate persuasion, he altered his apparel, yet after the example of that holy martyr, Saint Cyprian, did he of that little money that was left him send one angel of gold to his executioner.

And so was he by Master Lieutenant brought out of the Tower and from thence led towards the place of execution. Where, going up the scaffold, which was so weak that it was ready to fall, he said merrily to Master Lieutenant: "I pray you, Master Lieutenant, see me safe up and, for my coming down, let me shift for myself."

Then desired he all the people thereabout to pray for him, and to bear witness with him that he should now there suffer death in and for the faith of the Holy Catholic Church. Which done, he kneeled down and after his prayers said, turned to the executioner and with a cheerful countenance spake thus to him:

"Pluck up thy spirits, man, and be not afraid to do thine office. My neck is very short. Take heed therefore thou strike not awry, for saving of thine honesty."

So passed Sir Thomas More out of this world to God upon the very same day in which himself had most desired.

Soon after whose death came intelligence thereof to the Emperor Charles. Whereupon he sent for Sir Thomas Elyot, our English ambassador, and said unto him: "My Lord Ambassador, we understand that the King, your master, hath put his faithful servant and grave, wise counsellor, Sir Thomas More, to death." Whereunto Sir Thomas Elyot answered that he understood nothing thereof.

"Well," said the Emperor, "it is too true. And this will we say, that if we had been master of such a servant, of whose doings ourself have had these many years no small experience, we would rather have lost the best city of our dominions than have lost such a worthy counsellor."

Which matter was by the same Sir Thomas Elyot to myself, to my wife, to Master Clement and his wife to Master John Heywood and his wife, and unto divers other his friends accordingly reported.

Finis. Deo gratias.

Index of Names